The
FRENCH
SQUADRONS

The
FRENCH SQUADRONS

A True Story of Love and War

Barbara Rigby's Diary

1944–1946

Including letters of Francis Usai
translated from the French by
Michel Darribehaude

Edited by
Barbara Harper-Nelson
and
Geneviève Monneris

AMBERLEY

First published 2014
This edition published 2016

Amberley Publishing
The Hill, Stroud
Gloucestershire, GL5 4EP

www.amberley-books.com

British Library Cataloguing in Publication Data.
A catalogue record for this book is available from the British Library.

ISBN 978 1 4456 5538 3 (paperback)
ISBN 978 1 4456 3951 2 (ebook)

Typeset in 10pt on 12pt Sabon.
Typesetting and Origination by Amberley Publishing.
Printed in the UK.

Contents

To Barbara and Francis,
with my deep affection.

To their dearest friends, Henri and Pat Martin,
and Jacques Leclercq.

In my heart forever.

In memory of all the French airmen of the Heavy Bomber
Squadrons.

346 'Guyenne' and 347 'Tunisie'

To my father, André Guédez, who was one of them.

With much love

Geneviève

Acknowledgements

On thinking about these events, both happy and sad, which now seem so far away, I think that 'the past is another country', as L. P. Hartley has said so well in his magnificent novel, The Go-Between, and I am happy to have found the perfect go-between in Geneviève Monneris, whom I thank with all my heart.

In order to retrace this story, Geneviève and I have exchanged an enormous number of letters in the old-fashioned way, but also numerous messages over the Internet, thanks to my dear friend Ruth Bale, who has greatly helped our correspondence between Australia and France, so willingly and so faithfully, and without whom days would have been weeks.

I would also like to express my sincere thanks to Ian Reed, the Director of the Allied Air Forces Memorial and of the Yorkshire Air Museum in Elvington, who, by a happy chance, rediscovered the famous photograph of Francis with his three best friends, Henri and Pat Martin and Jacques Leclercq, taken on 3rd October 1944, and without which this story would not have become known.

It is with great affection that I dedicate this book to him who was my dear Cis, he who loved me so much and whom I have never forgotten.

Barbara Harper-Nelson
Lesmurdie, Western Australia, 2011

They for us fight, they watch and duly ward,
And their bright squadrons round about us plant;
And all for love, and nothing for reward.

'The Ministry of Angels' from *Faerie Queene*,
by Edmund Spenser (1552-1599)

In seventy years [...] people will talk about Barbiche who saw England invaded by all those weird foreigners who stole girls' hearts.

Francis, RAF Elvington, 2nd November 1944

Preface

346 'Guyenne' and 347 'Tunisie' were the only two French heavy bomber squadrons of World War II who fought with RAF Bomber Command from mid-1944 until the end of hostilities. They carried out all their missions from RAF Elvington, near York, the only station operated by French personnel in UK, and now the home of the Yorkshire Air Museum and Allied Air Forces Memorial.

Their role is little recognized, yet half of their young aircrews lost their lives, and today's generations have been able to live during the longest period of peace in European history simply because of what they, and thousands of others like them, did. One can only be humbled by the sacrifice they made for us all.

In 2009, Geneviève Monneris was searching for related documents for the film she was making about *Sergent* Henri Martin and Pat, his young English wife. By an extraordinary coincidence, I found an old damaged photograph showing a young lady surrounded by three French airmen. On the reverse was the date, 3rd October 1944, and the names of Henri and Pat Martin, Jacques Leclercq and Francis Usai. The photograph had been sent to the museum in 1995, from Western Australia, by a Mrs Harper-Nelson. The chances of her still being at this location after so long were slim, but I wrote to her and was overjoyed to receive a reply just a week later, and from this first contact, the hundreds of letters of *Sergent* Francis Usai were revealed to us.

By donating this correspondence to the Yorkshire Air Museum, Barbara Harper-Nelson gave us an immense gift. From a historical perspective, it is probably one of the largest collections of its type, exceeding 2,000 pages, and it was with great pleasure that we formally loaned the originals, written in French, to the '*Service Historique de la Défense*' to become part of the French National Collection.

Coinciding with the letters from her sweetheart, Barbara revealed that she had written a diary during those wartime years, and when she discovered the richness of those exceptional documents, Geneviève Monneris managed to convince Barbara into making her story known and pieced it all together with her.

As a love story, Barbara's diary and Francis' letters, gathered together so many years later, are extremely emotional, and as a social history document, they are highly significant for our two countries. Their personal perspective on the main events and daily life from 1944 to early 1946 particularly strikes a chord with us today, and it is such an amazing coincidence that Francis wrote in one of his letters of 1944: '*In seventy years… people will talk about Barbiche who saw England invaded by all those weird foreigners who stole girls' hearts.*' – a prediction now come true!

Amongst the many wartime love stories, this one is incredibly special because it is one story written from two sides at the same time by two quite different hands. It was then lovingly kept for all those years until now, by a lady who had no idea that what she had lived through as a young student in Liverpool, would be revealed one day and would revive the memory of so many of the people she had met. All this, just by coincidence and the discovery of a single photograph.

We are very lucky Barbara kept her personal diaries and preserved Francis' letters for so long. I am very grateful to her and also to Geneviève Monneris, whose sheer determination, perseverance and meticulous researching work made this project come to life, so that this extraordinary story can now be told.

Ian Reed *FRAeS*
Officier de l'Ordre National du Mérite
Director, The Yorkshire Air Museum and Allied Air Forces Memorial

Liverpool

I met Francis on 1ˢᵗ January 1944 at the British Council in Liverpool, on the occasion of the New Year's reception organized by the AVF, the Association of Friends of the French Volunteers, of which I was a member. The *British* was a welcome centre for the Allied Forces' servicemen in Great Britain. Almost every night you could dance there and for those young men, who had just arrived in Liverpool, it was an essential place for entertainment. For me, like for many other young women, it was a chance to meet young foreigners who dazzled us with their uniforms and made us laugh in trying to speak our language, which most of them could not manage yet.

I had left my boarding school in Wales only a few months earlier. I had neither brother nor cousin. I had just gone to university and suddenly met lots of boys. I was under the spell of those young servicemen coming from Allied countries to fight with the Royal Navy or the Royal Air Force. I was filled with admiration for their involvement and their courage. It was a real wave of foreigners which flooded into Liverpool port, and here, at home, in Great Britain, we all thought that, thanks to them and our own forces, the war would finish at last. We were happy to welcome them as our own children or our own brothers, they who had left their native country, their families and all their loved ones thousands of miles away.

I had the feeling that we were living through extraordinary events and that a different world was going to be born. That's probably why

I noted every day in my diary what I lived through during all those wartime years, and especially during the last two, which influenced my life as a woman for always.

Francis had arrived a few weeks earlier, on 9th December 1943, on board the *Scythia*, with his friend Henri and other comrades: François, Roger, Maurice, and many others. They were part of 'Guyenne' and 'Tunisie' Squadrons' aircrew reinforcements, the only two French squadrons integral to RAF Bomber Command under the names of '346 and 347 Squadrons'. Liverpool was their first contact with Great Britain. Having left Algiers ten days earlier, Francis and Henri stood side by side on the deck when the ship came into the port. The city seemed dull and cold to them. They, coming from a sunny country, thought they didn't like the look of England at all. They had not yet the least idea of what was coming to them.

RMS *Scythia*: British Cunard liner, launched in 1920 for voyages in the Atlantic and Mediterranean, requisitioned and converted into a troop and supply ship at the end of 1939.

1944

January

Saturday 1

Went to the AVF. *Mme* da Horta charming said she remembered me. She introduced me to Francis Gilbert? I couldn't grasp his surname. He stuck to me and was very charming – dark, greenish eyes. He's from Marseilles and arrived from Algiers. He has a little brother called André and two sisters, Marie-Rose and Marie-Jeanne. He speaks very little English and that was very funny. He liked dancing and was quite musical. Has seen Charles Trenet and says he looks anything but glamorous in uniform. Tino Rossi is small and unattractive. Asked him to tea tomorrow.

AVF: *Amis des Volontaires Français* (The Association of Friends of the French Volunteers) at the British Council in Liverpool.

Mme da Horta: president of the AVF and French wife of M. da Horta, the Portuguese consul in Liverpool.

Francis' surname was Usai. In order to respect the wish of Barbara, who always wrote his surname 'Uzay', the reader will find two different spellings in the text.

Sunday 2

Francis came to tea. He immediately found his way; he's very sweet and easy to get on with. His father is one of sixteen children and works in a factory. Said in Algiers the Arabs set on people and stripped them of their clothes because stuff was short. His English was most amusing; we taught him some more. He wears a dyed British battle-dress. He is going to London for a medical inspection and then to the north of Scotland. He finds English girls very free because they smoke! He sang *Elle pleure comme une Madeleine*. It's funny; the French are great ones for little songs. He called Wiener '*Globule*'. He stayed quite a long time and seemed grateful for our welcome and a bit of companionship. He's typical *Midi*: black hair, greenish-hazel eyes, lovely white teeth and a very olive skin. Told me pointless stories about Marius and is very fond of animals. I took him back to the tram with my torch. He recommended me to use it as a baton whilst returning if necessary. He kissed my hand and said: '*Goodbye Princess!*'

Il pleurait comme une Madeleine was sung by Maurice Chevalier in the film *Pièges* directed by Robert Siodmak (1939).

Barbara did not smoke.

Wiener Schnitzel, usually called Wien, the family's Dachshund.

Marius: a famous character from Marseilles in *Marius*, a play by Marcel Pagnol (1929) and a film by Alexander Korda, written by Pagnol (1931).

Monday 3

Poor little Francis, he hadn't even any handkerchiefs!

Wednesday 5

I received a letter from him today. '*3rd January 1944. Dear Barbara, as I said to you yesterday evening, no sooner have I arrived than I hasten to write to you, so you can't say that I have forgotten you, and that the French are ungrateful (Oh! A slap on the face!). I can't say much about the town, because I don't know it yet, but in any case I can tell you it looks rather gloomy. Perhaps that is only a first impression, but in any case I'll tell you about it in person. With that, I will end this masterpiece of calligraphy, begging you to excuse my handwriting, because I'm*

using my suitcase as a desk. Please don't forget to thank your parents
for the delightful evening which we had together. Say hello to Globule
and Grimalkin. *My best* 'fromages' *(Sorry!* 'hommages') *to* Mademoiselle
your sister. Hope to see you again soon. Your Francis.' He is at West Kirby
camp: that's where all the French airmen disembarking at Liverpool are
staying. I find it much easier to talk to Frenchmen. Most Englishmen only
want to talk about themselves. F seems to me particularly interesting.

Fromages and *hommages*: Francis keeps making puns; this one is about '*hommages*'
    (regards), which almost sounds like '*fromages*' (cheese).
Camp located near the village of West Kirby, north-west of the Wirral
    Peninsula, between the rivers Dee and Mersey, some twelve miles
    from Liverpool. The RAF had made it a camp to welcome and train new
    recruits. When arriving, the French had to undergo interrogation by British
    intelligence officers.

Sunday 9

I went to the *British* and there was Francis, back from London. He
prefers Liverpool infinitely: '*C'est plus familial!*' He dances quite well
and does not hold one too tightly. He likes English girls, who take no
account of rank. He now has his golden stripes. He saw me home.

Francis was just back from London where he had undergone the standard RAF
    medical examination for all flying personnel, at Abbey Lodge. He had just
    been appointed *caporal-chef* (corporal) and wore two red stripes and one
    golden stripe on each sleeve.
'*C'est plus familial*': 'It's more family-like.'

Friday 14

Got another letter. He has given me such a funny name: '*Barbe à ras*
de mon coeur'! They had two lectures on Monday and Tuesday, and
when he got to the *British*, the office was closed. He hopes to see me
again on Thursday. '*My regards to your parents, and say hello to*
your little menagerie for me. Your devoted and very well-behaved
(hum!) Francis.' I wrote to him, enclosing a letter from Joan to *le*
Vicomte.

'*Barbe à ras de mon coeur*': another pun; literally: shaven beard of my heart, but
   he means: 'Barbara in my heart'.
Le Vicomte (*the Viscount*): nickname given by Barbara and her friend Joan to a
   warrant officer, member of ground-crew.

Wednesday 19

He had to go and get my letter at the post orderly's. '*Princess of my
dreams [...] When I read your letter, I was furious with the English
Post Office. Don't be offended at this, because it's a characteristic
of the French to get hopping mad easily like this.*' He hasn't seen *le
Vicomte* yet. '*It's as if he had vanished into thin air! [...] My regards to
your parents and to* Mademoiselle *your sister. A brotherly kiss on their
muzzles to Puss and* Globule. *Goodbye Princess and think sometimes of
your Francis.*'

Thursday 20

Went to AVF. Found the ubiquitous Francis: he was his usual gay self and
very possessive. Asked him for my birthday on Saturday. He introduced
me to his friend François, who is from Marseilles like him, a very nice
boy.

Friday 21

I read *Le Silence de la mer* by Vercors. I liked this book very much; it
was sensitive and very well-written.

Saturday 22

19 today. Francis arrived very gay, having had a letter from his family.
It sounds like his sisters used to clean his shoes before the war and they
now eat cats in Marseilles! He told us about having been entertained at a
feast by an Algerian chief at the camp in North Africa. He acted the fool
about washing up, pretended he was a butler getting ready for a party
and then at supper he was 'the father of the family'! The time passed
very pleasantly and we did enjoy having him. He really is a dear and not
at all forward. Uncle Max said that all the French have caressing voices,
or could it be the French language? It was a lovely birthday. His friend
François' surname is Saytour.

Sunday 23

Went to the *British*. F there pretending that he had been to Buckingham Palace! François and F talk in incomprehensible language, a kind of slang I think. They call poor Hannah '*the spectacled snake*'. I introduced Joan to him; he found her charming and vice versa. He told me a bit about his childhood when he played cowboys or when his mother sang him to sleep. He confessed he hates tea although he drank some at home to be polite. He says he'll '*be getting more than enough*' in England! He grows on one. I find him very amusing but our points of view are quite different.

Wednesday 26

F came to the university. He's going away to Scotland on Friday to the air gunners' school at Evanton. We walked arm in arm decorously to the Pier Head. He recognized the place where they arrived in December in the *Scythia*. He is a dear and very funny about his imaginary driver he calls 'Joseph'. We'll see each other at the *British* tomorrow.

Pier Head: famous group of buildings of the early 20th century along the River Mersey at Liverpool (Unesco World Heritage since 2004), an important connecting place for transport by tramway, bus, train and ferry.

Thursday 27

F couldn't come. He asked François to telephone, but I was already off to the *British*. Mummy answered the phone. She said he was very amusing.

Saturday 29

F was confined to barracks on Thursday night because of his departure yesterday morning. He sent me a little note saying he would be travelling all night long and would write to me as soon as he got there. '*Light of my dreams. I am so sorry not to have been able to see you yesterday evening. [...] However, there you are, that's war for you. I must say goodbye now, because I haven't much time to spare. [...] It's time to go and I'm leaving you. For the first time, I embrace you (French style) because I am sad to leave you, and now I shall have no-one to tease. However we shall see each other soon, I hope. My regards to all the*

family and to Puss and Globule. *With my most sincere thoughts to you.
Your Francis.*' I am sad that he leaves too.

February

Wednesday 2

At last I've heard from Francis. '*Fisherwoman of Iceland of my dreams,
as I promised you in my last letter, I am sending you a few words on my
arrival here.*' He turned up at Evanton station in Scotland on Saturday
night after a long journey by train. After having left Lime Street station
on Friday night, they travelled overnight, took another train at about
6 am, and then had to reverse because of a derailment. They arrived
starving and black with smoke at Inverness where they had some food
at last in the city's restaurants. Then they got on yet another train to
Evanton where they eventually arrived at 10 pm. He already wants
to know all about what I've been doing since he left. '*Did you have a
good time on Sunday evening? I hope so, but look out; you know that
I am very jealous and that I'm quite capable of committing a crime (!)
when I'm angry. That's it, angel with star-like eyes (hum!), that's all I
have to say to you tonight and, anyway, my eyes are closing in spite of
myself, and perhaps I'll be able to dream of you tonight (a nightmare).
I think that if I go on like this, my Princess will be annoyed with me,
so I'll hurry up and say goodnight to her before she is angry with me.
Goodnight, Barbara, and think of me a little sometimes.*'

'*Fisherwoman of Iceland*': referring to *Pêcheur d'Islande*, a novel by Pierre Loti
    (1886) which Barbara was reading.
Lime Street station: a railway station in Liverpool.

Friday 4

His letter of 2nd. He says he is not allowed to give any information about
his training. These are the rules. I only know he must get up at 6.30
am and he works from 8 am to 6 pm. This RAF station is better than
the camp at West Kirby. A jazz band plays during lunch time. Many

WAAFs work on the station, which of course is rather to the liking of that great seducer. He's going to send me his picture. I definitely find him very funny, perhaps even a bit dotty. '*I hope that you are enjoying yourself and that your studies don't bother you too much. Please receive*, Mademoiselle... *no, that's too formal – Goodnight, Barbara of my heart, from your quite mad and very affectionate Francis – that's better, isn't it?*

    P.S. My usual greetings to your parents, Patsy, and Joan, as well as the menagerie, Globule *and Sabu.*'

WAAF: a member of the Women's Auxiliary Air Force. Francis always referred to 'Waaf' in his letters, rather than using the usual upper case.

Patsy: Patricia, Barbara's younger sister.

Sabu: Siamese cat.

Saturday 5

I received a little note with his photograph. I find him rather attractive in his uniform and airman's peaked cap. On the back of the picture he wrote: '*With best wishes from your boy-friend Francis. Evanton 3/2/44.*' I didn't know he was my 'boy-friend'! I've replied and sent a photograph of me too.

Tuesday 8

I read *Les Yeux d'Elsa* by Aragon and *Tartarin de Tarascon*. I found that story very amusing. It takes place in Provence, in Francis' area. I've heard a French song which tells about a horrible old castle and a rich uncle's legacy.

Tartarin de Tarascon: a novel by Alphonse Daudet (1872).

Le Vieux château: sung by Mireille and Jean Nohain, and also Charles Trenet.

Wednesday 9

Another letter. '*Good evening, heartless Princess. This name definitely suits you very well, and I shall adopt it. I have just had your long letter, and I was delighted, because I was beginning to despair! Do you realize that it is eight long days since I heard from you, enough to make me commit suicide three times at least. Thank you so much for the charming photograph. It really is a good one of you, and you have that expression that I like so much (Princess!) [...] In a few days' time, I will send you another of me in flying kit and then your collection of monkeys will be complete!'* They've started their training. The Scottish winter is dreadful; I bet he will finally enjoy very warm tea. *'This morning, I went for a practice shoot quite a way from here, and much farther north. I was so pleased to get back because, in spite of my boots and flying suit, I was almost turned into frozen meat. Scotland is a really cold country. The poor French exiles from tropical countries ought to be put into warm greenhouses, so that their poor bodies won't suffer! I am very angry, because we aren't going to fly before Friday, when I believed that I was going to get into a taxi (pardon!) a plane as soon as I got here. I have been really taken in. Anyway, I will give you my impression of my first flight in the skies of England soon.'* On Sunday he got on a train from Evanton to Inverness, which takes three hours. He went to the swimming pool, had lunch in a restaurant, and then went to the cinema. *'In a restaurant, I found it difficult to read the menu, so I took a chance and it turned out well.'* It is strange they don't have English classes; he's glad I can give him some lessons.

Taxi: French aviation slang for 'airplane'; the equivalent in 1940s RAF slang would have been 'kite'.

Saturday 12

I got a letter. *'Actress with the eyes of a vamp* femme fatale, *[...] I went to a dance in Evanton, a charming little town, which has about fifty houses in all, and about three hundred inhabitants. Important buildings: the church, a pub and the dance hall, all in the local style. At first, I took the church for the dance hall and vice versa. I'm not saying this to flatter your English girl's pride, but the girls are much prettier in England than in Scotland, and here the girls are all country lasses and when you look at them, you expect to see a flock of sheep appear behind them (shocking!). Don't forget, though, that there are charming shepherdesses, since kings married them! Another thing, at the end of the evening, the band started up with a Scottish tune and all the dancers began to utter such cries that I thought that they had all been smitten with a collective madness [...]*

I think if this goes on, I shall become a real Scot, and when I get back to Liverpool, it will be in a skirt. [...] At last I'm flying tomorrow and it won't be too soon as I have begun to despair. But since it will be in an English plane, I haven't a great deal of confidence (oh, oh, don't be angry, I was just joking, I assure you, and I won't do it again, as I don't want to get to know your torch). Goodnight, beautiful Princess – no: darling little Princess – no, that's not right – that's it, I've found it: sweet phantom who haunts my nights. I am going to sleep with the adorable vision of your dear face [...] Goodnight, sweet dreams. Your very bad Francis.' I had asked Nelly, who is a Catholic like him, to find me a medallion of the Blessed Virgin to protect him. She gave me one, which I've sent to him.

Nelly: the charlady.

Monday 14

His last letter is melancholy. *'Good evening, sweet light of my soul. My sad and wandering heart has come to visit you this evening. I don't know why, but such black thoughts have been in my mind all day. I think it's the first time that I have really felt lonely and cut off in this huge country where everything is so strange. I do so wish that you were here, so that I could hear your calm gentle voice (hum!) – perhaps you would be able to soothe my heart. You'll be thinking that I am not very amusing today, but this sometimes comes over me, this feeling of depression. Don't be frightened by this, it passes away quite soon and nobody really notices, because I am always as cheerful as ever, in spite of the huge bitterness of my soul. You know, it is such a long time since I have been wandering, going from one country to another, without even having the time to experience any genuine feelings, so that sometimes I feel like doing stupid things. It's always leaving, going away. In Liverpool I had almost found that healing atmosphere which could comfort my heart, starved of affection. But I am stupid, Barbara, and I must be boring you with my stupid sentimentality. Let's talk of other things. I promised to tell you about my first flights in English skies. Everything went well, except that I looked like a bear in my flying kit, and the shivers down my spine, Brr! When I think that in Morocco I flew in shorts and singlet! I did my exercise without much difficulty in spite of my ignorance of the English language, and I landed about an hour afterwards, after having been able to admire the wonderful woods which surround the district. I was lucky because it was good weather, and it was a real pleasure to glide in the endless blue sky. Oh, this morning I was a bit worried because we had an inspection, and the* colonel commandant *of the station closely examined the haircuts of his subordinates. As mine was rather long, I was a bit apprehensive, however he said nothing to me and that was the main thing. I won't tease you this evening as I haven't the heart to do so. I hope that you will forgive the beginning of this letter. I was stupid, but it was too much for me. I needed to unburden myself. I promise that I won't do it again. I leave you now, because it's lights out; good night and, once again, forgive your Francis, who would be very unhappy if he thought that he was upsetting you at all.'* Poor little bear, he seems suddenly lost and fragile. I've written him a little note during the Social Sciences class.

Friday 18

His letter of 16th. He is back in a good mood again and in his usual brilliant form. He is beginning to find that time passes by so slowly and says his head has been crammed full with theory. His instructional training course is ending; he will eventually be able to fly every day. They lost a football match against the English. He was aching all over because he had not played for years. I'm pleased he liked my medallion. *'It's beautiful and I'll keep it near my heart; no doubt it'll bring me luck on my trips over Germany.'* That's exactly what I wish for him. I still dare not think of the day when he will set off to bomb Germany with his crew, although I know that day is coming. *'Good night, my dear little friend, your crazy Francis, who may be forever joking but is very serious when he says he is very fond of you.'* What a strange boy! I find him endearing and very tender. I know when his birthday is: he will be 22 on 24th April.

Saturday 19

I've posted him a parcel with oranges, a fountain-pen and a little sewing-case.

Monday 21

I got a letter. He was glad to hear from me. '*I've just received your short note probably written at the university, and I'm as happy as a lark for I can see that even in those tragic moments when you're studying, you can still spare some time to think of your little bear. Yes I have pulled myself together, angel with star-like eyes, and I'm jolly and cheerful again. As I've already told you, those things don't last long with me.*' It snowed in Scotland; the mountains are all white. He says he is fond of skiing and regrets not to be able to slide on the snowy slopes. He talks about leave. '*At long last the days go by and soon, I hope, an airman will be walking into the railway station of that welcoming city named Liverpool. I hope neither journalists nor photographers will be informed of my arrival because I hate publicity. A police cordon will also be needed, if not, all the young ladies in Liverpool would invade the place. Good night, Princess with eyes of fire that have branded my heart. [...] My regards to His Majesty Sabu and his accomplice Globule.*'

Friday 25

'*Buenas tardes mi senorita de mi corazon!*' He was delighted with my parcel and told me off for the oranges as he knows they are rare and so difficult to find. They had a swimming session at Inverness where he saw a gift for me; he wants it to be a surprise, and I wonder what it is. On Tuesday he had a night exercise. At the beginning he used to complain about not flying and now it's the contrary. '*The French character – never content!*' He's given me another strange name again. '*Good night dear Barbiche! Your Francis who felt like giving you a piece of his mind yesterday evening. I'm hoping to do it soon in spite of your frightening torch. Regards to your parents, and a kiss between the eyes of my friends the dog and the cat. Say hello to Joan and le Vicomte, and also to Sheila whom I do not know but whom you often speak about and above all don't forget to kiss Miss Barbara for me.*'

'*Buenas tardes mi senorita de mi corazon*': 'Good evening, girl of my heart!'
'*Barbiche*': 'Goatee' in English instead of 'Barbara' is another of Francis' puns.
Joan Hughes and Sheila Smith were Barbara's two best friends.

Monday 28

His letter of 26th. It snowed again; all is white around the camp. His exams are starting tomorrow; he's a bit anxious. He thinks we will see each other again in twenty-nine days' time. He wrote a very funny little dialogue between him and me about English girls, which reminds me of a conversation we had in Liverpool! I have offered him to come and spend his leave at home with us. Daddy and Mummy are very pleased to have him. They found he was very sweet and behaved like a gentleman. I can't wait to see him again.

March

Wednesday 1

I got a letter. He called me '*Sweet fairy of my heart*' and '*Bébé Rose*'. Monday was his day off but he stayed at the camp. He says the French took their revenge against the English. '*We had a snowball fight with the English cadets and nevertheless they could not do anything against French might, they had to find refuge in their huts, like rats in their holes, and we didn't lift the siege until they hoisted the white flag of their emissaries which, in this case, meant the white flash on the forage caps of all English cadets and was held out when they cautiously half-opened a window for fear we should bombard them again. There you are Mademoiselle, you may take this as an example and tremble in your shoes for I am now running wild. I wish you had been here for me to see on your face that haughty look of yours when you react like an offended princess.*' Yesterday he probably went to the dance organized by the station WAAFs. He heard there were air-raid warnings on London and hopes nothing happened in Liverpool.

Saturday 4

He's glad about my offer but wouldn't like to be seen as bad mannered. He hopes to be able to arrive on 27th with his air gunner's wing just sewn on his uniform. Evanton is buried under the snow, and they continued their battles. '*By the way yesterday evening we joined forces with the English*

*cadets and attacked the station erks. It was splendid; such fury! Faced
with us screaming and as frantic as Indians on the warpath, the enemy
was forced into withdrawing to their fortifications, where they remained
in hiding until suppertime. I definitely believe that if we stay a little longer,
these young Englishmen will become more spirited and smarter. (Take
that! Serves you right!) [...] Good night Princess of my heart, it breaks
my heart to leave you, but I'm pleased I teased you a little. I kiss my
Princess's fine lily-white hand with all due respect. Good night Barbara,
Your Francis. [...] Kisses to our two little companions.'* He dreamt I was a
woman gangster and him a detective that I had held prisoner!

Erks: RAF slang for 'ground crew'.

Saturday 11

He couldn't write to me earlier because of his exams. *'I passed my
first test, with flying colours moreover, and left behind quite a few
Englishmen who were not wary enough of me and my unhurried ways.
At last you can be proud of your bear! He deserves a kiss on his muzzle
(how horrible!)'* As for my French he finds my spelling is very good but
the grammar a bit faulty. *'One thing that delights me is that you are the
only English girl who can understand French jokes.'* He would be closer
to the truth if he said the only girl to understand *his* very own jokes!
*'Goodbye my 'Barbe à ras', the vision of you will remain with me all day
long, bye, bye, my dear baby, see you soon! I leave you with a broken
heart but with a happy stomach since it's dinner-time and I'm off to see
the Waafs at the mess (Oh! How shocking!) Your Francis. [...] With a
few pats on the backs of our four-legged friends.'* On the radio I heard
Pierre Pucheu was condemned to death in Algeria for collaboration
with the Germans.

Pierre Pucheu: Home Office Secretary of State of the Vichy government from
July 1941 to April 1942, shot in Algiers on 20 March 1944.

Wednesday 15

His letter of 13th. He'll be here soon. *'Only twelve days left and I'll be
saying goodbye to Evanton with no regrets. Oh Princess, at last I'll be*

*seeing your sweet face again, your eyes so pure and your heavenly hair.
Many's the time, at night, when in my reverie I have thought of that
blessed day when I'll be able to tell you again: my heart is at your feet,
Princess, take care not to trample it. […] By the way, I am not even sure
that you will recognize me because I've put on weight, or so I've been
told, so it won't be a problem to show off with a big watch chain across
my belly that now looks like an airship.'* Patsy sometimes writes to him;
he finds her very funny and her French rather good. *'Goodbye sweet
heart […] I respectfully kiss my liege lady's dress. My warmest regards
to your parents, and a kiss on the noses of my four-legged friends. And
regards to Joan.'*

Saturday 18

He wrote to me. *'My dear Barbiche […] Right now I'm in the reading
room and on the radio they're playing a song that I find quite amusing.
It's sung half in English, half in French and the combination is very
funny. It's called* Darling, Je Vous Aime Beaucoup. *Maybe you've already
heard it? At any rate I'll have to learn it so I can sing it to you when I
arrive.'* His Morse test was rather difficult but he thinks he did well.
He says he has made progress in English – I can't wait to hear that! As
for me I have lots of work too and I have less time to write to him. *'I
suppose you're just as preoccupied with your exams as I am, for it's five
days at least since I last received a letter from you – or this time have
you found a Russian and forgotten me? But be warned: Russian is even
more difficult to learn than French!'* French officers visited them. *'It has
cheered us up a little because we felt somewhat left out of it in this place.
Flying is over for us, at least here, and the birds in Evanton can now
sleep in peace. It's crazy how the days are hurrying by now and I always
have the impression time flies too quickly: if it goes on like that, I'll be
old before I can say Jack Robinson! But I'd be very interested to see you
again because I always think that you've most probably changed. Who
knows? By the time I see you again you may have become a quaint old
lady with a moustache, or perhaps the typical Englishwoman, just as
we imagine her in France, with spectacles, large teeth and a face as long
as a month of Sundays. Maybe I won't recognize you at all! Ah well,
at any rate I've still got a photo of you and I'll keep it handy so I can*

compare the two.' How Francis exaggerates! I must take my revenge for his jokes, although they really make me laugh!

Darling, Je Vous Aime Beaucoup: sung by Hildegarde.

Monday 20

His letter of Friday was short as he still has much work. He asks me not to write to him at Evanton any longer as he will be away on 25th, the day he will finish his training period. He was so proud of telling me that he has got three stripes now, but sorry not to have been able to send me another picture as he didn't see the photographer again. '*Goodbye love of my life. See you soon, your Francis.*' He wishes Patsy a happy birthday. Only one week and I will see him again.

Friday 24

I've received a telegram: '*Cannot come. Will write. Francis.*' I wonder why. I'd been so much looking forward to seeing him again now that it's two months since he left. Can't wait to hear the explanation.

April

Saturday 1

News at last. I've received a postcard from Inverness and a letter from Lossiemouth. He continues his training on another station in northern Scotland. I now know why he wasn't able to come to Liverpool. '*Of all the Frenchmen at Evanton only four were due to go on leave and I was one of them. Then this was countermanded: only two could go, and I still was one of them. But at the last minute there was a misunderstanding and your countrymen mixed up my name with another, and just as I was about to dash off, I was informed I wasn't going after all. I think I nearly choked at that moment. But I pulled myself together and since we were not due to leave until later, I had my revenge by going to Inverness for three days. That was the reason for sending the card. I'm not complaining, for I got to know the Scots a little more, and I must say my first impression was wrong, because they're much nicer than I thought, and just as pleasant as Liverpudlians in fact – and that's saying something.'* He's now condemned to stay two more months in the freezing cold of northern Scotland and in that little village of Lossiemouth. The only consolation is that they are served wine at meals! *'Goodbye sweetheart, hope to have better luck when this course is over. My usual regards to your family and Joan. Francis.'*

RAF Lossiemouth was home to 20 OTU (Operational Training Unit), whose mission was to train full crews minus the flight engineers.

Monday 3

I received a lovely little tartan purse that he found at Inverness. *'Good night, love of my life, before going to bed I'm sending off this short note with a humble purse. It's not worth much but I hope you will be pleased to receive it. It's a souvenir from Scotland and it'll even bring you luck. Please treasure it, and think of its sender who feels so lonely while he's so far away from his beloved Princess. Goodnight Barbara, dream of your Prince Charming, and try to imagine that he is a bit like me. Goodnight. Francis.'*

I am very touched. I wrote to thank him and posted a parcel to him.

Tuesday 4

It's done! Francis got his air gunner's certificate in the RAF. He says he's now both a French and English air gunner. He is very proud to wear a wing with the letters 'AG' on the left side of his chest. He often now flies, that's what he wanted. *'At long last I can see the moment when I can get even with the Boche for all the evil they have inflicted on France, and are still doing right now.'* He wants to know if I liked his little purse. *'I want my liege lady to be the proudest of all the damsels in Liverpool because she deserves it for being so very kind to a poor French airman who's all alone in this vast foreign land known as England.'* I can now imagine what Lossiemouth looks like. *'It's a fairly big market town nestling in a cove, and it's probably the wind coming in from the sea that makes it so freezing cold. But it's very neat and pretty, with lawns everywhere. All day long noisy flocks of crows and seagulls fly to and fro across*

the cloudy skies and their calls echo all around the neighbouring hills.
A bitter north wind blows in every day, which is not very pleasant for
visitors. [...] As for the locals, they're very nice but rather uncouth like
all Scottish people, and what with their old customs and country habits
they remind me of the peasants of our old French provinces.'

Saturday 8

He got my parcel. *'Since you're probably as pig-headed as I am, I know*
perfectly well that I'll be wasting my time if I tell you off again, so I'll
simply send my biggest 'mercis' *and promise I'll kiss you on New Year's*
Day – as you can see, I'm very generous, aren't I? Seriously, I do want to
thank you from the bottom of my heart and I'm quite embarrassed for I
can never be as kind to you as you are to me. Your Fanfan who thinks a
lot about his Princess.' He enclosed a stamp from Canada for Patsy.

Wednesday 12

His letter of 9th. He sometimes goes to a dance at Lossiemouth. Dances
seem to be even more terrible there than at Evanton and there are even
more people. His suitcase is starting to fall to bits. I must inquire about
finding another one for him. He will send me money. He sounds very
enthusiastic. *'It'll soon be springtime, the flowers in the meadows are*
blooming, and the little bear, as you call me, is in a warlike mood. Sadly,
I think of all the poor people in France who won't be enjoying a happy
Easter like me, and this puts a damper on my good spirits, but I hope it
won't take long now before those lousy Boche are driven out of 'la belle
France'. *When that day comes and if – God willing – I'm still alive, I feel*
I'll give the moon to anybody who wants it; but now whatever she may
say I'll kiss Mademoiselle Barbara, *I'll nibble her nose, I'll pull her hair,*
in a nutshell I'll torment her till she begs for mercy!'

I wrote to him. *Le Vicomte* left Liverpool. I think Joan broke his
heart!

Saturday 15

I heard Alice Delysia singing *J'attendrai* with much feeling, it was
exquisite. I thought of him very much. I saw *La Fin du Jour* at the
Philharmonic; I like French films very much.

J'attendrai: also sung by Rina Ketty and Jean Sablon.

La Fin du Jour (*The End of the Day*): a film directed by Julien Duvivier (1939).

Philharmonic: a concert hall in Liverpool where the Merseyside Film Institute
    also showed films.

Tuesday 18

I got a letter. F gave me a little French lesson because I had mistaken
'*oursin*' (sea urchin) with '*ourson*' (bear cub). '*In order to improve your
fluency in French you must learn that an* 'oursin' *is a shellfish, which
lives in the sea and clings to rocks, and just like a hedgehog its shell is
covered with spines – and I believe I am not like an urchin, unless you
were alluding to my hair!*' As for the suitcase I'll have to sort it out myself!
'*Oh! Yes, the suitcase! Well, it ought to be roughly 0.70 m long and 0.40 m
wide, which makes it 2ft 10 and 1ft 5 – or so I believe, for your measures
are so weird that I'm at a complete loss when it comes to converting them.
Oh! Why don't you use the metric system, so simple and convenient? But
never mind. You see, I need a case that's neither too big nor too small. I'm
relying on you to choose one, because in spite of all my sarcastic remarks
I know that I can trust you.*' He doesn't give any details about what he's
doing at the station, all that seems very confidential. I saw a red signature
at the end of his letter, probably the mail control. It is soon his birthday.
I found him a little cuddly dog, shaving cream and a book. I posted the
parcel.

Mail control: the censor.

Sunday 23

On the radio I listened to *Les Français parlent aux Français* and heard
French songs: *Voulez-vous danser Marquise?* by Charles Trenet,
L'Ombre s'enfuit and *Darling, Je Vous Aime Beaucoup*.

Les Français parlent aux Français: from '*Ici Londres! Les Français parlent aux
    Français…*' ('This is London! The French speaking to the French…'), the
    opening sentences of *Radio Londres* (Radio London), i.e. the daily broadcast
    from 1940 to 1944 from the BBC studios in London, under the supervision of
    Jacques Duchesne and his crew.

'Voulez-vous danser Marquise?': the first line of *La Polka du roi,* sung by Charles
   Trenet.

L'Ombre s'enfuit (also entitled *Tristesse*): sung by Tino Rossi and based on an étude
   by Chopin (in English: *So Deep Is the Night*).

Monday 24

Francis is 22 today. I hope he received my parcel on time.

Thursday 27

His letter of 23rd. The mail is irregular; he hasn't received any letter
from me for eight days and asks me if I liked his purse again. '*By the
way you'd better be nice to me because you're no longer dealing with
caporal-chef but sergent Uzay. [...] Tomorrow at exactly 5 pm I'll be
22 and that'll be one more reason for you to speak to me with all due
respect.*'

He enclosed two stamps from Algeria for Patsy's collection and a
message for his parents. I offered him to send it through the Red Cross
office of Liverpool.

News could be sent to prisoners of war but also to families in occupied
   countries.

Saturday 29

He wrote such lovely words to me on Thursday, he had just received
my parcel. '*Thank you so much for the parcel, Barbara, and above all, it
makes me so happy to see that you thought of me. It's a long time since
my hardened old heart has been so touched as it was today. Thank you
with all my heart, Princess, please believe me that, in spite of my rather
flippant exterior, I do really appreciate all your kindness to me, and I'm
a bit worried that I don't know how to repay you. However, I will keep
the shaving cream to remind me of you. And I shall take the little dog as
a mascot. He will be with me flying in the skies of England, and perhaps
later in those of Germany. I have already read half the book, and am
enjoying it very much. In spite of its amusing style, it's a vivid description
of the magnificent effort that the English, whose habits and customs
I make fun of, have made. The book also shows how they welcomed*

*people from all the countries occupied by the Boche who arrived here
without arms, without a roof, without family, with a single idea in mind
– to fight, to go on fighting, in the hope of one day putting the invaders
of their countries to flight –and that day won't be very far off, at least
I hope so. And if I live to be a hundred, I will tell my grandchildren, if
I have any, how one day, at a little gathering in Liverpool, I met a girl
who was called Barbara who, under a rather stiff exterior, hid a heart
of gold. Au revoir, Princess, and thank you again. Yours affectionately,
Francis, your bear cub.'*

And as for me, if I can bring him some affection and comfort before
what he can expect, I am glad. I'm aware he misses his family; it is
such a long time since he has seen them. We'll be looking for a new
suitcase when he comes to Liverpool; in the meantime he can still
cope with the old one. He lost his wallet with his identity card and the
photograph I had sent him at Evanton. I'll have to send him another
one.

I studied *La Mort du loup*. Our French lecturer gave a very interesting
lecture about Alfred de Vigny.

La Mort du loup: a poem from *Les Destinées*, by Alfred de Vigny (1864).

May

Tuesday 2
I received a second small Scottish handbag with bright red and green
tartan colours. It is lovely. I wrote him a little note to thank him during
the Psychology class.

Friday 5
His letter of 3rd. '*So the* Marseillais *are chatterboxes – you ought to
know*, Mademoiselle, *that if God has given us a tongue, it is for us to
use it, and above all to annoy little girls like you, so I shall lose no
opportunity to do so, given half a chance.*' He dares not give me a date
for his next leave for fear something should come up. I don't have much

time to write to him at the moment, I have a lot of work as my exams are approaching. I sent him another photograph of me and also postcards from Liverpool.

Monday 8

Patsy is going to a new school; she's a bit anxious and sad about leaving us. I think F likes her. Honoré went to the south of England; Joan is sad. Only fifty Frenchmen remain in West Kirby now. His letter of 5ᵗʰ. *'Well, you know, I wasn't able to do much for my birthday. A few of my friends and I got together and they drank to my health, but not too much. In our Air Force slang we call it a 'watering'.'* F remains very discreet about his activities on the station. *'I can't tell you much, but I am working hard at the moment; I can't tell you what I am doing, or 'the Lady with the Scissors' will perhaps be angry with me, given that at present she is very strict about it.'* He goes to dances three times a week; he finds Scottish waltzes less terrible than before, and says one gets used to everything. *'If anyone had told me that I would drink at least a litre of tea a day, I would never have believed it, but at Evanton, if there wasn't any tea at lunch I was the first to shriek like a stuck pig having its throat cut. This is a purely French expression.'* I didn't know that in France they call the Germans *'Globules'*. It's because they are as numerous as red blood cells!

'The Lady with the Scissors': the censor.

Saturday 13

He did receive my postcards and my photograph. *'This time, I promise you that I will look after it as the apple of my eye. I also got the picture postcards of Liverpool, which gave me great pleasure because they reminded me of the good times when I strolled through the streets of this dear old town with a girl-student, whom you know. I hope that I can do so again, and that you will soon be able to show off your 'little bear' in the streets of your native town.'* Nothing special at the station, for him it's the usual routine; he says he now works at night and sleeps during the day. He forgives me for not writing to him as much as I used to, and hopes I am not overworked. *'It is enough that you are thinking of me to make me happy. With the affectionate thoughts of your little bear. Say hello to all those I know, your parents and my four-legged friends.'*

Friday 19

A passage in his letter of 16th was cut out. I was able to see the work of 'the Lady with the Scissors' with my own eyes. Difficult to understand what he meant: *'Please forgive me for not having written for so long, but as I told you before, I am now working at night, and I sleep all day. So in the evening, when I wake up, I've only got enough time to go to... and later on, like an angel... (Hum! A rather dark angel). But today I made a great effort and got up at 3 pm, so I had time to send you this short letter.'* In Scotland spring is intermittent, lilacs are starting to bloom and the meadows are covered with daisies. He hopes his pal François will soon join him and they will fly together in the same crew. He again enclosed some stamps he got from his French and English comrades hoping that *'they will please the avid collector,* Mademoiselle *Patsy Rigby, the hockey champion'*. At the *British* I had heard a Frenchman saying about a girl that she had *'le cerveau en chaise longue'*. F explained what it meant. *'This is a sort of slang expression! Someone is said to have 'their brain in a chaise longue' when they are slow on the uptake; that is to say that they only grasp something five or six minutes after it has been explained.'* He has improved his English but he can't write properly yet. *'You wanted me to write a phrase in English in each of my letters: Well! My Princess, I am going to tride, but I don't know if you can understand me. The English ise terrible language and I think all peoples must speak French. Now I must closed my letter here because I don't want to give you the opportunity to make fun of me.'*

'*Le cerveau en chaise longue*': literally 'her brain was (at rest) in a *chaise longue*'. The final passage is left as written by Francis in his shaky English.

Monday 29

I've received a telegram: *'Coming Tuesday by train at 6 am. Francis.'* Will he really come this time? How I wish it could be true.

Tuesday 30

He called me from the *British*. Their training period at Lossiemouth is over now. He is thrilled to bits as they have a ten-day leave and he won't be going back to Scotland any longer. He came home: he seems more serious and is really sweet; I do like him.

Wednesday 31

Sheila also thinks he's very sweet. I went to university. F stayed at home to rest, and then came to fetch me. He looks older and much more serious than before. He talked about politics and their operations, which will soon be starting.

June

Thursday 1

F stayed at home while I was at university. Before leaving I gave him a translation to keep him busy and improve his English, a text from *David Copperfield*. He did very well. He worries a lot about his family. He has sent them another message through the Red Cross.

Friday 2

At the *British* we met Phyllis Pattimore who is engaged to his friend Henri. Both Henri and F were born in Marseilles and have known each other for several years. They were together in the FAF in Algeria. Pat is a very sweet girl. She lives in St Helens but comes from Jersey. Her family escaped just before the German invasion. Henri and Pat first met at the *British* like us. They really love each other now, they're even thinking of getting married soon. Hope the marriage comes off. Then we went for a walk in the park. Francis is as charming as ever and he always behaves like a gentleman.

Pat: Phyllis Joyce Pattimore. Pat worked at the censorship department of the Ministry of War in Liverpool. She was also, occasionally, a SOE (Special Operations Executive) courier. Before she met Henri Martin, her missions

had involved being parachuted into occupied Normandy at night to deliver
messages to the Resistance.

FAF: *Forces Aériennes Françaises*, i.e. French Air Force.

St Helens: a fairly large town near Liverpool.

Barbara and Francis used to walk in Calderstones Park.

Saturday 3

Ran some errands with F who caused a sensation with his uniform and
his dark, Mediterranean complexion. Thanks to his good looks and
charm, we were able to get some tomatoes. Went to the *British* and met
Maurice Bordier, one of his comrades. Sheila invited the three of us to
her place. We listened to records and had great fun. Back home, Francis
said: '*I'd like to kiss you.*' Our first kiss: very sweet and tender.

Maurice Bordier was a mid upper gunner in the crew of *capitaine* Stanislas (347
'Tunisie' Squadron).

Sunday 4

F went to Mass. This afternoon he gave me an FAF button. He says it
represents '*the star that guides us, the wings we fly with, and the crown
which awaits us*'. All his crew are also staying with English families
while they're on leave. From now on we've decided to say '*tu*' to each
other. He says he loves me. He helped me to wash my hair; we had a
good laugh. Went to see Gran who gave me 10 shillings.

In French, '*tu*' is more familiar and colloquial than '*vous*'.

Monday 5

F met me at the university. We walked to Pier Head. After supper we
went for another long walk and he sang a sweet little song, *Je suis seule
ce soir*.

Je suis seule ce soir: sung by Léo Marjane.

Tuesday 6

We were doing the washing up when we heard the news on the radio:

the D-Day landings have started in Normandy! F was terribly pleased but a little sad too. I haven't worked much today. He met me at the university again. At home we drank a toast to the invasion. F and I have agreed on a little ruse so I may know when he has started to fly on operations. He will write: '*I've been to town for the first time.*' I do so wish his mother could know we're taking good care of him and he has all our affection. He repeated a number of times that he loves me, even if he thinks it is hopeless.

On the night of 5/6 June 1944 eleven crews (out of the thirteen that took off) of 346 'Guyenne' Squadron, based at RAF Elvington, took part in the operations for the D-Day landings by bombing a German heavy artillery battery at Grandcamp-Maisy (Calvados).

Wednesday 7

Francis met me at the university. At the *British* we met Pat again. We then took the ferry across the Mersey to Seacombe. F found it looked a bit like Marseilles. We saw the *Louis Pasteur*. He said he wished his leave could last longer because he loves me passionately and never wants to leave me. He was so gentle when he kissed me.

The SS *Pasteur:* French liner launched in 1938, requisitioned in September 1939, then seized by the British in August 1940. She was then given to the British Cunard-White Star Line and converted into a troopship from 1942. Liverpool became her new home port. She was returned to her French owners in early 1946.

Thursday 8

We visited the cathedral, and then walked to Pier Head. F was sad, since this was his last day. We played records, and he didn't talk much. He said his leave was wonderful and he loves me but thinks it is hopeless. I'm sure I am not worthy of his love. He laid his poor head on my bosom and said he wanted to be cradled like a child.

Friday 9

F packed his things in the new case Uncle Max gave him. He was very quiet and sad. We went to Exchange station where we met Maurice Bordier. F gave me his mother's address so that I should write to her in case something happened to him. His heart seemed full of tears. We kissed without a word. I said to Maurice: 'Take care of him!' The train left; F looked so miserable. Oh! my poor darling, may your mother know one day how happy you were here. I feel weary but I'm pleased to have made you happy somewhat, at least I think so.

Monday 12

He wrote to me as soon as he arrived at the camp at Acaster Malbis, near York. The full crew is now together, including the pilot, *sergent* Jacques Leclercq. '*Bébé, Barbiche or Barbara, choose whichever name pleases you. [...] I had a strange feeling when the time came to leave: although my face was wearing a smile, I felt as if my heart and soul were staying with you and my mind was a great blank. [...] Now I shall have to resume my life as an airman and forget those few days when I was so perfectly happy. By the way say 'Thank you' to your parents once again because I can never thank them enough, but don't worry, I think it'll be another month before I go to town for the first time.*' He thought of me at 2.30 pm whilst I was having my German exam: we'll see if it brought me luck. '*Give a kiss to your grandmother and Mummy and Daddy, and tell your uncle I literally swelled with pride in York station because everyone was gaping at my suitcase. [...] If you assemble all the letters I've underlined, you'll read something that'll make you say: 'Oh! He is off again!'*'

I found the enigma: '*I love you less than tomorrow, more than yesterday and each day more.*' I wrote to him and sent him a parcel.

Formation of the crew (347 'Tunisie' squadron): *sergent* Leclercq, pilot; *lieutenant* Cottard, navigator and captain; *adjudant* Adaoust, bomb aimer; *sergent-chef* Morel, wireless operator; *sergent* Dufaure, flight engineer; *sergent* Usai, mid upper gunner; *sergent chef* Aubiet, rear gunner.

Jacques Leclercq joined the FAFL (*Forces Aériennes Françaises Libres*, i.e. Free French Air Forces) on 26 December 1941, aged 17. He started his training at RAF Camberley and then trained as a pilot in Canada until October 1943, before coming back to complete his training in Great Britain.

Wednesday 14

I miss Francis. I realize how much his absence makes me feel melancholy, he is always so gay. His black thoughts never last very long. I feel lonely without him. I didn't believe straight away that his love was sincere, but now I'm sure it is. It really is terrible because there is no hope. Mrs Dick likes Francis; she tried to cheer me up yesterday at the canteen, saying I would see him again soon. I received a letter. On Saturday afternoon he had gone to York where he met Canadians and Frenchmen. They spent all night together. He also met François in the city's most famous ballroom. He says York is a nice old city with a beautiful cathedral. Henri had gone off to meet Pat on the day F arrived at Acaster, and he has just arrived back. He says hello and hopes to see me, and so does Pat.

Mrs Dick: a lady at the canteen of the YMCA at Lime Street station where Barbara served food and drink to servicemen from midday to 5 pm every Tuesday for her national service.
De Grey Rooms: a dance hall in York.

Saturday 17

His letter of 15ᵗʰ. He seems so cheerful and relaxed. He has moved to yet another station. He's now at RAF Rufforth, again near York. During the day they are given classes and lectures. They are allowed to go out in the evenings but he arrives in town too late to phone me. They even seem to be having a great time. *'Great excitement last Tuesday: a telegram from Pat told us she'd be arriving at 8 that very evening. So at 5 we started looking for a hotel room for her and another also for the two of us. After making enquiries at about fifteen hotels, we were exhausted and reeling as if we were drunk, but managed to find one. Pat arrived at 8, we dined at the Grand Hotel near the station, and I nearly fainted when I saw the bill. Afterwards, as might well be expected, went to a dance-hall where I was a good boy because I was too afraid you might meet Pat and learn that I hadn't behaved myself. We went to bed at 2 am, got up at 7, and lorded it by riding back to the camp in a taxi, just as the lectures were about to start. I didn't learn anything that day because I was half asleep all the time, much to the shock of the instructors, who glared at me but failed to keep me awake. On Wednesday evening, went back to York and met Pat again, then went dancing again, too, in spite of the three of us being dog tired. [...] Then, since Pat was due to leave at 11, we went to the station, stayed in the waiting room until 3 and when we woke up the people were slightly amazed and stared at us because we had all slumped together and fallen asleep one on top of the other so you couldn't tell which arms or legs belonged to whom. Well, we got back this morning, dead-tired this time, and after having listened to those horrible lectures for six hours on end, just when we thought we could get some rest, we've just learnt we've got to pack our kit bags because we're due to leave tomorrow morning. [...] Goodnight Barbiche, have pleasant dreams, I've finished my diary (but he only wrote ten pages!) and I think it'll take you a whole day to read it. Kisses to Mummy, Daddy, and grandmother, and a vigorous (and oh! so very English) handshake to Uncle Max. Kind regards to Nelly. Don't forget to shake paws with my friends Sabu and Globule. Goodnight and mind you don't have nightmares just by looking at my photo. My sad and forlorn heart does so want to find comfort with your arms round me. Your Cis. Your crazy Cis.'* At the railway station he gave Pat a book for me.

HCU (Heavy Conversion Unit) at RAF Rufforth: conversion of the full complement of crews on to four-engined Handley Page Halifax bombers. Another training period started there.

Sunday 18
I heard Lord Vansittart of the Foreign Office appealing for donations to the AVF and asking British families to play host to 'these boys' when they're on leave.

Wednesday 21
His letter of 18th. *'Life here is as regular as clockwork, and you may not believe me but I haven't been out of the camp since I last wrote. And I also have to get up at all hours – 7 am! Do you realize how I suffer like a martyr? This is not due to strict discipline, but only because*

it's rather a long trek to the mess and at 8 the cruel Waafs refuse to serve the poor airmen who arrive late.' He doesn't seem to be much interested in the lectures at the station *'after those eight days in heaven'* that he spent with me. *'The usual regards to your family, my student friends and the Menagerie. Goodnight Mrs Noah, Mr Noah sends you a kiss.'* I also received a very nice letter from Pat with the book Francis handed over at the railway station. He signed it with these words: *'To Barbiche, my Princess with eyes like the moon. Francis.'* Pat says he never stops talking about me to Henri. I got three razor blades for him yesterday!

Saturday 24

At 11.20 last night, someone knocked at the door; it was him! He had not told us and was a bit embarrassed at arriving so late. He said he had a thirty-six-hour leave and had come by train with Henri and Maurice. It was such a wonderful surprise. I made his bed in a hurry. This morning he came downstairs, singing a Tino Rossi song, holding his old cutthroat razor, with his dark face covered in white shaving cream. Mummy, Nelly and I roared with laughter. In the kitchen he imitated Mummy and pretended he was speaking on the radio, holding a spoon as if it were a microphone. He asked her very seriously: *'What's a love of bread?'* and we doubled up with laughter. He often tells Marius jokes and keeps saying: *'Peuchère'*, *'Horreur et putréfaction'*, *'Mektoub'* or *'Inch' Allah'*. He loves teasing me and often says: *'Bébé, how silly you are!'* We tried to listen to Radio Toulouse but it didn't work. I lent him *Les Fleurs du mal*. We went to say hello to Gran; she was really glad to see him again. We had a walk in the park. There was a thunderstorm, we sheltered under a tree. He was so sweet and tender as usual. He kept saying silly things with a Montmartre accent. He also told me about his family. His father is a Socialist and a trade unionist. F was spoilt by his grandmother. He was keen on cowboy movies when he was in France. While trying to kiss me he burnt my finger with his cigarette and also bit my lips unintentionally. He was so sorry and so painfully embarrassed. A little later we visited our neighbour Beryl Lunn whose brother has just been killed in Burma. F loved her little daughter Elizabeth, who gave him flowers from the garden. He'll soon be taking part in 'leaflet raids' over France and in a fortnight he'll be flying his first operational sorties. May God protect him! I'm so scared death might be his fate, though he loves life so much. Tonight we had supper and played records; then he had to go and catch the train. He looked so sad and miserable.

'*Peuchère*': in the Provence region, an interjection used to show compassion, the equivalent of 'Poor thing!'. '*Horreur et putréfaction*': 'Horror and putrefaction' (instead of 'Horror and stupefaction' – yet another of Francis' puns). '*Mektoub*': 'it is all written'. '*Inch'Allah*': 'God willing!'

Les Fleurs du mal: a collection of poems by Charles Baudelaire (1857).

Sunday 25

I have passed my exams! So have Sheila and Joan. Pat Moore's failed. I immediately wrote to F and told him the good news. He was afraid he might have distracted me and prevented me from working when he came in early June. I sent him photographs of us which we took in the park with *Globule*.

Wednesday 28

He wrote me a wonderful letter just before going to bed. He slept throughout the journey, so he didn't even hear Henri getting on the train at Warrington station; they arrived at York at 4 am and then jumped into a taxi. '*I haven't much to say about my trip back, since it can be summed up in two words: sadness and sleep. It was a vague and somewhat uneasy sadness, or to put it in a nutshell, a very confused sort, mixed with regret for having left behind people I am fond of, for not having uttered all the words I had repeated to myself so many times before arriving, and for having left the arms of the loved one who knows so well how to soothe me. On oh! so many days that count for ages, I also wished I could see, and not just think of, the one being for whom my heart beats so fast and her wide eyes in turn so gentle, so joyful or so angry. And above all this, there was the overwhelming wish to get some sleep, to live apart from this earthly planet, for only sleep can provide oblivion and is full of dreams that allow you to forget the ugliness, the ordeals and disappointments of the chaotic, topsy-turvy world that we're living in right now. [...] I love you but wish never to see you again, for one day of bliss is followed by endless suffering that reminds me that my hopeless love is a dead-end. I love you and wish that I could let the whole world know; wish I could also tell the swallows, the trees in the park, the sun and the moon. [...] But today I feel strong, and will confess all, by telling you about the hurt inside when I have to leave, the incredible bliss when I'm back at your side, and the delightful emotion when I can almost feel you quiver beside me and feel your heart beat in unison with mine.'* I feel so sad.

Thursday 29

I've read that letter again and again since yesterday and I cried. I think he wrote it because he will soon be flying his first missions and might never be able to write again. How I wish he'll escape with his life! I received another little note with two songs he had forgotten to send me. One was *Lili Marleen*. He dreamt the Boche had taken him prisoner.

I went to buy some bread this morning. The baker's wife asked after him. She said he was a nice boy, and very funny too. It was this woman whom he asked for '*a love of bread*' when Mummy sent him out for some errands the other day!

Lili Marleen: sung by Lale Andersen and also Marlene Dietrich.

July

Saturday 1

His letter of 29th. He hasn't received mine yet, probably due to his changes of address in quick succession. He worries about the effect his last letter may have had on me and fears I found it too sentimental. It was just marvellous! It rains every day and the camp has turned into a real sea of mud. He gets bored. He thinks he will go on his first mission next week. I'm so sad for him.

Monday 3

He wrote to me on Saturday just before going to sleep; they had landed a short time before. '*Sweet friend with eyes like the moon, today I received your two letters and all at once the sun seemed brighter, the sky clearer and the young Waafs' smiles more enchanting. [...] I do wish that you who have done your utmost to make me happy and soften my life here, you whom I want to see smiling all the time, should not be bothered or troubled by the ranting of a young idiot who cannot hide his feelings when he is in low spirits. [...] I roam the skies of Yorkshire, thinking of another sky where I wish I could be. The invasion seems to be holding, the Boche are beaten more and more, and I hope that soon I'll be able to invite you to my home so you can taste our famous aioli!'* He congratulated me on my exams. He liked *Les Fleurs du mal*. At the end of his letter he drew a face, mine I suppose, with a moustache and a small beard (*une barbiche*)!

Monday 10

He wrote to me on Saturday from the mess bar at 7 am once back from a flight. *'This is a very spacious room, well-lit, well-ventilated, with big armchairs (ideal for lazy me) and a big table in the middle with a bunch of flowers on it; the young Waafs on duty regularly look after these flowers. Then there is a piano, and in the back of the room, where all the airmen's eyes eventually turn, there is the bar, that place where peace, dreams and pleasure, in the form of cigarettes, wine, beer, and other more or less noxious beverages, are provided.'* He still hasn't been 'to town' and can't wait. On Friday, after a training flight I suppose, they set off to the village inn. *'The whole crew went on a commando raid. We started off on our bicycles along the rather pretty road leading to the nearest village and there, to the great astonishment of the villagers amazed at our shouts and laughter, we invaded the public bar, or rather the very nice, well-kept inn, built and decorated in a fairly old-fashioned style. The beer was good, Jacques played old French songs on the piano, and so in short we spent a very pleasant afternoon, in a truly delightful atmosphere of comradeship and friendship.'* He doesn't know yet if he'll be able to come to Liverpool on 14th July for the big AVF party. I'm pleased he likes my idea of a date. *'Nine o'clock is fine with me, and I shall be starting this very evening. It really is a lovely idea you had and I send you my sweetest thanks for that. There's a little word that I liked at the end of your letter, all the more so since it's the first time you have addressed it to me, you know, the one starting with a capital 'C' and ending with a small 'i' – I couldn't believe my eyes when I read it!'*

It's true, it is the first time I've called him '*Chéri*'.

Chéri: darling.

Thursday 13

I got a letter. On Tuesday he flew above Liverpool. '*I am now back after spending six hours in the air and I flew over Liverpool, but we were too high above the city to distinguish anything. Just the same, it came as a sort of shock to realize that a brief jump with my parachute was all I needed to drop in and say 'Hello'! I even smiled to myself while imagining the scene: imagine an unshaven man in his flying suit, dragging along his parachute and knocking at the door of No.2 Gwydrin Road. I wonder if Globule could have recognized me.*' He still didn't know if he could come tomorrow.

Friday 14

Francis couldn't come for the *14 Juillet* party, what a pity! There was a big reception at the AVF with a crowd of sailors with their red pompoms. I talked to André Boucher, a Breton who was torpedoed in the Gulf of Mexico. He's married and has a little 5-year-old boy who was two months the last time he saw him. He studied mathematics at *La Sorbonne*. All the French hope to be back home for the next National Day. I sent F a little flag and a tricolour pompom.

14 Juillet (14 July): National Day in France.
La Sorbonne: famous University of Paris, founded in the middle of the 12th century.

Monday 17

The phone rang. When I got on the line, I really was afraid that something had happened to him. He was ringing to let me know he's arriving tomorrow. He said he was supposed to go on a sortie today. I think Henri will take part in the mission too. Can't wait for tomorrow!

Tuesday 18

He turned up at about 1.15 pm. The mission had turned out well. He even brought some sweets he hadn't eaten. He'll soon be going to RAF Elvington, which is in the same area near York. It will be their permanent station now. He said he had waited four years for the liberation of France. I broke the record *Pigeon vole* that I liked so much! F looked very sad. I hope it isn't a bad omen. We visited the crèche where I am going to do war work for a month; I start on Sunday. He found it quite funny to see me surrounded by children. This evening, we walked in the park with *Globule*. F held my hand; he hugged me very tight in his arms and we kissed. He is so much in love; I'm afraid of disappointing him.

Pigeon vole: sung by Charles Trenet.

Wednesday 19

Francis dug up potatoes from the garden: Mummy was delighted. He finds the English are very nice people but their lifestyle is terribly boring! He says it does him good to come to our house because it is calm and quiet. At the railway station he told me I was an angel and he could never thank me enough. I also was told it was not the role of a woman (not a *bébé* this time!) to make declarations of love, but I never made any. We promised to think of each other every night at 9 as we have already started to do. On the platform he looked awfully miserable; his eyes were full of sadness. I couldn't help but cry, thinking we might never see each other again. I'm sure that was also on his mind.

Thursday 20

I feel a bit upset. Time is so short and precious that you must do everything you can and never say anything you might regret. I must learn to control my emotions. He said he's always upset and feels helpless when he sees a woman crying. When I cried at home he imitated Serge Lifar to make me laugh. I wrote to him.

Serge Lifar: French ballet dancer from Russia.

Saturday 22

His letter of 20th. Another address again; when he had just got back to the camp on Wednesday, he had to jump into a military truck which took them to Elvington station. I probably won't be seeing him again until our holidays at Kirkby Thore. '*Now, my darling little girl, I don't think I'll be able to see you until my next leave. This will be a six-day leave, but by then you'll most probably be on holiday in the town with such a strange name. I will travel across England, however, for in spite of my rather long stay here, I know practically nothing of your country. And I can assure you that I'll be coming your way. [...] I also had a strange feeling during the day I spent with you, especially in the evening when we went for a walk with dear* Globule *as our chaperon. I felt how much I really loved you, but you seemed totally beyond my reach and more unattainable than ever before. It's strange but there are times when I feel that you are willing to show something of your real self, something that lies deep down in your heart, something that you keep to yourself; sometimes I even believe that you are on the point of weeping, but no, you don't: you just make a little moue, wrinkle your little nose and become your usual self, the Barbara that intrigued me so much right from the very start. In such moments I have a mad desire to hold you and crush you in my arms, such a strong and overpowering wish to be able to protect the fragile being that you have shown yourself to be, and then two minutes later this feeling is all gone, and I'm more stupid and awkward than ever before when I try to find some diversion by telling you in a pompous tone about the big issues in life.*' He has decided to adopt a slightly different lifestyle, not to please me but in order to be up to his job. '*I'm just a small part in the great machinery of war, but if I make just one single mistake because I have overindulged in this or that, I may cause the deaths of six of my comrades. And after all there are far more interesting things to do than go dancing, run after flighty girls, or indulge in drinking or any other of those things that are nowadays called 'the pleasures of life'. On this station there is a splendid library that's looked after by our padre and I'm sure it'll more than satisfy my needs whenever I'm bored or looking for distraction.*' He also reads English books now and has made great progress: '*I was walking* *yesterday from York to Rufforth but my feet are so tired that I can hardly bear to wear shoes. It would be marvellous to be one of the Natives of South Africa, for then I could go out without anything on my feet!* Phew! Hope you can understand this gibberish. I'll leave you here, Bébé darling. But I'll write to you again tomorrow, since I'm so glad to be able to speak to you even by means of a humble letter.'*

On 15 May 1944, the first 346 'Guyenne' Squadron crews had arrived at RAF Elvington (six miles from York), followed, a month later, by 347 'Tunisie' Squadron. The station, commanded by a French Air Force group captain, colonel Bailly, was part of Station 42, 4 Group RAF Bomber Command. Until October 1945, it was almost exclusively operated by some 2,300 Frenchmen, including air and ground crew. After arriving there on 20 July, Francis and his crew kept on training, night and day, for another two weeks.

Kirkby Thore: a village in the Lake District (Cumbria).

* This passage was written in English by Francis.

Sunday 23

Patsy is now home for the holidays. I started my job at the crèche. I hope everything will go well. I have to look after about fifteen children. I shall have to feed, bathe and dress them, and play with them as well and take them out. I saw *Marthe Richard au service de la France*. I sent Francis the cinema programme and also a road guide, which will help him if he comes to see me at Kirkby.

Marthe Richard au service de la France: a film directed by Raymond Bernard (1937).

Thursday 27

His letter of Tuesday. He wrote to me at about 9 pm. It was raining and he was not going on a sortie. *'At the very moment when I'm writing this, my heart missed a beat, as I realized that this is the time when you are thinking of me and it gives me much comfort. What are you doing right now, distant angel? Are you in your bedroom wearing that long, flowery dressing gown of yours, the one that gives you the look of a Chinese mandarin, and are you thinking of that rascal called Francis? Or are you in the dining-room in deep conversation with Mummy, or perhaps in the park walking* Globule, *thinking with some relief – but also with some regret, I hope – that I'm not with you to either give you a sudden, passionate kiss, or launch into a long dissertation on the origins and species of the trees around us, or on the love affair between Napoleon and Maria Walewska? As far as I am concerned, I can see the walls of my room and the photo of the queen of Iran that you sent me; the suitcase that I'm using to write also comes from you; the pen with which I'm writing on this paper is a present from my Bébé, and even the ink that's committing all my thoughts to this very paper I also owe to Barbiche! How could you expect that all this… what I mean is that with all this before my very eyes, added to all the feelings that jostle in my poor heart, how can you expect me to forget you one single minute? Even if I wished to, I simply couldn't.'* He regrets that François is not in his crew and says *le Vicomte* still hasn't recognized him. Elvington is farther away from York than his previous camp but they have better meals since the food is cooked the French way and they are served wine every day! He says the station is entirely French and the only two WAAFs are in fact French officers. He has already done three sorties. May God protect him! *'If I told you anything more it might excite the 'Lady with the big scissors', and as you know, she uses them not only to cut the letters of NCOs who can't hold their tongue, but also to snip the stripes on their sleeves, which is not so funny.'* He doesn't expect to have any leave before 5th or 6th September, so I will be back in Liverpool at that time.

The queen of Iran: Princess Soraya.
There was actually only one WAAF at RAF Elvington: *sous-lieutenant* Plunkett, a French woman married to a British officer. She was deputy intelligence officer.

Friday 28
'From Planet Mars, 26/7/44, Hullo Barbiche!' His letter is rather short as he was due to go on a sortie. I hope everything turned out well. He

knows the exact date of his next leave; it'll be on 25th August, the day we're going on holiday. We'll find a solution. He sent me a photograph of him taken in France – he's in his swimming trunks, and looks like Tarzan! – and also a message on behalf of his wireless operator. He doesn't want to send any more to his family for fear that it should cause them problems. '*A thousand kisses to great, fabulous, gentle, sweet Barbichette. From your mad bear cub Francis – called Cis by all close friends and ladies.*'

Let's hope he came back safe! I wrote to him.

Saturday 29

Daddy's birthday. On the radio I heard General Valin, commanding the FAF in England. I had nightmares last night and have dark thoughts.

General Valin: in command of the FAFL (*Forces Aériennes Françaises Libres*, i.e. Free French Air Force) from July 1941 to July 1943, then of the new FAF (French Air Force) stationed in Great Britain, after the FAFL and the FAF in North Africa merged on 1 August 1943.

Monday 31

His letter of 29th. They had to land in Sussex when returning from their sortie last Wednesday. They spent three days there before they were able to get back to Elvington. '*Do you remember that in my last letter I told you I planned to go out for… a drive. On the way back our car (!) broke down, so we had to stop near London, more precisely at Ford, in Sussex.*' F and Jacques made the most of it and went to London. They spent one night in a hotel, had scrumptious macaroni in a French restaurant, then went dancing in a club. There were air-raid warnings but they didn't hear any explosion. The day after, they went down to the coast and visited Brighton and Littlehampton. I believe they had a very good time after all.

RAF Ford, in West Sussex: formerly RNAS (Royal Naval Air Station). HMS *Peregrine* converted back to RAF use in 1940, following a major attack by the Luftwaffe during the Battle of Britain.

August

Thursday 3

Despite my apprehension, all goes well at the crèche until now and I find the children more interesting than I had imagined and so endearing. I'm pleased Cis takes an interest in that. He likes children very much.

His letter of 1st. With Jacques they went to see *Hamlet* in York. They also contemplate buying a car which costs £75. He hasn't gone on a new mission since they returned from Sussex; he reads and rests. He wrote to me from the mess. Henri was beside him writing to Pat. '*Thanks to your little flag I was able to take revenge, because when he arrived back from Liverpool and showed me his own flag he looked blissfully happy, but now we're even.*' It's funny, whilst he was writing to me, the mess band was playing *Amor, Amor*, the same tune I heard on the radio whilst I was also writing to him. He thinks happiness is worth it only if we have suffered before. '*Darling, I feel so light-hearted and carefree this evening. I want to say crazy things and tell you 'I love you' thousands of times in every possible language, then go and dance some frenzied African dance on top of the mess table. [...] It seems to me that everything is beautiful, that the world is kind, that men are at last behaving like human beings, that women deserve paradise and that the little photo I keep next to my heart is going to smile and say: 'Come into my arms, darling!' [...] I don't always see things that way, and wonder what I'd do if I didn't know you, for whether it's out of pain or for joy, expressing one's feelings is always soothing for poor human beings like us. [...] Life is a perpetual race whose goal is forever changing, and what ultimately happens? We return to the ashes and dust we ought never to have left. Everything is more elusive even than smoke, and just when you think happiness is within your reach, it flies away like a bird, and the wheel of fate starts turning round once more until you think you have found happiness again. [...] But keep smiling in all circumstances, Bébé, even when you are in a sombre mood, for it'll keep your friends and family happy, and maybe life will be kind to you – that's my dearest wish. Good night sweetheart, I'll be thinking of you at 9 as I do every evening, and tonight my thoughts will be sweet. Keep your beautiful soul untroubled, and please keep me in your thoughts.*' A cigarette ash made a hole on a page of his letter; he says it will remind me of a certain time when he burnt my little finger! I wrote to him.

Amor, Amor: sung by Tino Rossi.

Monday 7

I received two letters of 4th. He first wrote me a little note at 2 am, just before going to bed back from a sortie. It seems '*it's getting more and more interesting*'. He sent me chocolate and tells me to enjoy it, for it went the same way as the sweets he had brought me to Liverpool. He wrote me the second letter as soon as he woke up. '*Don't be too cross about the time I spend on you, I think you ought to know that I'm fully capable of writing six or eight pages of nonsense in less than twenty minutes.*' He gave me some other details about the night he spent in London with Jacques. '*In London I never went to a shelter, and no-one did in fact. However I saw quite a few poor women together with elderly people and babies sleeping in the Underground, and felt both great pity for them and at the same time increasing hatred for the Boche, even though I already hated them so much. At any rate the end is very near for them and they'll have to pay dearly for all the evil they have inflicted on both our countries, without mentioning all the others.*' He thinks Henri and Pat's wedding is due at end of October or early November. They sent her a card for her birthday.

Until 3 August, Francis' crew had only flown on training missions. Their operational missions started on 5 August 1944.

5 and 6 August: attack on a V2 flying-bomb launch site in the Forest of Nieppe (Hazebrouck) in Flanders.

7 August: attack on concentration of troops at May-sur-Orne, in the Caen-Falaise area.

Tuesday 8

Met Pat with her mother in town; they were choosing dresses. Mrs Pattimore has a broken accent; she is French. Pat invited me to the wedding. They have already made the cake. She says Henri is more serious than Francis and not so dark. Got a letter from Pat Moore, she's been in the ATS in York for a month. F may meet her one of these days.

ATS: Auxiliary Territorial Service. The students who failed their exams were not allowed to stay at university, and had to do full-time war work.

Wednesday 9

Antoine de Saint Exupéry reported missing.

Antoine de Saint Exupéry: French writer, poet and airman, who went missing over the Mediterranean on his last reconnaissance mission (31 July 1944).

Thursday 10

His letter of Tuesday. '*Sweetheart, [...] it's easier for Henry to travel to Liverpool than it is for me, because he's not yet caught up in the war machine and is therefore free to go wherever he wishes. He plans to get married around September 15th and he and Pat are adamant that you go and see them on that day, even if you don't go to the ceremony.*' There was a sultry heat at Elvington, a storm was threatening and everybody was dozing in the room. They had gone to bed at 3 am and were supposed to go out again at night.

8 August: attack on a VI flying-bomb launch site at Fromentel (Boulogne). *Lieutenant* Balas' Halifax (347 'Tunisie' Squadron) was shot down; all seven crew members were killed.

Francis always referred to Henri as 'Henry', so the reader will find two different spellings in the text.

Friday 11

They eventually only went out the day after and even then had to get back because the weather was too bad. Nostradamus did his first journey. It's a little cuddly-toy rabbit that Francis bought for the crew's mascot. I had never heard of that name. It seems to be the name of a famous astrologer from Provence in the 16th century who made predictions. Let's hope it brings them luck! They were taught some German words in case of necessity but he hopes never to have to use them. He's also aware that we'll have to part one day although we don't want to think about that. '*Yes, our love inevitably leads to our parting, but maybe that's the reason why it is so strong, and darling, whatever happens, you will always stay in my heart; in any situation whatsoever my thoughts will be with you and my sweetest words of love will be for you, since this is the most I can give you now that I know you.* [...] *Right now I'm on my own and yet you're here with me, you inhabit my thoughts and the air that I breathe, you're in the light that shines in through the windows, you're everywhere, in all that I see, and this is the way it shall be for as long as I live. With all my heart and soul I wish I could be with you, I love you and know that I shall lose you, but better than anybody else ever could, I'll be loving you forever.*' I hate the sun because I know the risks are even bigger when they fly in good weather. '*No, don't hate the sun*, Bébé, *we have a task to accomplish, and faced with this all other thoughts must take second place; even without it, nothing would be different, only our working conditions would be a little harsher. Remember that each day thousands of young men peer at the sky to see if they'll have the opportunity to strike once more at the Boche.*' He won't have leave before a month, in other words ages.

II August: attack on marshalling yards at Somain, near Douai. '*G for George*' hit
   by flak.

Saturday 12

F is really sentimental; he wrote me a long declaration of love again, rather funny and cheerful this time. He sent me *La Chèvre de M. Seguin*, a book by Alphonse Daudet that he found in a bookshop at York and that he had told me about when he came last time. At the end there is a little sentence in *Provençal*: '*e piè lou matin, lou loup la mangé*' with the translation in French: 'And then in the morning the wolf ate her up.' Henri must have done his first 'sortie to town' on 10th or 11th. Francis says Pat's worries are only just beginning. And what about me? I know that terrible anguish already. Jacques and F are inseparable and seem to have the same passion for books. '*At the mess a legend is being born about these two fellows – one a giant of a man and the other so small – and about how both of them always carry a book under one arm, and hardly speak to anybody apart from the barman when they order beer and cigarettes in a distant voice.'* They intend to go and see the car they want to buy again, a two-seater black Morris. Meanwhile he bought a bicycle!

La Chèvre de M. Seguin: one of the short stories of *Les Lettres de mon moulin* (1869), by Alphonse Daudet, who was from Provence like Francis.

Monday 14

His letter of 11th. Henri and he went to see the station chaplain who promised to do what needs to be done for the wedding. It sounds as if we'll both be their children's godfather and godmother. They flew on the same sortie on Friday. He seems tired, his ideas are a bit confused as the sorties come one after another and often by night. '*My life is now totally unsettled, and it's almost as if I didn't know whether it's daytime or night time; so I assure you I need to think twice before I can put a date on my letters whenever I set about writing. But I know that you will understand this without even explaining, so there's no need to dwell on the matter really.*' On the radio I heard General Leclerc, F's hero, who sounded very optimistic. I offered Pat to ask Marjorie to lend her her wedding dress.

Leclerc: *nom de guerre* of Philippe François Marie de Hauteclocque in the Free French Forces, one of the most prominent military commanders in those forces during World War II. He was in command of the famous 2e *DB* (2nd armoured division) which was sent to Normandy in August 1944 and liberated Paris on the 25th.
Marjorie Wilson: a friend of the family who married in July 1939.

Tuesday 15

At 12.30 pm they announced on the wireless the invasion of the *Midi* between Nice and Marseilles. Dear Cis, how happy and proud he will be! I sent him a telegram saying how overjoyed I am. I asked him to try to telephone me at 9 pm. At the canteen I met a French merchant seaman who was from Arles. He was astonished hearing I was allowed to go out by myself! Apparently they don't have the same customs in his native city!

Thursday 17

His letter is ecstatic. '*From 'Seventh Heaven', August 15th 1944, My Love. First of all I must give you the news – that's it, my darling Princess, My 'everything': my native city is about to be liberated, so it will again bask freely in the sunlight;* Notre Dame de la Garde, *from the top of her hill, will again be blessing the free ships that sail into the old Phoenician port, the* vieux port *will again see its small pleasure boats which, for 5 or 10 francs offer wonderful, magical trips within sight of the coastal road and to the* Château d'If, *and* Massilia *will again be the peaceful gateway to the East and Africa. I wish I could cover your beloved face with wild kisses, dance with you in a wild circle – in fact anything wild would do. [...] I heard the news this morning and when I walked into our room I just couldn't help whooping with joy and ruffling Jacques' hair; the tall man was totally stunned! Then I started some horseplay with our all-too-serious bomb aimer and tickled the feet of our wireless operator, then asleep. And two hours later the six bachelors were seen again around a table in York, celebrating this happy event. [...] Please send my regards to* papa *(known to all the ladies as* Riri*), to your Uncle (the very epitome of elegance), to Mummy (who makes such good desserts), to Gran (with a good old-fashioned, 1870s style bow), without forgetting a grandson's resounding smack on Nelly's cheek (but please do ask her to keep quiet about it). Oh, sorry! I almost forgot Miss Chewing-Gum (so as to appease her, tell her I'll try and get her some for my next leave). For the Menagerie, let me stroke Sabu so he'll keep purring and Globule will growl. As for you my darling, words fail me to express what I feel, but tonight let me hold you tighter and kiss you more tenderly than usual. May your dreams be happy ones. With billions of kisses from your bear-cub Francis. 'J. t'a...' (I'll let you guess the meaning).*' He did a sortie on 14th. I received a nice letter from Pat who is overwhelmed with gratitude about the dress but she doesn't want it. Very warm invitation to the wedding.

Riri: nickname of Henry, Barbara's father.

14 August: attack on concentration of troops north of Falaise (Operation

Tractable: last offensive by the Canadian and Polish troops during the Battle of Normandy).

16 August: raid on Kiel, North Germany.

Saturday 19

Cis was very pleased with my telegram. '*Dear little pet, [...] I couldn't give you a ring because here, each time something's on – I'm sure you know what I mean – that's to say almost every day, the telephone is disconnected in order to prevent young French (and English) blabbermouths from revealing the RAF's big secrets to their girl-friends in York.*' He doesn't know if his parents stayed in Marseilles. He came back at 5 am and got up at 2 pm still pretty tired. On the day before, with Jacques, they had gone to a sports meeting at the station, as spectators only, laying on the grass. He says their favourite sport is resting! He hopes to be able to arrive at Penrith on 27th evening or 28th morning; he'll send me a telegram. Jacques will also be at the wedding.

Penrith: in Cumbria, Lake District, near Kirkby Thore.

Sunday 20

Heard radio Brazzaville. De Gaulle in Cherbourg. Our troops can see the Eiffel Tower.

Monday 21

His letter of 19th. I can understand why they were so happy on 15th August. '*There's only one* Marseillais *in us seven bachelors, but four of us are southerners. The bomb aimer is from Toulon, tall Jacques lives near Nice, the rear gunner near Montpellier and the flight engineer hails from Avignon.*' They don't have the funds to buy the car yet. I sent him *France Magazine* with a little note from Mummy and a box of matches. He was supposed to do a sortie that night.

Wednesday 23

At 12.45 pm we heard the latest news from France: Paris is being liberated by the FFI who began to fight on Saturday. They have now gained control of the whole city. General Koenig is the new governor. I'm very proud to hear that students are taking part in the liberation of Paris. We have asked the Parisians to hold out till we can get food to them.

After having been overjoyed the last few days, his letter of Sunday is rather sad. 'Ma tendre amie, 'il pleure dans mon cœur comme il pleut sur la ville' *(Verlaine)*[...] All this greyness has found its way into my soul, all the more so since we're unable 'to go to town' and inaction means the days seem longer until I can be with you again. [...] Only one month, one short month, so insignificant in a man's life, but it has seemed as long as a whole year – no, as long as a whole century, in fact. [...] I can picture you in your long Chinese dressing gown, kissing me and telling me off at the same time, crying over a broken record as if your heart was broken, or now my imagination is taking over and I can see you in your canteen looking like the princess you are and serving those poor soldiers, sailors and airmen, who, in addition to the ritual cup of tea that I don't envy them, are blessed with the sunshine of your eyes and a smile. [...] Why do all my thoughts always go to you even though I wish they didn't? Am I afraid of thinking that I may be able to love you, am I scared lest I will have to go sooner or later, and then – no, don't protest – I should never see you again? Knowing that we'll be seeing each other again makes parting painless, for as soon as we do, we start thinking of our next rendezvous. But it seems to me that to leave, knowing that we'll never meet again, has got to be utterly impossible.'* He finds Sundays even drearier than the other days. The only consolation is that he can get up later without running the risk of missing breakfast! He had time to read two books and began a third one about Marie-Antoinette. He gave the farm's address at Kirkby for his leave. He'll telephone me this evening at 6 or tomorrow morning at 10; it'll depend on his sortie. '*Good night*, Bébé, *in one hour's time I'll be seeing you again* – '*absence makes the heart grow fonder': I love you, and send you a planeload of kisses.*' He drew a little heart with wings dropping kisses on '*target Barbiche*'. In six days' time we'll be together again, at last.

FFI: *Forces Françaises de l'Intérieur*, i.e. the French Resistance.

General Koenig: commander in chief of the FFI in 1944; he had become famous during the Battle of Bir Hakeim (Libya, June 1942).

*From *Romances sans paroles* (1874) by French poet Paul Verlaine: '*It's raining in my heart, As it rains on the city.*'

Thursday 24

The liberation of Marseilles started yesterday, not long after Paris, again by the FFI. Dear Cis, how pleased and proud he will be! He'd been waiting for this day for so long. I received a little note dated 22nd, the last one before our respective departures. '*See you soon Barbiche! Your Francis.*' He was setting off for a '*little ride*'. I can't wait to meet him again. He didn't telephone.

22 August: bombing training and air to sea gunnery.
Paris was eventually liberated on 25 August and Marseilles on the 28th.

Friday 25

General de Gaulle walked down the *Champs-Elysees*. We're told the Americans got to Bordeaux.

I've received a telegram from Inverness: '*Arrived safely. Shall be with you on 28th, hope you had a good journey. Kisses. Francis.*' He's spending two days with Veronica's family whom he met in Scotland. They are very kind people; he had promised them to go back and see them again.

Saturday 26

Leclerc entered Paris with his Division for mopping-up. We reached Kirkby Thore tonight for our holidays. I wish Francis was already here.

Sunday 27

Fighting outside *Notre Dame*. Maurice Chevalier may have been arrested. Big raids on Germany by Halifaxes.

Tuesday 29

Francis turned up. How I missed him! He looks extremely tired, he had already done seven sorties, Hazebrouck, Caen, Kiel …

Wednesday 30

Walked to Appleby. Cis said he hates '*the Macaronis*' even more than the Germans; that's what he calls the Italians. He says they are only fit for singing or farm work. We got to the riverside and there I told him that I loved him. He looked so happy. His face lit up and we kissed each other.

I do love him and I want to do all I can to help him. We had dinner at the local pub, then we came back in the dark, very happy. It was all so strange. There will be six more weeks of separation again, six weeks during which he'll still have to endure flak or German night fighters, let alone the risk of collisions between bombers; they sometimes are a thousand flying by night without lights, side by side each other, above and below. What terrible danger, what torture! Why do I have to love an airman?

Thursday 31

Went to the village again. Standing on the bridge we threw stones in the river, then went for a walk on the moors eating wild strawberries. We talked about pleasure and joy, our Easter and Christmas customs, and also about the AVF where we met. F is very worried about his family, who matter more than anything else to him. He's afraid of perhaps not finding them again on his return and says he couldn't get over it. He may go on leave home in two months' time. He says how his youth has been shattered and how he will not be able to settle down again. His father was in the *Chasseurs Alpins* in the last war, on the Austrian Front. I suddenly burst into tears in his arms, thinking of what could happen to him and also of the day when we will part. My darling, I can't really help you at all. He was very sweet and so understanding. He never grumbles and never annoys me. He gave me *Le Livre de mon ami* by Anatole France with such a tender dedication. '*I'm all alone tonight with my dreams, I'm all alone tonight without your love. Francis.*' It is so sweet, it's just like him! He has the sun in his heart.

Chasseurs Alpins (Alpine Hunters): élite mountain infantry of the French Army.
Dedication inspired by *Je suis seule ce soir*: sung by Léo Marjane.

September

Friday 1

Went to the village and then sat by the fire. He talked about his plane 'G for George'. He said he never forgets to take Nostradamus when they go on a mission and they were given little buttons as compasses. Went to Bolton for lunch; he was very quiet. His imminent departure hung over both of us. He said he would come back after the war, perhaps, but I don't think so. We had dinner, then went to the station where F said he wanted us to be only one person. He asked me only one thing, which was to smile when he left, which I did, and not to worry about him, but I can't help it. When the train left and he wasn't there to see me anymore, I burst into tears. My heart was broken.

Bolton: in Cumbria, Lake District.

Saturday 2

The last few days passed like a dream. He told me I was the sweetest girl in the world and nobody had ever done as much as I had done for him. He's got such bright and tender eyes. I felt like breaking all the watches and clocks of the whole world, but time never stops. He seemed to me so tired during his leave, not very lively and almost sad. At least now he is sure that I love him.

Sunday 3

We heard Sabu had died. It's stupid but I cried. I hope he'll go to the cats' paradise. Five years today since the war started. Will it stop at last one day? I don't want anything to happen to Francis. God protect him!

3 September 1939: Great Britain and France declared war on Germany, following the invasion of Poland by the German troops on 1 September.

Monday 4

His letter of 2nd. He wrote it as soon as he got back at the station. '*My darling, it is raining, hopelessly raining, and the whole countryside looks as if it was drowning – is it rain or sorrow that's flooding my soul with melancholy? It breaks my heart and I'm unreasonably scared as I sit alone in our hut – I'd managed to keep it out of my mind for a few days, but now just like the raindrops tears keep falling on my poor love. […] The last few days were the most marvellous in my life. It was near the* bridge, when you were afraid someone might have seen us, and I knew our two hearts were beating in unison. It was the same near the river when you said 'I love you' and I stood like an idiot, or when our hands were clasped together under the table during all those hours when only the two of us mattered – no-one can ever take them away from us. And finally there was this small, ivy-covered station in the countryside, my Bébé walking alongside the train as it started moving, then a last kiss, and the dread in your eyes when I said 'adieu' – but don't worry about that, in France we say 'adieu' as often as 'au revoir'. And then you are only a silhouette that says 'See, I'm smiling!' You are indeed smiling, and so am I, but our smiles probably look like grimaces. Then my Barbiche is receding in the distance and she's smaller and smaller, until everything becomes blurred. Am I going to cry? No, she wouldn't like it if I did. And so there I am, all alone in this unfriendly compartment – was it all a dream? No, I've got everything that proves it wasn't, I can even smell your perfume all around me. […] I've left the best of myself with you and now I am a body without a soul. I left my heart in a small village, and all my love is over there in a village where there runs a little river, where flowers seem to be in bloom all the time, because there it stands, that old church that inspires poems and where one day we held each other's hand. In this hamlet is my darling, the one that I truly love and cherish. But why should I mention all this, it can only make you sad again, darling, and I would give my life for one of your tears.' All that makes me feel immensely nostalgic and so sad as well. I do wish I was still there with him. He'll have his next leave on 17th October. This evening the telephone rang: it was him! I was surprised; he said he just wanted to hear my voice. He sounded sad and a bit lonely. He thinks the English worship Shakespeare, but he doesn't know anything about English literature. He also thinks that French parents have more sympathy with youth and love.

Tuesday 5

We all came home. I can't stop thinking of him. I wrote to him to tell him how much I miss him and that he is always in my thoughts. I've spent such lovely holidays, unlike any others. I enclosed two postcards from Kirkby in the envelope; he hadn't had the time to buy some. Here

the blackout is to stop at last. Concert at AVF to celebrate the fall of
Paris. His letter of 3rd is nostalgic again. It hasn't stopped raining at
Elvington. '*Why am I so melancholy and pensive when I hear the drip of
a raindrop? It's an indescribable and intangible sort of feeling, a kind of
fog in my soul where images dance, with either sad or joyful memories
of two large eyes in turn smiling or upset, of the moue of a princess, or a
little nose in the rain under a large monk's hood, a path lined with plane-
trees in the friendly dusk, where two young people walking together
and talking about serious matters suddenly embrace for no apparent
reason while a soaking wet, sad-looking little dog is looking up at us
reproachfully and you start with fright with each clap of thunder. All
these thoughts keep rushing through my mind in a sort of magical dance
and as soon as I try to catch one, they vanish in the haze. I listen to
that rain, that September rain which seems to mock me. Outside, the
corn stalks quiver and look as though they have been weeping, probably
because autumn is coming, and because it is the end of a summer that
for me only lasted three days. [...] Maybe this evening the rain which had
rekindled my turmoil will be far, far away, and flying in the cloudless sky,
my triumphant thoughts will come to you, bringing you love that grows
with each passing day. Perhaps I shall be near you in the evening, like
a shadow that's no longer afraid of being happy because of you, whose
love will seem so sweet. The scents of the woods will be in your hair, and
your eyes will reflect the wide expanse of the sky. I shall take your hand,
and we will be silently sharing the sweetest emotions. Only you and I will
matter, and we shall suddenly see a great hope light up, Hope, the god of
lovers, the god that keeps the world alive. And holding hands we shall
make a nightly visit to the land of happiness, walking on air along the
Milky Way to see the sky and gather stars. Together we'll go towards that
shining world where our dreams will become eternal. On our way there,
we'll stop on Mars or Saturn to try and understand what the sky rests
on.*' As for me I like the rain for I know that when it's raining he doesn't
fly. Fortunately he ended on a bit more of a cheerful note. '*Tomorrow
we'll be able to baptize my rabbit and his name has already been chosen:
Nostradamus. I'm sure you'll find this an awful name but the decision
was made by the 'Grand Council of the G's' called for this purpose.
And the rabbit's baptism will be even more magnificent than the king of*

Rome's. But I fear that before arriving at the church (in this case Betty's Bar) he might well be seriously drenched, and baptized, by the pouring rain!'

Referring to *Il pleut dans ma chambre*, sung by Charles Trenet and *Voyage dans la lune*, sung by Reda Caire.

Betty's: famous bar and tearoom in York.

Wednesday 6

I saw wonderful pictures of the Paris rising at the cinema.

Thursday 7

His letter of Tuesday was short as he was supposed to go out the day after. It was cold; they made a fire in their room. He heard a Belgian on the wireless. '*He's yelling for joy because his country is free after five years of slavery, and he's yelling for hatred against the abhorred Boche, but such great joy leaves me perplexed: what will be the result of such general hatred when Germany capitulates and joy and hatred all combine? What will be the reaction after the storm? When I think that some people are afraid that poor Germany may be too severely punished, I can't help but feel a little angry. If we don't want our children to go through the same horrors as we have, we have to act without mercy, but I trust our leaders and believe we won't be making the same mistakes as in 1914, for it would mean heading towards an even greater catastrophe, twenty or thirty years hence.*' I don't think a whole nation can be so bad. How could Schiller's, Goethe's and Bach's Germany have become so barbarian? They must be fanatics, made so by their leader, who made war and committed all those horrors. Civilians, women and innocent children shouldn't have to pay the price of such crimes.

Packed Pat and Henri's wedding present, a pretty tablecloth. Pat sent me a letter with all the details for getting to St Helens and being at the ceremony. Cis telephoned. They eventually didn't go out because of rain. So he went to the pub with Henri and Jacques. He was sorry to hear Mummy was ill.

Friday 8

His letter of 6th. '*Good night, Bébé, I have kissed this corner here tenderly just for you.*' I also put my lips to it like a long kiss. He woke up thinking of me and arrived late with Jacques who was waiting for him for the lowering of the flag. They were reprimanded by their *lieutenant*. '*But what do the petty worries of this life matter, when one can escape from them to the marvellous fairy tale of dreams? What does it matter if the sky is black if I can dream of you? If I can rest my poor tired head on your kind shoulder, if I can dream of your arms, which are such a sweet circle where my heart beats faster as soon as it enfolds me? Your arms which intoxicate me as no-one else can, your arms where, calmed, loving, I will stay forever because they are my supreme sanctuary, where the hours are so short, where life passes like a fleeting dream, and if I hadn't the distraction of my work, I would doubtless be very unhappy. But the minutes when I can think of you are so brief that I savour each one as a huge happiness. And now I understand why medieval knights could fight so gaily when they knew their sweethearts were waiting for them. Yes, darling, you're right, your heart was torn apart when I left, because I was taking it with me; yes, I was taking that little heart of yours that seemed so sensitive and complicated when we first met, and now I'm jealously watching over it, just as the ancient vestals had to do with their burning fire. I'm watching over it because it is the most wonderful present anybody has ever offered me. And even if one day life should separate us, I'd never give it back.*'

Lieutenant: flying officer.

9 September: attack on the German defences near Le Havre. The mission was abandoned on the Master Bomber's orders over the target, as it was hidden by clouds. The bombs were dropped into the sea. When landing, the Halifax of lieutenant-colonel Venot, commanding *346 Guyenne*, burst into flames as a bomb still attached exploded, killing six crew members. Seriously wounded, Lieutenant-colonel Venot was the only survivor.

During a raid, a Master Bomber in a Pathfinder aircraft indicated the target and gave directions by radio.

Monday 11

Another letter. *'Just like you I thought of you during the whole journey and it made me quite incapable of reading the small book you'd given me. Why was this so? I haven't a clue; I was in a kind of nebulous dream in which all my thoughts, no matter what they were, were leading me back to you. [...] It was a kind of vague feeling on which my whole mind was focussing, forever returning to the same starting point: 'I love her, she loves me and we're apart.' And all the while the train was moving and taking me farther and farther away from you.'* He was surprised to hear Sabu died; he liked him very much too, and vice versa. Sabu always used to jump up and purr on his knees, and he found it amusing, seeing him sleeping in the same basket as Wien. *'So poor old Sabu has died; I shall never have the pleasure of stroking him again, and Wien will have no reason for being jealous when I return to Liverpool. Poor Wien! He, too, must miss his old friend. But as you say, Sabu certainly will have a special place in his cats' paradise. And actually I'm both shocked and saddened by the news, so I don't find it ridiculous at all that you cried.'*

Tuesday 12

I saw an English film by Marcel Pagnol with Françoise Rosay, *Halfway House*. Cis told me Pagnol has big studios in Marseilles where he made films with Fernandel.

Wednesday 13

Heard General de Gaulle speaking from Paris, rather exciting. He promised a general election and spoke of French reconstruction.

Thursday 14

His letter of 12th. He received the two newspapers I sent him and had fun decoding my message. Jacques and he have now got a greyhound which they called 'Lady Grey'. They bought her from a woman who lives in a disused wagon near their camp and who almost starved her to death. They did a sortie on 11th in the afternoon. *'The weather was beautiful and I believe the sun wanted to annoy you.'* He took Nostradamus with them and said it was *'very, very interesting.'* I'm a bit frustrated that he can't tell me everything; but on the other hand it's perhaps better not to know everything, I'm already afraid enough as it is. Cis has been exactly like me since we're back from holiday, sometimes overjoyed, sometimes terribly sad. '*And now that I know, ever since we stood together on the bridge (no, not the Avignon bridge!) I've been utterly confused. One moment I feel like singing and whooping with joy, and then suddenly, for no particular reason I feel sad, desperately sad, and wish I could die; I don't know why at all, and I have vainly tried to analyze my feelings and thoughts, but I can't. Yet I mustn't be like that, I've got to be happy and sing for you, so that some happiness may shine in your heart and soothe your pangs of fear if you have to have any, for my only wish is to see you perfectly happy until the moment when I leave you. And when that day comes, remember that I love you and that despite my grief, I'll be going away for your own sake and to let your life resume its course.*' Why did I tell him our love is hopeless? I am stupid and he must find me really cruel. He doesn't know if he will be able to come to the wedding yet; his *lieutenant* promised him a twenty-four-hour leave, '*well, you know, if … make it possible.*' He will send me a telegram. I will be so disappointed if he doesn't come.

Sur le pont d'Avignon: one of the most famous popular songs and nursery rhymes in France, said to date back to the 15th century.

11 September: raid on a synthetic petrol factory at Gelsenkirchen in the Ruhr. Several crews, amongst them Francis', were severely hit by flak. *Capitaine* Hilaire's Halifax (347 'Tunisie' Squadron) was shot down. Six men were killed, plus the bomb aimer of another crew from the same squadron; his comrades managed to return to England.

Friday 15

Got his telegram at noon. '*Can't come tomorrow. So sorry. Henri's been informed. Kisses. Francis.*' I couldn't help crying. I'm really upset. We won't be able to be together tomorrow. It must be a big disappointment for him too. He was to be the best man. It is really unfair, it is too sad!

His letter of 13th. 'The lady with scissors' dared open my letter! All we write to each other is read by the eyes of a stranger: I hate that. He gave me a long lecture about passions: '*Is it better to experience moderate feelings or none at all?*' He quoted the Stoics and other Greek authors. For someone who hasn't studied much, he really is very well-read. At the end of his letter he drew bombing of kisses above Liverpool. I am so disappointed that he cannot come tomorrow. My train leaves at 9.15 from Lime Street station.

Sunday 17

It was such a beautiful wedding and I spent a wonderful day at St Helens yesterday. It would have been even more beautiful if Francis had been there with us. I took the train in the morning as planned with several girls from the *British*, including Mrs Manson who likes Pat very much. Henri was superb in his new navy blue uniform and Pat wonderful in her dress of white satin with a long train and a long veil, her hair up à la Edwardian. Brian, Pat's cousin, was the best man instead of Francis, and her cousin Sadie was the bridesmaid. The wedding took place at St Mary's Lowe House. The marriage ceremony was very short and then they had a Nuptial Mass. The old priest couldn't speak French. I hoped with all my heart that they would be happy and Henri would be safe. He and Pat constantly kept looking at each other from their prie-dieux.

When they came out, seventeen heavy bombers dipped in salute. The carillon played *La Marseillaise*. The wedding breakfast was at the Fleece Hotel. Among the guests, there were Henri's three crew members (Auguste and two Jeans) and also André. Brian made a speech and read the telegrams. Afterwards we drank toasts, and Jim, Brian's friend, passed round cigarettes and chocolates. Pat changed into a very nice grey suit and a pink blouse; she looked so sweet. They then went to Blackpool for their honeymoon. Dear Pat and Henri, they've got all the cards stacked against them, so perhaps they'll be happy after all. After their departure, Sadie invited us all back to her house. Pat's father, from Jersey, was very nice. We had tea and sang *La Madelon*, *Parlez-moi d'amour* and *Lili Marleen*. Then all ten of us washed up in the tiny kitchen, with a bit of flirting. There was another Jean, a Belgian sailor, who seemed to be a friend of Pat from the *British*. André and he sang *Tout va très bien Madame la Marquise*. Auguste seemed sad. He spoke no English at all. I tried to cheer him up. He has a wife and three children in Algiers, two of them twins. The two Jeans, André, Auguste and I came back to Liverpool by train. I arrived at home at midnight to find a frantic family!

La Madelon: very popular song in World War I. *Parlez-moi d'amour*: sung by
Lucienne Boyer. *Tout va très bien Madame la Marquise*: a hit by Ray Ventura's
band.

Lieutenant Auguste Hyenne: a navigator, Henri Martin's crew captain (346
'Guyenne' Squadron). *Sergent* Jean Reynal, a rear gunner, and *sergent-chef* Jean
Laherrere, a flight engineer: also in the same crew. André: unidentified. The
Belgian was Jean Dahnen.

Monday 18

Packed up a piece of wedding cake for Cis and wrote him a seven-page
letter.

Tuesday 19

He wrote to me as soon as he could. He wants to know everything: how
Pat was dressed, if there were many people, how Henri was. What a
disappointment for him too! That wedding would have been such a chance
to meet each other once again. At the time of the ceremony he was sleeping
as he had done a sortie by night. Jacques couldn't go to the wedding either
of course; I did look forward to meeting him. Cis was awarded the *Croix
de guerre*. I'm really happy and proud of him. He is too modest: he says he
didn't do very much to get it. He sent me a ribbon to sew it to the *Croix*. I
went to the Post Office quickly to send him a telegram of congratulations.

The *Croix de guerre* 1939–1945 (War Cross 1939–1945): a French military
decoration, a version of the *Croix de guerre* created in September 1939, to
honour people who fought with the Allies against the Axis Forces at any time
during World War II.

Wednesday 20

All the family was delighted for Cis; even Nelly was thrilled. She takes such
an interest in him and says the 'Miraculous Medal' protects him. I sent him
her congratulations. Mummy and Patsy each wrote him a little note.

Friday 22

Letter from F. He cannot give me any details regarding his '*little ride*'.
He'll tell me during his leave as it seems to be worth it. No sooner were

they back than they had to go out again in the afternoon. He was very pleased with my little parcel. Jacques also tasted the cake. I finished sewing the ribbon to the *Croix* and sent it by registered post.

17 September: bombing and air to sea gunnery training. 18 September: night flying training.

His crew should also have taken part in the bombing of enemy positions at Sangatte on 20, but the mission was cancelled for three aircrews, including his own.

Saturday 23

He's very touched by all the signs of friendship and congratulations that he had, which he didn't expect. He seems to have taken it good-humouredly that I went out to the cinema with Michael, an Irish airman I met at the canteen and who said to me 'I love you' the next day! I found it so funny that I told Cis. I think he's a bit jealous though.

Sunday 24

F rang. He was in York with Jacques, Henri and Pat who're back from their honeymoon. He said he was wearing the *Croix de guerre* ribbon and they were going to have dinner in a restaurant to celebrate the wedding. I wished I could have been there with them. The call was cut off. It is really annoying and frustrating not to be able to have a chat as long as we'd like. Sometimes Cis says he would like to punch the telephone employees, and so would I! I showed a photograph of him to Marianne; she thinks he looks like a film star. I do love Francis, but all that is hopeless and time is so short.

Monday 25

His letter of 23rd. '*My darling, my love, the apple of my eye, my everything.*' He did receive the ribbon and the *Croix* and said he will be able to wear it on and in his heart. He promises to improve his way of dressing because he loves me and I made him see that he's sometimes a bit sloppy! I know he is sensitive about it. '*I hate people who are dressed up to the nines and the way I dress is a sort of challenge to all that is too stuffy. [...] You know, I'm a bit of a bohemian at heart and sometimes I'd like to walk into a grand hotel, while dressed in the most shabby clothes, in order to show all the stupid upstarts who dine there that one may be unconventional in outward appearance, yet have better manners than some of them.'* It's all the same with his hair: he hates going to the hairdresser's!

Wednesday 27

In his letter of Monday he described their dinner in town. '*Yes, Henri is back, and so is Pat, and I think they're going to live here. And yesterday we had supper together to celebrate this gathering. [...] We went to all the smart places in the city and shocked all those big, fat, overbearing head-waiters by ordering the most improbable beverages and adopting angry looks when they answered that they could not provide them. In short we had good fun. We then went back to the camp quietly, while the couple stayed in York.*' He wrote me words of love again. I sometimes wonder if, by being said again and again, they don't lose their sense. I wrote to him from the university. Classes have started again and every Tuesday afternoon I'm at the canteen at Lime Street. I will have less free time. I hope he won't hold it against me if I write to him a little less often.

Thursday 28

His letter of Tuesday. '*Barbichette of my dreams.*' He told me a strange story; I'm not sure I guessed what it is about. Henri also did the same sortie. They stopped '*on the other side*' and drank a delicious white wine. He enclosed two little flowers with his letter, '*picked on the continent*'. So they must have landed in France, but I don't know where or why. I'm pleased that he thinks of our 9 pm date every day. '*Just as it does every evening, my love, this little bird with the golden wings has flown off to tell his beloved one that I'll never ever forget her. At the time when birds go to sleep, when darkness falls over the fields, a light starts shining in my heart, it comes from my dearest star, and it's the light of our love. At the time when daylight is fading, I know a house where someone lives, where someone breathes, where someone who beckons me is waiting for me with a heart full of passion. When we are apart, you're never closer to me than in those moments. It really seems that our thoughts unite – and maybe my heart does have seven league boots.*'

'At the time when birds go to sleep': referring to La Maison sur la colline, sung by
   Rina Ketty.

Saturday 30

A letter again. '*Yes, the evening with Pat and Henri was splendid, but
the financial arrangements of our great lords Jacques and Francis were
seriously undermined, all the more so since, by a strange coincidence,
these things always present themselves at the end of a meal.*' It's really
him who picked the two little flowers. '*I've been at least three times
to the place where they grow. One day I'll tell you why and under
what circumstances.*' He sent two letters to his family through London
Headquarters and is waiting for news. If he doesn't hear from them,
he'll try to get through via the Red Cross as I told him he could. '*I've got
to go, Bébé, Jacques is asleep and I'll soon have to wake him up. Lady
Grey is stretched out near him; what a touching sight, I wish you could
see them, they look like lovers.*'

In the newsreel they showed an FAF Heavy Bomber Squadron.
September is ending and we haven't been able to see each other again.

October

Monday 2

I got a letter. He also is sad that a month has passed without being able
to put his arms round me. '*So it's true that a man can live without seeing
the sun, and that time has gone by – a whole month… How incredible,
and how shall I cope later on? Oh damn! I've used the forbidden word!
But because a month is such a long time when I'm hoping to see you
again, how shall I be able to face all those years when that hope is
gone? Oh bother, I don't want to go on writing like that, let's change the
subject… No, unfortunately, Bébé, the flowers don't come from where
you imagined, but just a little further up – just think of the first letter
of your name and you're bound to guess.*' I was wrong; it was certainly
in Belgium that they landed. But why? He eventually went twice to the
hairdresser's within four weeks. It seems that the boy was shy and only

cut off a bit of hair. F must have terrified him! He telephoned tonight; he was in York with the gang. Fortunately I was at home. I spoke to Jacques: he has a deep voice and speaks very quickly with an Oxford accent. He sounds very nice and said he wished that he could see me. Also spoke to Henri. They all sounded to be having fun. I couldn't speak to Pat as we only had six minutes. Cis had been to the North of France. He sounded in a marvellous mood and announced that there was a pretty waitress! He always notices them!

From 25 September to 2 October 1944, the two French Squadrons flew eight missions transporting petrol to Brussels Melsbroek airfield, in Belgium, to supply Montgomery's 2nd Army in their advance through Belgium and the Netherlands towards the Rhine, in the immediate aftermath of the Battle of Arnhem in the Netherlands. Francis' crew took part in it on 26, 27, 28 and 30 September.

Tuesday 3

He rang from Pat and Henri's: they live in a little flat in a house. We had six minutes again. I spoke to Pat, this time; she said she bullied Henri as he forbade her going back to her job. Jacques was in York. Lady Grey had stayed at the camp; she was so dirty that Cis had to wash her after he took her out for a run.

Friday 6

His letter of 4th. All about their time out in York: they apparently had great fun. '*Two nights ago, the famous quartet was seen wandering in the streets of York, singing and almost dancing while the flabbergasted passers-by looked on. It was a wonderful evening – but without you it was incomplete. We first went for aperitifs at about 6. Once these had made us joyful, being in high spirits, we headed for the Grand Hotel and sang* Ma pomme *and other melodious ditties of that sort. Pat was singing, too. Our arrival in the hall caused quite a stir: a porter came rushing up, but we refused his help in a very dignified way, and then I gave him 20 francs – I'm sure he's still wondering who were those weird fellows who insisted on carrying their belongings and yet tipped him just the same. We drank another aperitif there, a complicated concoction made with port, sherry, pepper and a drop of orange juice. Then in the*

*dining room there were some pretty but rather stupid waitresses totally
lacking in style, and we naturally asked for the wine list. There wasn't
much choice, but just the same we managed to find some Algerian wine
that wasn't bad. Poor Pat was begging for mercy and drank with her
eyes closed, as if she were drinking cod liver oil. No sooner had we
started eating than I got up with great dignity and said that I had an
urgent phone call to make. This was followed by general mayhem, and
eventually the two famous sergents followed me to the phone booth to
the great distress of the head-waiter, who imagined we didn't like his
cuisine and were just about to leave. You know the rest: I phoned, we
phoned, you spoke to Jacques for the first time, and we then returned
to our table while all the diners gazed at us wide-eyed. The meal itself
was nothing to write home about, but it was passable, and we then
had black coffee with rum, exactly the French way, and we left but not
without looking down as scornfully as we could on all those stupid
people who seemed so shocked at seeing others who were quite simply
happy. We found ourselves in the streets again, walking towards the
dance-hall, locking each other's arms and blocking the whole width of
the pavement, so that no-one could pass in the opposite direction. And
I'm sure that some people must still be wondering what was that troupe
with such a small man on one side and such a tall one on the other. At
midnight, after dancing again and again – only dancing, believe me – a
taxi took us back to Henry's, where we had some more coffee. And
when the couple retired, Jacques and I went sadly back to Elvington.
[...] Yesterday morning we slept until 10 and I had to throw a glass
of water at Jacques' face to wake him up. I received your second letter
while I was at the mess; indeed we had lunch because not having had
breakfast, we were literally starving. Back in the hut I slept a little, and
I had started writing to you when those two oafs forcefully interrupted
me. Whether I liked it or not, I just had to resign myself. Once in York,
we went to fetch Pat, who was not ready of course, and the four of us
went together to have our picture taken.*

*That was when another funny incident happened; first I was adamant
that the female photographer should stand with us, under the pretext that
having three men for one woman just wasn't done, and then, in despair, I
held Jacques' hand while looking tenderly into his eyes; by that time Pat*

and Henry were having the giggles, and finally the young girl who was taking the picture just pressed the button when she burst out laughing, and it all had to be done all over again. Finally three-quarters of an hour later, we managed to have the photo taken and left the poor photographer in the grip of what looked like a fit of delirium tremens, so much so that I'll end up thinking that we actually are funny. For the umpteenth time, there go the four lunatics in the streets again! This time we walked past a fruit shop, and we rushed inside because we'd seen beautiful pears in the window; after buying some, there we were in the avenue, each holding a pear and eating it while a despairing Pat threatened never to speak to us again. We strolled along, saying 'Good evening!' to all the passers-by. At 6 Jacques left us and the three of us had tea at Henry's, like a little family. We listened to music for a while, I rang you up again, and afterwards we returned to the dance-hall. There I met a young girl who insisted that she knew me and said that my name was Francis and she'd first met me about two months ago. Since Pat was around, I told her: 'Don't you say a word to Barbara' and I smiled and whispered confidentially in the young lady's ear: 'Hush! This is my wife, you see!' with a knowing look. She must be rather bright because she never spoke to me again. And this was how the evening was spent; I danced with Pat and even the three of us did, all together, and I went to bed at one in the morning.'

He telephoned me again tonight. I felt rather ill. He said: '*Oh darling! You sound so poorly.*' He sang *I'll See You Again* to me, one of his favourites.

Ma pomme: sung by Maurice Chevalier.
20 francs: 6 pence.
I'll See You Again: sung by Noel Coward.

Saturday 7

He rang up from the mess. Jacques was in York. They had been on operations last night and got in about 9 am. I didn't get any letter. Luckily he can telephone, otherwise I would be worried to death.

6 October: bombing of a synthetic petrol factory at Scholven in the Ruhr. '*G for George*' hit by flak.

Capitaine Hablot's Halifax (346 'Guyenne' Squadron) was attacked by a German
   night-fighter. All the crew baled out and were made prisoners, but several
   were wounded.

Tuesday 10

At last a letter today, a beautiful love letter. '*Maybe in a hundred years'
time, a young girl will discover a book bearing an inscription to Barbiche
and she'll tell her boy-friend with a thoughtful look: 'In those days
girls really had quite funny names!' She may also pity those two poor
young lovers and think that Francis had a strange way of expressing his
feelings. For the time being I don't need pity, I am happy, terribly happy,
but I must only think of one thing, the present, and for the time being,
the present is marvellous. I don't want to think of anything except that
you love me, I don't want to dream of anything apart from your eyes
and smile. Nothing else matters, nothing except that I love you, I love
you, do you understand? You may think that I keep repeating myself,
but I don't care, I'll never tire of telling you that I love you. Words are
quite inadequate to express this, but how meaningful they are when
one can understand them. And I'm sure that you can, my marvellous
darling!*'

   Had solitary lunch, weeping over *La Dame aux camélias*. Cis rang;
he didn't go out last night for the weather was bad. Jacques was playing
the piano. I'm so pleased that I can hear him every night, at the moment.
I sent him a lock of my hair. Met another *Marseillais* at the AVF.

La Dame aux camélias: a novel by Alexandre Dumas' fils (1848).

Wednesday 11

He rang from the mess and said to me '*Je t'aime*' very softly. Hasn't
been out much lately as the forecast is too bad; he gets bored. The fog
covering the camp reminds him of Liverpool last winter.

Saturday 14

He was very pleased with my lock of hair: he wants to put it, tied to a
golden thread, in a frame! '*You know, I went to Pat's yesterday evening,
and you must avenge me. She and Henry tickled me so much that there I*

was lying breathless on the carpet, but then for my part I pinched three apples, the best ones, and ate them right under their noses. Pat then saw me off when I took a taxi and asked lots and lots of questions about you and our respective feelings. Poor Pat, she's so kind, and I believe she's very fond of you. I saw your photo at the wedding, but they wouldn't give it to me.'

Sunday 15

He rang: sounded tired. He had been on operations lots the last two days and had to make a forced landing. He may come tomorrow.

14 and 15 October: two successive raids on Duisburg in the Ruhr.

Monday 16

His letter of Friday. Private calls were not allowed that night or the night before. He was supposed to do a sortie on the day after. *'Nostradamus is very well, he's blooming, he's a lord of the skies, and he must look down on his mates who are not so lucky as he is.'* I'm very touched by what he says about my letters which are not so interesting though. *'Oh! Bébé, but to me every one of the words that make them up sound such sweet music, they're so soothing and comforting. How can anyone find anything stupid when it comes from their loved one? What could be more enchanting than evoking such sweet memories? Each letter that you write is one more link in the chain of our beautiful love. At times I'm even afraid I might become conceited when I read them, because in each of them I find something close to admiration, and I believe that admiration is one of those things that go straight to the hearts of men. But I only want to see in them the reflection of your innocent heart and that wonderful love you have given me. I want to repay you a hundredfold. Maybe I'll succeed. I only want you to be happy and I'll do my best for that in spite of all the odds. [...] My warmest regards to Riri, Mummy, your uncle, Gran, Sheila and Joan. Remember me to Nelly. Kisses from Lady Grey to Globule. Good night Barbiche, 'see you' at 9! Tonight again my dreams will be about 'Princess Barbiche'. Good night again. With a thousand mad kisses from your Francis.'* He rang and said: *'I will kiss you tonight.'* Jacques is going to London.

Tuesday 17

He came late last evening. He looks quite well and even in very high spirits. He now has an *étoile d'argent* for his *Croix de guerre*. The petrol tank was damaged on Saturday, so they had to land at Foulsham. They were narrowly missed by a nasty piece of flak. Brought me a Focke-Wulf shell case as a souvenir! Has been to Brussels and found it was lovely. He met me at the canteen this afternoon and created quite a stir. He then bought me violets, his favourite flowers, and pinned them to my collar. We then went to the *British* as I had tickets for the dance. Jean Dahnen (from the wedding) was there, watching us closely. Walked to Pier Head and came home. Then I worked in my room for a while. We went for a little walk again; we kissed each other such a lot. I think F will never come back.

Étoile d'argent: silver star.
Foulsham: RAF station in Norfolk.
Focke-Wulf: German fighter plane.

Wednesday 18

F got up late, as usual. We did chores together, peeled potatoes and did the washing up. We went to town; he bought some gloves. We went to see about buying records. The assistant was very gloomy, saying they weren't making any more French ones. I bought *Lili Marleen* and F bought *Loin des guitares* for me. Afterwards, we went to see Bing Crosby in *Pennies from Heaven*, but we didn't pay much attention to the film… How I love him! At the *British* we met *adjudant-chef* Jean Chabroud, Henri's crew's bomb aimer who was very nice, and then three other boys from Elvington, not so pleasant. F, *sub rosa*, bought some black-market clothing coupons. Bad luck! Lost F's tricolour for Nostradamus.

Loin des guitares: sung by Tino Rossi in the film *Au son des Guitares*, directed by Pierre-Jean Ducis (1936).
Pennies from Heaven: a musical comedy film directed by Norman Z. McLeod (1936).

Thursday 19

F bought a raincoat: he looks quite smart. Went to the *British* but did not dance a great deal. F said he began to love me as soon as he wrote to me: but he wrote to me immediately after our first encounter! Walked to Pier Head and watched the river with so many coloured lights. He kissed me with a mixture of passion and tenderness.

Friday 20

Went to the university whilst F stayed at home. Met him outside beneath the clock and then we had lunch with Mummy and Uncle Max at Reeces'. F and I met Antoine Morel, his crew's wireless operator, who is very nice but seemed a bit lonely. We went and bought some shirts, a scarf, shoes and a tie: the assistant thought I was *Mme* Uzay, which amused me! At the *British* we saw Mrs Manson; she likes Pat very much and had enjoyed the wedding. Joan said we looked too happy: it made her cry. And *Mme* da Horta said we looked a sweet couple! We bought some flowers for Mummy. After supper, we sat in silence, me darning. He put his head on my shoulder and fell asleep. He said he didn't want to go back to Marseilles any longer because he could be there for years without being able to talk to me, which made me so sad. And then he said that he hoped that God would grant him the blessing of dying, which made me feel even more miserable. Poor children, what's going to happen to us? There is no future for both of us.

Saturday 21

We dusted, then took Wiener out. Pat said she hadn't fallen in love with Henri at first. She also thinks that we ought to get married. It's sad as we both feel how hopeless it is. We discussed the different ways of bringing up girls and he talked about his family. He thinks I am very self-controlled. Then I darned socks for him. He said he is unhappy when he is away from me. He gave me a lock of his hair.

Sunday 22

No Mass at 9 am; so he went later. Drank F's health for the *Croix de guerre*: he seemed very pleased. He said he got it because the plane was hit and damaged before the mission was completed, and they did it all the same: not bad! He told me that he hadn't thought much of me to begin with, as I was a bit stiff and he wanted to change me, which he has, I think. He telephoned Henri and Pat. Henri comes on leave on Wednesday. Went to see Mr and Mrs Dick who asked us to come again.

Monday 23

Went to university. F met me there and we had tea in the Students' Union. We discovered a marvellous book about Henri IV at a second-hand bookseller's. Cis was longing to buy it but he didn't have money with him. Went to see *In Our Time*, then walked home, seeing thousands of stars. Sweetheart, where will you end up?

Henri IV: King of Navarre (as Henri III de Navarre) from 1572 to 1610 and King of
　　France from 1589 to 1610.
In Our Time: a film directed by Vincent Sherman (1944).

Tuesday 24

F came to meet me at the canteen; I was allowed to leave early. At the *British* we met some French boys from the Merchant Navy who have come en route to North Africa. They came from Normandy. I think it is the first French ship that has arrived at Liverpool since 1940. They had no uniforms and wore poor clothes. Cis was sweet to them and gave them money. Said things were very bad in France, especially shoes. They seemed amazed that they could have as many sandwiches as they wanted. They gave me a 100-franc banknote that they all signed. Took Rufus and Wiener for a walk. Cis seemed very angry that he couldn't do anything against the forces of the world and he felt like rebelling against it. He was trembling with passion: it was a bit frightening. It's all so complicated. Why is he French and me English?

Rufus: Barbara's grandmother's Cairn terrier.

Wednesday 25

Went to have our photos taken together: the photographer told Cis to put his arm round my waist. Then went across the river; walked along the shore at Seacombe and traced hearts in the sand. Then went to the *British* where F met some friends from 'Tunisie' Squadron and some of Henri's crew. We met the boys from Normandy whose clothes were better; F gave one of them a shirt. I couldn't eat as I felt so miserable, and F too. Home for dinner. Pat and Henri came in the middle of it. They were very affectionate; Henri obviously adores Pat: she is so lovely. Pat had trouble with her landlady. Played records and drank a toast to the bride and the groom. Henri had been to Essen and had an awful time: his squadron leader was missing and he was very upset. As for me, I had tears in my eyes, I didn't know how to hide my anguish, my sadness. On the contrary, Cis seemed quite at ease, even very excited. I think he tried to entertain us. The four of us walked to the tram stop at Penny Lane. Said farewell to Cis and I cried; he was not far from tears either. Henri and Pat were very sweet. I burst into tears on Pat's shoulder. Cis asked me yesterday if he had been able to make me happy during this leave, and I said he had.

23 October: *Commandant* Simon, commanding 346 'Guyenne' Squadron's A Flight, and his crew went missing on the way back from Essen, probably due to a collision with another aircraft above the North Sea. The seven crew members, plus a co-pilot, who was with them as an observer, were all killed.

Penny Lane: in Liverpool; made famous in 1967 by The Beatles.

Thursday 26

Cis rang. He had travelled all night and arrived at 10.30 am. He and Jacques were late. They had an argument with their squadron captain; fortunately he showed mercy. He wasn't 'going out' tonight. He asked me how I was. I was ashamed of having upset him. Packed up parcel of his shaving things: he left them, as usual! He says once you are in the air, you never think about things on the ground. He was so excited when Henri and Pat came home yesterday: you would have thought that he owned the place! If only he could be safe! It is so terrible to be on edge all the time. I have such black thoughts. I wrote him a long letter.

Friday 27

He rang. He should have gone out today, but didn't. Sounded a bit better, but not much. I do so miss him.

Saturday 28

I received the letter he wrote to me as soon as he got at Elvington. Henri
and Pat took the train with him to St Helens where they got off. '*Dear
sweetheart, yesterday seems so close and so distant at the same time,
where is your tearful little face, where are your large eyes that seemed so
blurry, as if they were drowned in tears, and how I wish I could kiss you
a thousand times. I wished so much I could comfort you, one moment
I even thought of not leaving and forgetting everything else in order to
cradle you in my arms, to think only of you and you alone. [...] I assure
you quite shamelessly that I, too, felt like crying, but only when I had
got on the train, and I suddenly felt so lonely and sad that it was as if
something had been torn away from me; I was all the more shattered
since I had to laugh and joke all evening, even though I'd had to bear
looking into your sad, tearful eyes without even being able to give you
one word of solace. But I can assure you that Henry and Pat did have
some comforting words for my poor aching heart.*' I replied to him and
enclosed a little tricolour ribbon for Nostradamus in the envelope. Met
Henri and Pat with Jean Chabroud at the *British*. Henri wanted to go
to the State Restaurant which was full, so we went to the Adelphi where
we had a drink. Henri was very edgy and nervy; he must have been so
affected by his last raid on Essen and the loss of his squadron leader.
He was almost angry because we were not waited on quickly enough.
Jean asked: 'When will you be getting married?' Pat said Francis isn't
worth my worrying about and that she was annoyed with him for even
thinking of other girls for consolation! She said also he is always quiet
at 9 pm: he sits in front of the fire, quite quiet. So I told her of our date.
Henri was telling me about his travels and his boarding school. He is
apparently of very good family, especially his mother. He wasn't well:
his eyes were bloodshot. Pat wanted him to see a doctor. Jean left us
after having eloquently cursed Blum and his government. Pat and Henri
came home to stay the night at home. I was awfully sad about Cis. Pat
was very sweet to me.

The Adelphi: the biggest hotel in Liverpool.

Léon Blum had been Prime Minister of France (Popular Front government) in
    1936–1937, then in March–April 1938.

Sunday 29

They took ages getting dressed; I was afraid that they might miss the train. Uncle Max came and took Henri's watch to be mended. I went to the bus with them. Henri said F is from a real Marseilles family and he speaks with a strong accent (which I can't hear). He never quarrelled with him and has looked after him for four years. Apologized for having been a bit sharp yesterday. Pat thinks Henri and F will be ok. I hope she's right.

Monday 30

Had lunch with Joan, Beatrice and Olga. They were sweet when they saw how depressed I was. Poor Beatrice, her John is in the RAAF and she feels she will soon have the same worries. Pat said the best thing would be to forget F, which is easy for her to say! However I believe that he does love me and that's one thing I can't be cynical about. Got his letter of Saturday. He says he hasn't done anything since he came back three days ago and he is furious. He couldn't ring me that night as they were supposed to go out, but the others eventually went off without them. 'No Bébé, *the season's not over, or rather, if it is indeed over, it will come again. There has never been an eternal spring, but neither has anyone ever seen winter end without another spring taking its place. Life would not be what it is if it were only nice, and maybe it'll be nice enough for us not to feel how nasty it can be. Darling, I've read your letter four times at least since midday, and each time I discovered something new that filled me with wonder. You know, there are times when I wonder if this is not a dream – can she really love me? Can she really write all those words to you? What have I done to deserve such love? Nothing, except making her unhappy. And in those moments I'm both ashamed and annoyed with myself. But soon all of this is swept away and I can only see these words: I love you – it's such a short but wonderful poem! I love you and everything smiles on me, I love you and the future doesn't seem so bleak. I love you darling, and nothing else matters. [...] Good night, darling, a very good night while my love is watching over you. With a billion kisses. Your Cis.*' The moon is almost full tonight and the night so clear. I'm thinking of him so much.

29 October: training cancelled. 30 October: raid on Cologne.

Tuesday 31

Cis rang. They bombed Cologne last night and everyone got back ok. Lovely! He sounded very cheerful. Had given Lady Grey some of my biscuits. He wants me to ask Daddy what happens to the poor pets whose masters are shot down. Tomorrow I will send him some chocolate I was given at the canteen. With Mrs Dick we spoke about English girls who fall in love with foreign soldiers.

Mr Rigby, Barbara's father, worked for the Ministry of Food, supervising the purchase of animals and the abattoirs.

November

Wednesday 1

All Saints' Day. Cis rang: phone very faint. He murmured something about his flight engineer and the *British*: I couldn't understand. He and Jacques were going to a concert in York.

Assassination attempt on General de Gaulle.

Assassination attempt in Vitry.

Thursday 2

He rang. He was smoking those abominable Turkish cigarettes. So glad he wasn't 'going out' tonight. His letter of Tuesday. He regrets that he was sad in the last letters for he doesn't want to upset me; I didn't sound very cheerful the last few days either. He's going to send me money so that I can buy the big book *Henri IV* at the second-hand bookseller's. '*Thank you ever so much for the ribbon, my darling, Nostradamus now looks so proud with all his lucky charms [...] I've also received your parcel, Bébé, and I'm very sorry for all the trouble that I once again put you to, but each time I have to leave you I'm so upset that when it's time to go my mind's a blank and all I can think of is that I'll be away from you for another long month – what else can I think of? [...] So, Pat and Henry took your mind off all this for a while, I'm glad they did, and am very grateful to them, particularly to M. Chabroud, who was kind enough to keep you company, but please forgive Henry for asking too much from you, he most certainly thought he was doing whatever was best. [...] Thank you, too, for having them to stay for they must have been quite tired. [...] Ha! Ha! So Henry tickled you, and pinched you, too! Well, Pat will have to pay for all this teasing; you'll have your revenge darling, yes, there will be blood on the floor! [...] Yes, Pat and Henry are truly wonderful and you know, you really ought to consider them as more than friends. I think that when I said they were my brother and sister, I wasn't too far off the truth.'* I like the way he writes the 'M.' I cooked macaroni this evening, one of his favourite dishes.

Friday 3

His letter of Wednesday. *'I'm sorry the line was so bad when I rang this evening; you sounded slightly disappointed but I can assure you it was not my fault. I was phoning from the mess so that I might speak to you for six minutes instead of three. [...] If I can, I'll try to call from the village tomorrow, but at least this evening I was able to tell you 'I love you' and you were able to make out what I was saying, and that's what matters most. [...] It's funny,* Bébé, *but I also looked at the moon on the evening of the 30th, and it crossed my mind that you could see it too; even if I was so far away, it brought us together for a minute.'* They enjoyed the concert the other night very much. The orchestra played *Pavane for a Dead Princess* and the *Bolero* by Ravel. *'Jacques was ecstatic and didn't utter a single world throughout the concert. [...] My most tender kisses, not for you, but for my Barbiche, my angel, my darling, my one and only love.'*

Saturday 4

His letter of 2nd. *'Darling Barbiche [...] I do aime you very beaucoup. [...] That's life, as you say, and maybe in seventy years from now a little English girl will say the same words that you use about yourself – people will talk about Barbiche who saw England invaded by all those weird foreigners who stole girls' hearts, and maybe they will say it regretfully.'* He says he tried to persuade Henri that Pat would be better in St Helens but he didn't want to hear of it.

At the *British* charity sale, I bought a little cockerel with an inscription on its back: 'When this cockerel sings, my love will end.' Met Vivien Kane; she's engaged to Charles, a Parisian who is the 46th Frenchman to have joined de Gaulle. There were other boys from the *Maquis*. Cis rang and told me: '*Chérie, there will be a little Martin soon!*' I think it'll be a boy! Do hope Henri will take care of Pat. F said the '*G*' has been badly smashed up; so they are having a new plane. Was going to a dance tonight.

The Maquis: rural guerrilla bands of French Resistance fighters in occupied France during World War II. Barbara meant 'from the French resistance'.

Sunday 5
He didn't call today.

Monday 6
Dreadful day. Cis rang at about 8.40 pm to say Henri has been missing since Saturday: his plane didn't get back from the mission to Bochum. Cis was terribly upset; he said he was dancing at the time the plane was shot down. He murmured something about Henri being a prisoner but didn't believe it anymore than I do. Said Pat was very calm. Poor Pat, seven weeks of happiness to the very day, with a baby on the way; to be all alone in that dreadful lodging. They looked lovely together, almost too lovely. Why didn't he go to see the M.O.? Then he would not have been flying on that day. I hope F and Jacques spend a lot of time with her. Cis was so sweet and said: '*I didn't really want to tell you before you went to bed*'. I suppose that he feels it is his turn next; and Henri was his one link with home. I knew all that crew too. Poor Auguste, the two Jeans, and the boy we met on the stairs at the *British*.

M.O.: Medical Officer.

4 November: Bochum in the Ruhr. Five crews from 346 'Guyenne' Squadron, out of sixteen detailed for the mission, were shot down: *lieutenant* Hyenne's, *capitaine* Baron's, *capitaine* Beraud's, *lieutenant* Dabadie's and *lieutenant* Vles'. Twenty-four Frenchmen were killed on that mission, amongst whom were *lieutenant* Hyenne and all his crew.

6 November: Gelsenkirchen. '*G for George*' severely hit by flak.

Tuesday 7

His letter of Sunday, written just before midnight. '*My beloved, [...]*
I'm so shattered, my darling, and I'm probably going to upset you,
but I can't conceal the news from you. I didn't call you this evening,
but I'm sure you'll understand when I tell you why. But why should
I hesitate? To put it in a nutshell and tell you the plain, brutal truth:
Henry is reported missing. He failed to return yesterday evening. We
haven't heard from him and can only imagine the worst has happened.
I only found out this morning and immediately phoned Pat. Poor Pat,
she was so brave, so wonderful, but we should not despair, all hope is
not lost, on the contrary, and maybe I was a bit of a coward, but I didn't
dare to tell her anything definitive, and in any case it's true that I do not
want to think that the worst has happened as long as nothing has been
confirmed. But this is so shattering, my darling; he's my best friend, and
Pat seemed so calm that I was a little afraid. Write to her, Bébé, comfort
her, for I feel so unequal to the task, you must help me darling, I need
you for that. My God, what shall I do, what can I do? I just don't know,
no, I simply can't think straight. Life really is unjust, isn't it? And to
think that Pat will have a baby in a few months. It's a good job Jacques
was with me because if I'd been on my own, I never could have carried
out that horrible task. When I knocked on her door, I felt like running
away, I didn't want to see her cry. But I'm also thinking of you, darling,
how are you going to take the news? You're so sensitive. But don't dwell
too much on all this: as I said, I hope he's now a POW. So darling,
please don't be annoyed with me if I don't spend much time with you
in the next few days, as I'll have to find out a lot of information, and
above all I'll have to keep Pat company: if I leave her alone, she'll go
crazy. Oh! Bébé, how I wish you were here with me; right now I feel so
overwhelmed and awkward when I have to talk to her. We insisted that
she take sleeping pills this evening, but how will she react tomorrow?
It also breaks my heart to think that once again there's nothing I can
do, nothing at all, except try and comfort her. But even when I feel so
helpless at least you're here, darling, your love is with me and I promise
I'll be strong. Don't be cross if I broke the news rather abruptly, but in

that sort of situation tact is out of place. I'll leave you now, to try and get some sleep, for it is midnight and I'll have to get up early. Good night darling, this evening again you'll be sleeping in peace since you'll only get my letter tomorrow. With all my best, most tender kisses and all my love, Francis.'

He rang from the mess; I couldn't hear very well. He went to Gelsenkirchen yesterday. Said how upset and useless he felt; and how my love helped him. He sent a cable to Henri's parents: he was an only child. Called him '*my brother*'. He has a lot of details to attend to. He is a bit frightened for Pat who is too rigid. Told him to stay by her as much as possible. I do hope Pat's family have reached her. I feel awful and so do Mummy and Nelly. If only nothing happens to him! But I haven't much hope. Wrote him a long letter.

Wednesday 8

His letter of 6th. I wonder how he will get through this ordeal. '*Oh my friend, my brother, we had such wonderful plans for our next leave. I feel so lost now. Fortunately Jacques is here, but it's not the same for we haven't been friends for as long. Pat feels much better than yesterday evening, she's hoping against all hope that all is not lost, and I don't want to discourage her, I simply can't, for it would be a crime. And if there really isn't any hope left, she'll only know for certain in a month or two, but in the meantime her grief will have calmed down. Darling, tell me, have I done what's best, or have I done something wrong? I'm so afraid I might say, or do, something stupid. It's so difficult to behave as one should in such a situation. But what's most annoying is the bunch of idiots around us; I admit they're like all human beings, but they're all such morbid nosey-parkers and hypocrites, and they keep asking what's the latest news I have, as if they didn't know that in such cases it's better to say nothing. Please forgive me if I'm rather bitter, but anybody would be. Poor darling, this is one more reason for you to worry, forgive me for that, but, you see, it's still the same, all I can offer my sweetheart is worry and tears. Now, Barbara, I feel that I love you more than ever, and I feel more than ever how much I need you, how much the whole of my soul is in harmony with yours. In happy times just as in dark ones I can only think of you. Your love is the light that will help me through the darkness. But right now we mustn't think of ourselves. Only Pat matters and we must help her; yes, we must, we simply can't let her feel lonely one single minute; I just don't want her to feel that way, and that's why I need you. I know it'll cause you to worry a lot, and I ask you to forgive me for that, but I know how kind-hearted you are, and I believe that you'll do it both for her and for me. Besides, for the time being we must make it impossible for her to think too much about the worst, for if the worst does come to the worst, we'll have to help her to accept this little by little. So if you do write to her, please mention this event very superficially, try to take her mind off it. We have to keep her in good spirits, because there'll be her child with her, and I think that if outwardly she is very brave, the pain inside must be terrible and by all possible means we mustn't allow it to wear her down because hidden pain is the worst. I know you darling and trust you'll do what's best.'*

He rang from Pat's flat; sounded better and even joked a little. Jacques was there as well. Spoke to Pat who is really marvellous. She wants the baby to be a girl and she will call her 'Suzanne'. Her mother is there, and she's going home with her at the end of the week; then F will have nowhere to go. Poor F, I do love him and I would do anything for him.

Thursday 9

Our neighbour said Pat and Henri should have never got married. Cis' last letter is still very sad. *'My darling Princess, [...] I still feel quite helpless when faced with adversity, but you know, although I could cope with any obstacle I'm not up to losing you and facing up to what has happened. You may think I'm a very weak sort of man, especially if you consider my job, but I can't think of it without having a dreadful sense of crushing defeat. Forgive me, darling, I don't wish to hurt you, but I can't help feeling sad. Jacques insisted I go to the cinema tonight and I managed to take an interest in the film, but as soon as I have nothing to think of, it's awful. Oh darling, how I wish I could be with you and stay in your arms like a little child with nothing to worry about! What a coward, indeed, but what use is courage when it's no help at all? Why, oh why did fate have to strike at two of the persons I am most fond of?*

Do you think I can have faith in anything now? But how stupid I am to complain, you are mine, my darling, aren't you? So what more do I need? I'm lost, there's nothing, absolutely nothing left, only emptiness, darkness, and you, for whom I must be brave, whom I love and who is still here with me. But as for Pat, I tremble each time I have to speak to her, I tremble and wish I could run away – how can I take her mind off this a little while? I'm so scared that when I try to smile, it looks like a grimace, but that's all I can do. I didn't go and visit Pat today, because I was on duty with the squadron, but I phoned her at noon and I went, sorry Jacques went and inquired from the administrative personnel about… – well, what I mean is, like it or not, one has to think of money matters, but everything is all right as far as this is concerned. I won't be answering your letter now because I need to write to Henry's parents in Algiers.'

He rang but I was at the *British* as I had told him. Daddy answered the phone. He's 'going out' tomorrow. I do wish I'd been in. About the middle of the dance, I felt so unhappy, thinking about him. I felt like throwing myself into my beloved's arms, but it was impossible.

Friday 10

His letter of 8th. *'I've just arrived from Pat's where I saw her mother, who was very kind. Everyone was almost cheerful this evening. But I'm starting to worry a little that I may have given her too much hope, and if the worst has happened, I should always feel guilty. Nevertheless I think I did what was best, and it wasn't a lie either, because what I told her remains quite possible. Thank you for your letter, which I received this morning: you're so tactful, your words were just the right ones to soothe my heart. I am deeply grateful to you and if you were not by my side I just don't know what I'd do. But everything is all right now, I feel a little braver and, after all, one has to face up to difficulties, and this I must and will do. Now that I've pulled myself together I must think of Pat's circumstances before anything else, especially the child's, but I think everything will work out fine, because the French Air Force are still providing Henry's pay as if he were here. Apart from this, still talking about the baby, there's the AVF and Jacques above all will be able to ask for plenty of stuff from America; as you can see, the situation is*

*not that bad. But I believe it'll be better for Pat to go back to St Helens;
she hasn't made up her mind yet, but she'll come round to it. We spoke
about you this evening and Mrs Pattimore is fond of you; by the way, her
French is rather funny. We spent the whole evening trying to find a name
for the baby, a boy's name and a girl's name. My darling I've got to stop
already, I'm tired, morally and physically, and I may have to get up early
tomorrow morning. Good night, Barbiche, go to sleep, sweetheart, and
forget this world, sleep well, and don't let even the gentle ghost of love
disturb your dreams, for love is yet another worry. Good night darling,
my thoughts and my love are with you. With all my best and sweetest
kisses. Francis.'*

He rang up. Pat was playing Patience and Jacques was reading. Heard
the *Aubade* from *Le Roi d'Ys*, which F sings while washing up. He's
horrified that I don't know anything about operas, and especially *Le
Roi d'Ys*.

L'*Aubade du Roi d'Ys*: sung by Tino Rossi. *Le Roi d'Ys*: opera by Edouard Lalo
   (1888).

Saturday 11

When I answered the phone, he said: '*I have marvellous news.*' I thought
he meant about Henri, but no; he had heard from his family. They are
all well and still living in the same place. Jeanne has grown a lot and is
engaged. Dédé was in the countryside and is very well. F was so thrilled,
and so was I. I'm so glad he has heard from them at last. He sounded a
bit bewildered, but he was teasing me: so that's a good sign. He hasn't
done any sorties for a few days, as the weather was too bad. Finally, Pat
didn't want to go with her mother: that's what he says in his letter of
Thursday. '*This evening I went to Pat's at about 5, we saw her mother
off, then we took a taxi and went back to Elvington to pick up Jacques.
From 7 to 9 we talked a little, Jacques played the piano and at 9 he left
us – why? That's a mystery. We then had a snack with Pat, and then guess
what? Can't you guess? Well we played with a jigsaw puzzle, and when
I left at 11.30 we hadn't finished it yet. [...] To say that I'm cheerful
would be something of an exaggeration, but I'm now able to control my
thoughts, and that's saying something. All the more so since, strange as*

it may seem, I'm now just as hopeful as Pat is because of me.' I wonder what the end will be. Not what happened to Henri, I hope!

Monday 13

His last letter is more cheerful as he had just got the one from his family with some photographs. The letter he sent them took a month to reach them. They got all his messages and replied to them, but he never received anything. They are all safe and sound. The Germans had told the inhabitants that they were going to blow everything up before leaving; luckily, they had the time to go to a safe place. His little brother spent four years in the countryside. *'What a ray of sunshine amid all the darkness of the past few weeks. I'm glad that at long last I've been able to give you some news that won't make you sad. What a pity this news comes at such a time, but maybe it's just as well because it's cheering me up a little. You see, all is not lost, there is still some happiness left on this earth. [...] Yes, Pat is very brave and as you say her child will help her through this crucial period, should Henry never return – which is something I can't and just won't imagine. [...] It'll soon be a year since I arrived here, darling, but what a lot of things have taken place, happy ones, funny ones, but also sorrowful and painful events – I'm sure this year will have contributed much to shaping my character once and for all. And I also met you, light of my life, my love, my everything, and I've had plenty of opportunities to see that mankind is not wholly corrupted yet, since such a pure and wonderful love as yours can still blossom.'*

He rang. Pat has been sick and has fainted.

13 November: bombing training.

Tuesday 14

F rang. He wants me to write to his mother. He thinks Jeanne's fiancé looks a bit plebeian.

Wednesday 15

Cis and Jacques are spending much time by Pat; they do all they can to help her in her ordeal, they are wonderful. But Cis doesn't really know how he must behave. *'Do you really think I have given Pat too much hope?*

*This is bothering me so much, and when I see her smiling, it almost hurts
me as much as if she were crying, to think that all this is due to me. How
shall I cope if one day I have to tell her the worst has happened? Won't she
despise me for having maybe unwillingly lied to her? This is all so painful
it hardly bears thinking. I can only hope the future will prove that I was
right.'* He didn't ring: therefore out. I am so worried about him. The photo
of the wedding came; so ironical! Felt really upset to look at it.

Thursday 16

Cis rang at 8.30 pm. He had obviously been out today. It was the mess
telephone: we couldn't hear a word; it was distressing and infuriating.
Anyway I did know that he was ok. I hope he will get my parcel quickly.
Sent him shaving cream, the same one as for his birthday (he liked it
very much) and a box of matches. I wrote 'ILY' inside.

Reception in honour of the FFI girls at the *British*.

16 November: support to troops at Julich, in the Cologne area. '*G for George*' hit
by flak.

Friday 17

Got a letter. He goes to Pat's almost every evening and so can only write
to me during the day. I think he is better now. Anyway he avoids talking
about Henri. He's going to send me the photograph of the four of them
in York. I must send him a big envelope for that. He rang just after
9 pm; I was so thankful. Yesterday, he had telephoned just after he
had got out of the plane. He said the non-commissioned officers were
looking at him, flabbergasted, whilst he was shouting '*Je t'aime*' down
that silly telephone. Tonight, with Jacques, they were styling Pat's hair
and taking her to the cinema. I asked him if he didn't mind if I went to
the cinema with Robert too. It's John who introduced him to me. Robert
is an officer in the Merchant Navy. He was torpedoed and swallowed
a lot of oil; it's awful what happened to him. Cis said: '*Alright, I trust
you!*' Newsreels of Churchill in Paris. Paris looked lovely and the
Champs-Elysées so big and broad. General de Gaulle looked majestic.

John: Sheila's boyfriend in the Merchant Navy.

Sunday 19

Cis didn't ring up. I am very worried.

Monday 20

Met Mummy in town for lunch; she brought me F's letter with the photo.
It is really lovely. Jacques looks very English and is really handsome; he
has a frank well-made face. Pat looks lovely, just as she is. Henri looks
to be smiling crookedly. And F has had all his wrinkles erased! Then I
read his letter that I'm still quite shaken about. He blames me for having
been out with Robert. If I told him about that, it is because it didn't
matter, but he took it quite the wrong way. *'My love is so exclusive that
it hurts me just to think that someone else might be near you, and who
knows? might also whisper sweet nothings; even though I know you
won't listen to them, they hurt me just the same. [...] Pat thought I was
being nasty. [...] In spite of all her worries the dear girl was right and
I'm glad I listened to her [...] for you've given me so much proof of
your love that those feelings I expressed could only hurt you. But I'm
rather upset these days and more sensitive than ever. Please forgive me
for treating you thus, for I know that you love me and I know I'm a
fool to even think of you like that – how dare I? Goodbye my love, and
don't worry because nothing has changed, I love you just as much, no,
much more than before this little storm. [...] I love you, darling, more
than ever. Your nasty but loving Francis.'* He said he had even torn up
a letter he had written before this one. He wrote fifteen pages, amongst
which were eight on the cinemas in France to help me to prepare my
talk. This evening he rang up only three minutes. He was sorry that he
had blamed me; he didn't know how to be forgiven. As for me, I didn't
know what to say; I felt like crying. I told him he didn't love me because
he didn't trust me. But I forgive him: one dare not do otherwise. I know
how upset he has been since Henri has been missing. I don't want him
to be unhappy because of me. I wrote to him.

Tuesday 21

His letter of 19th. He says Pat seems in slightly better spirits, but he worries
about her health. *'She feels tired and her whole body is aching, just as if
she had been beaten.'* He and Jacques do all their best to entertain her a

bit. '*Three or four days ago we had a good laugh. Jacques and I insisted on doing her hair, pretending we had come over from* Maison Antoine, *the hairdressing salon in Paris. As she really didn't trust our skills, we had to use force, so as to make her look beautiful the way we wanted her. So we sat her in an armchair, and willy nilly we did her hair in such a way that even the queen of the Zulus herself would have been jealous. All that we could lay our hands on we used as an ornament, from the children's toys to the flowers on the mantelpiece. When poor Pat saw herself in the mirror, she almost fainted in horror; her landlady arrived just at that moment, and when we asked her what she thought of Pat's hairstyle, she admitted she'd never seen anything like it before. Was it a compliment? I've no idea, but at any rate I can understand how she felt.*'
He wonders how I reacted to his previous letter. '*Don't be too cross,* Bébé, *please, I didn't want to hurt you. [...] I'm so impatient to know how you felt when you read my letter; you know, no sooner had I posted it than I wished I hadn't.*' At the end of his tour of operations, he thinks that he will have a four-month leave in France; but before that, he must still wait at least for four other months. He can't wait to see his family again. '*Now that I know that everything is alright back home, I would so much love to see them again, especially Dédé and my dear mother. Now I can see how much I've been more than ever deprived of family love throughout those four horrible years, because there wasn't always a sweet and kind Barbiche to lift my spirits. [...] Goodbye darling, don't worry, I love you, I love you, and once again I beg for mercy. All my heart is full of tender kisses – may they revive your love. Your Francis, your foolish Francis, more loving than ever.*' He did not ring: must have gone out. I sent him a lock of hair with my letter.

21 November: raid on a synthetic petrol factory at Sterkrade-Holten in the Ruhr. The Halifax of *capitaine* Loew (346 'Guyenne' Squadron) crashed into the ground, following a collision with a British aircraft above Belgian territory. Both crews were killed.

Wednesday 22

In his letter of Monday, he asks me if I feel upset or cross. He doesn't know how to apologize for having hurt me. Like me, he heard on the radio that the Allies continue to progress. He will send some chewing-gum to Patsy. They write to each other once a week; he says she has really made progress in French. He didn't ring up tonight either: surely he wouldn't have gone out two nights running. Poor darling, we don't have time to waste in quarrelling. I do love him so much.

Thursday 23

His letter of 21st. '*My darling, you sounded so sad as I spoke to you yesterday evening, what can I do to try and atone for my foolish words? You know, I haven't much time to write for I've been on permanent alert for four days, but just the same I have enough time to let you know I realize how heartless I was, and to tell you how much I love you in spite of all that I may do and say. I haven't received a letter from you, I suppose you need to think it over before you can answer, but I'm so impatient to find out what you think of me.*' Pat wasn't at home on Monday evening when he wanted to telephone; she had been to a little concert given by children. '*So I rang you from a booth and hadn't more than 1/8 in loose change. But those three minutes were enough for me to realize how upset you were. How your voice made me sad and how I cursed myself as well is impossible to describe. I wished I could have paid with tears of blood all the painful intonations I could sense in your voice. Oh believe me, Barbara, I love you, I love you, nothing can tear me away from you, not even you if you should wish to. Think whatever you like, but please don't have any doubt about my love. Be kind and forgiving, darling, this is all that will comfort me and my heart will be at peace only when you have written that you do forgive me. You said yesterday evening that this was the least you could do; your noble soul didn't even think that you could punish me, for that's what I deserve it, and I deserve it simply for even daring to have such thoughts. […] Goodbye now darling, I must leave you because once again, I have 'to go to town'. Today the weather's fine, and I think that this time the show will be on. All my heart, my poor heart flies towards you and I kiss you hesitantly, darling. I love you, Francis.*' Gave my talk on the French cinema. My professor congratulated me; I should congratulate F as it is thanks to him. I also did Old French. He rang at last: it was wonderful to hear him. By a bit of charm, we managed to get nine minutes. Yesterday they went to the cinema. He and Jacques had hidden Pat's shoes. She was much better. He has sent some chewing-gum to Patsy. He said, if anything should happen to him (may God protect him!) he had told a friend of his to telephone. He also said: '*I'm fed up!*' He won't be able to ring me for three or four days. I wonder if they are going to do other operations in Belgium. Thank Heaven, he did ring up!

Friday 24

De Gaulle is in Marseilles. Henri's watch arrived. Must send it to Pat. How sad it is!

Saturday 25

He got my two letters and my parcel at the same time. I think everything is all right now. '*My beloved one… Brr! What an icy-cold message! First the name: 'Francis' and only 'Francis'. But even then I think you were too kind. Personally I would have started the letter with: 'You old rogue'! No darling, you are the most brilliant creature I've ever met, and compared with you I feel I'm such a nonentity.*' He is even grateful to Robert, '*the nice young man I'd like to shake hands with, for without him I couldn't have realized how stupid I can be at times. Indeed you need to take your mind off things, darling, so why don't you go out, and not unaccompanied? That's what I'd like you to do, and I promise I won't ever throw a tantrum like the last one. [...] Oh darling, darling, I can see tears have fallen on that paper, and I kiss them just as I would your eyes. I curse myself for causing those tears; what shall I do to atone for that? [...] Thanks for the lock of hair, nothing could please me more. But if you go on, you'll be bald and if I have your locks spun and woven they will make a splendid uniform.*' On Wednesday they saw *Escape to Happiness* with Leslie Howard and Ingrid Bergman; Pat cried. During his last leave, Cis said to me: '*Tu m'appelles ta vie, appelle-moi ton âme, car l'âme est immortelle et la vie n'est qu'un jour.*'

Escape to Happiness (also called *Intermezzo: A Love Story*): a film directed by Gregory Ratoff (1939).

'*Tu m'appelles ta vie…*': 'You call me your life, Call me your soul, For life is only for a day, But the soul is forever' from *Fantasio*, by Alfred de Musset (1833).

Tuesday 28

He wrote this letter on his knees on Saturday, huddling by the fire; outside it was freezing. On Friday they couldn't go out because of bad weather; so they took Pat to the cinema. '*But this time it was a film with plenty of shooting and gunfights and battles and so on and so forth. It was very exciting. Really, Pat reacts like a child; this time she kept clapping her hands and was totally engrossed in the film. I think she's actually better now, morally and physically. Poor Pat, I hope the future will be kind to her because she's in such a state it might be dangerous for her if it didn't.*' I still feel he is sad and nostalgic. '*They're playing My Heart Stood Still on the wireless, it's the tune you are so fond of and I don't know why but it makes me melancholy. It's the same each time I see or hear something that reminds me of you and you're not here. I feel so lonely when I can't nestle in your arms, when I can't hear your heart beat, or when I can't kiss your lovely eyes. I wish you were close to me, I need your tenderness, I need you. [...] Bliss came into my heart from the moment I started loving you, and when you said 'I love you' it was enough for our two lives to become one; I saw in your eyes that love is worth more than any fortune; no matter where I may go now, whether it's in the streets or in the foreign lands that all blend in the shadowy nights, I will take your love with me to any corner of the earth; that's all I need to make me happy, now that love keeps us together.*' He told me another tragedy: his friend François is missing too. It's dreadful! '*Poor François has met the same fate as Henry did about one month ago. Nevertheless I hope he's alright, but it's so doubtful that I fear it might be a sacrilege for me to say so. [...] I love you, Bébé, I love you, you don't know how much I do, but maybe one day you'll find out. Good bye, Bébé, and don't fret too much, for I keep thinking of you more than ever. My sweetest kisses go out to you. I love you, Francis.*' Who will be the next one? When will the war be over?

My Heart Stood Still: composed by Richard Rogers for the musical *A Connecticut Yankee.*

Sergent François Saytour: Barbara had met him at the British Council in January 1944. He was a flight engineer in the crew of *lieutenant* Condé (346 'Guyenne'

Squadron) shot down above Düsseldorf on 2 November 1944. François was killed with four other crew members.

Wednesday 29

Joan has heard from Honoré who's back in France; F had said to her: '*If he does love you, he will come back; believe me, love never ceases.*' His letter of 26th. Every day they're expecting to do a sortie, and in the evening it is cancelled because of the weather. '*My nerves are on edge, you can't imagine how this waiting all the time for so long is nerve-wracking; to me it's more tiring than having 'to go to town' every night. Tonight my heart is dark and gloomy, it's a shadowy night, almost tragic and desperate, and I'm almost stifling in my room where I feel so confined. What can I do except dream? But what kind of dream is it? It's a dream in which I've been walking up and down for hours with a bitter heart, without being able to ease my pain and I try to open my eyes and look at the bright moonlight. What can I think of to cure my fever? In the distance there floats a blue and brown mist over the fields, and like a happy melody with a pure, uncluttered outline, the crest of the indifferent hill draws on the horizon a wavy line that links the stars together. The air is alive with sighs, voices and beating wings and a loud roaring can be heard down below, revealing the presence of water. I look at it all, I listen and breathe, and amid this huge void in which I'm standing and which is so painful to my heart and soul, I feel like shouting abuse at the bright night that I've just imagined and keep smiling to, but the night ignores me, for yet again it's you that I see, my beloved darling. [...] No, don't say anything, Bébé, just stay there until the last star, faithless to the pale sky, flees into the new morning. Look, dawn is already breaking, and hands full, it is scattering new pink roses. I like to think of you at the break of dawn, and many's the time when I return from one of my trips and the pink rays of the sun light up your face in the pure, cold air, and in the lovely setting of the landscape, my eternal love, you are even dearer to me. Why can't you be here to share with me this intoxicating fever, when nothing, neither the joyful world nor the blazing sky, can distract our two hearts from our dreams, two hearts which in the growing sounds of daylight cry out in the silence of our infinite love? Love? I open my eyes again and look around. Everything is still dark. My shining love has not come and there I am, more lonely still than ever before. The voices that kept my senses enraptured were but an echo, and the long dream in this sweet hour was only the effect of desire, that master of illusion. So it's better to shut the window and give up hope, and since everything, even the art of dreaming, is false, to forget my wild pain, I'll go and seek the safe refuge where a man can escape from his waking dreams. I'm going to sleep, darling, and maybe tomorrow morning I'll see a better world. [...] Don't worry if I seemed rather melancholy, it's nothing, just a small dark cloud caused by all the waiting in the past few days, I suppose. [...] With a big, a very big hug, even if it hurts you. Good night my angel, with yet more kisses, darling. Your Francis.'*

He rang: only three minutes. He hasn't been out of camp since last Thursday. Jacques has been sent some money. They have both decided to stop smoking! F said: '*You are so precious to me.*'

Inspired by *L'Eros funèbre*: a poem by Charles Guérin (1900).

Thursday 30

Lovely letter from Pat. She says one has to pay for one's bit of happiness. Obviously she thinks Henri is still alive, and F persuades her that he does too.

December

Friday 1

He wrote this short note on 28th. '*My darling, just a note – a short note for I didn't sleep yesterday, even if I didn't go to town, and tonight it's the same again, but it seems that the weather's quite fine. So I'm writing this brief note to tell you that I love you, I adore you, and you're my only love. I've got to leave you now darling, be good and sleep well. I send you all my love. With a thousand tender kisses. Francis.*' I'm so afraid for him. He rang whilst I was out. Said he hadn't been able to write for four days and couldn't ring again.

28 November: Essen in the Ruhr. 30 November: Duisburg mission cancelled for Francis' crew, following a failure of the navigation system.

Saturday 2

Went to the *British*. Roger Bordelais was there with his fiancée Irene. He's very sweet and so nice; very understanding about poor Henri: said there sadly was no hope at all. However François had been seen parachuting, but was not saved. Roger is very fond of F; he says he's a good chap and does nothing but talk about me! He had such a wistful air: hope he's ok. Introduced me to his *lieutenant* and two more of his crew, one called Patry. Danced with Aristide who was very cheerful; said he would be able to tell F that he had danced with me. I know Cis likes him. He also flies in 'G' but in the other crew. He said 'G' was full of holes. He went to Bochum on 4th November too and said five crews out of their squadron were missing. It is such a strain. Said F was terribly upset about Henri and worried about lying to Pat. However he is much better now. I was so glad to see Aristide and talk about Cis to someone who knows him and is so nice. But the *pièce de résistance* was that I met a sailor from Berre, who went to school with F! I couldn't believe it, but he proved it by describing both him and his family. His name is Maurice Feriolo and he is on the *Felix Roussel*. He is extremely amusing and very nice: he said he was glad to have news of Cis and that he would write to him. They were in the same gang: said F always wanted to join the Air Force and it was funny to think of him as a *sergent*. I can't get over how queer it was to meet him, almost novel-like. He had been in Toulon until two days before the invasion. He talked about F's escapades and wanted to know if he had changed.

Roger Bordelais was a rear gunner in the crew of capitaine Stanislas (347 'Tunisie' Squadron) – same crew as Maurice Bordier.

Felix Roussel: French liner built in 1929, dedicated to long voyages in the Indian and Pacific oceans, requisitioned by Great Britain at the beginning of World

War II and converted into a troopship. Re-commissioned with a mixed crew of French and British volunteers, she sailed under the flag of the Free French Navy in 1942.

Sunday 3

Cis rang at 8.30 pm. Went out to Hagen yesterday. He was at Pat's. I spoke to her. She sounded quite cheerful and asked me to look after him during his leave. Her cousin Sadie was there. Cis was most astonished about Feriolo: asked if he had lost his accent (no!) and what he was doing now. He was thrilled to hear about him and could not get over my meeting him. Seemed amused that he was in the Navy. I was so glad to hear Cis: he was in a marvellous mood. Went out to Hagen yesterday and said it wasn't a bad operation.

2 December: Hagen in the Ruhr.

Tuesday 5

His letter of 3rd. Pat has received Henri's watch and all went well. She's been much better for the last few days. Cis had just got up at 2.30 pm and said they talked about them on the radio and about what they had done on Saturday. '*Please forgive me if I don't answer all of your letters in detail, but this would be rather difficult. Did you meet Aristide? By the way it's his fault or rather the fault of his whole crew if we're so busy, because now we're the only ones to fly on old 'G', we find ourselves in the thick of it each time something's on.*'

He did not telephone.

Wednesday 6

He rang: said he would possibly come tomorrow, if no operation and everything went ok. Bordelais had given him news.

Thursday 7

At 11.30 pm F arrived, looking tired, and rather grubby. I think he threw himself into the train without having had time to change his clothes. He is sad and looks older than ever. Thank God, he's here after all! I can hardly believe it.

Friday 8

Mummy cleaned his trousers because they were muddy. He seems rather low and spiritless. Says Pat is in a bad way: nobody wants her and money is rather short. Poor girl, she doesn't deserve any of it. Poor F, he is trying to convince himself that there is hope for Henri. Went round to Gran's, then took the two dogs to the park. Guy came with us. He's one of the ground-crew that I met at the canteen. They got on well together. Had a long argument about equality between men and women: F is very feudal! He sometimes has very outmoded ideas: he is a real Southerner.

Saturday 9

Cis came to England exactly a year ago. What a lot has happened since then! Poor soul, I only hope that he lives to get back home. Said, whilst approaching Liverpool, Henri and he stood on the deck, not liking the look of England at all. Met Sheila and Guy and went to see *Two Thousand Women*. In the film, a bomber crew, exactly like F's, was shot down. I had a premonition when I saw an airman parachuting. I wondered how the man I love, and who was just beside me, would cope with that if he had to face such circumstances. In the interval, an actress, Nicky Nicholson, spoke. Stranded in Italy, then interned in Germany, she escaped via the Pyrenees into Spain. She thanked the French for their help. I put my head on F's shoulder, which I've so wished to do for so very long. Then, went to the *British* to meet the famous Feriolo. They were overjoyed to see each other again and they gossiped a lot. Maurice has married a Polish girl who lives near Marseilles and has a baby. F had a nasty incident with a Canadian, which upset him: as if he wasn't stretched enough to breaking point! We all walked down to the Pier Head. F and I came home. Cis told me that I am a woman with whom he can talk about anything, which made me happy. I sewed the buttons back on his shirt. I can hardly believe he is really here and that I needn't worry, for a bit at least.

Two Thousand Women: a film directed by Frank Launder (1944).

Sunday 10

F went off to Mass. He came back late, just as it was starting to snow. He told me: '*You are my sister, my mother and my love.*' We tried to ring Pat but she wasn't in. It's odd, I can stay for hours with Cis saying nothing. Heard *I'll See You Again*. Went to Gran's where F talked quite a lot of English. It snowed quite hard but we took Wien for a short walk though. F talks quite gaily of his family now; the cat, Mickey, is still alive. But he also has moments of awful sadness. Made sandwiches. He gave us an imitation of a ballet dancer in a passionate love scene!

Monday 11

Went to buy toys for Pat's landlady's children, and bought slippers for her, after a long search. Met two of F's crew. Then went to second-hand bookshop where I bought *Pêcheur d'Islande* and Aragon's *Crève-cœur*. Uncle Max invited us out to lunch at Reece's with a friend of his, Mrs Rowe, who lived in Paris and speaks good French. Then went to the *British* for a dance ticket and had coffee. A year today since Pat and Henri met. Pat told F to try to forget it on leave. But he can't help feeling sad, even when I am so happy. He bought black-market clothing coupons, then we went to the tailor's. Hope F is still here to get the suit. Rang up Pat who seemed well enough; she's going to work. Jacques went to see her this morning. Listened to French wireless station with Jo Bouillon and Ray Ventura singing *Je crois bien que c'est l'amour*. Whilst I was darning, F sang *Ces petites choses*. Said he didn't think anyone could love as much as he did me. I am so grateful that he has come, but so full of fear for the future that I can scarcely be happy.

Le *Crève-cœur*: collection of poems by Louis Aragon (1939–1940). *Ces petites choses* (*Those Foolish Things*): sung in French by Jean Sablon.

Tuesday 12

F was very quiet. I asked him what was wrong but I could not get it out of him. A girl, in the fruiterer's, said '*bonjour*' to F and gave us some nuts. He bought a lighter. Went to the *British*. Maurice Feriolo turned up with his little friend from Rochefort; he was great fun and smelt of garlic! I telephoned Mummy and we all went home and had a higgledy-piggledy dinner. F and Maurice reminisced a lot. We played records and tuned in to *French Cabaret*. We accompanied Feriolo to the bus stop. It was a lovely day.

Wednesday 13

It was extremely foggy and very cold. Went to St Helens to see Pat's mother. Had to get the train to St Helens junction, as the others weren't running. We seemed to be the only people in the world: we could see nothing out of the windows, there didn't seem to be anyone else on the train, we could hear nothing. It was both unreal and wonderful. F was very funny and seemed very happy. We got to the junction where we took a bus to St Helens, and then got another. Mrs Pattimore was going out but seemed pleased to see us. She seemed more concerned about Pat's mental state than about her immediate needs. Poor soul, she does live in sordid surroundings. She said sadly that it would be her fifth Christmas away from home (Channel Islands). I don't see what she can do to help Pat. Mr Pattimore came in and seemed only half awake: perhaps he works at night. We had to leave in haste for the train and we only just caught it. It was very slow back. There were fog signals all along the line. We kissed each other as if we were the only ones in the world. We didn't talk much as there was nothing to say. Once back home we rang up Pat who had fallen on some ice, poor girl. She seemed pleased that we had gone to see her parents. Her position is so pathetic and one can do nothing. I do try not to talk about Pat to take F's mind off it. Went to see Mr and Mrs Dick. F pretended to court Mummy who was very amused.

Mr Pattimore was a policeman.

Thursday 14

We went to Exchange station to meet Patsy who was coming back from her boarding school. Had a bath and changed. Found F asleep in the armchair in the dining room: he tossed and turned and shivered; it was very pathetic. Poor boy, he isn't really well, especially in mind. I got dressed in my black frock to go out, as F had asked me to. It's a nice second-hand dress from an American parcel that Mummy gave me; I am very fond of it. Had dinner and then went to the *British*. Saw

Maurice, as gay as ever, and scented with garlic! They played *I'll See You Again* and *Long Ago and Far Away*. F and Feriolo bade an affectionate farewell to each other. Danced some more and then came home. F very sweet: said I looked very pretty. What he needs is a long rest, away from planes.

Long Ago (and Far Away): a song from musical film *Cover Girl*, directed by Charles Vidor (1944).

Friday 15

Went to town: F tried on his suit; it will be ready in the New Year. F bought me a lipstick *Passion*, which amused us very much. We had lunch at the Rest A While, near the *British*. As he was saying he liked intimate restaurants, we saw Mummy and Patsy coming in! Then we saw *French Without Tears*, extremely amusing, especially with a Frenchman, Claude Dauphin, who was very good and sang *Il y a de la joie chez moi*. Had tea at the *British*; it was a bit sad. F bought me some violets. I was saying how complicated things were and he said they could be so simple if I chose. Also went to the AVF to ask for help for Pat. *Mme* da Horta, to my great surprise, was really unwilling to help. There was another woman there, who said Henri had married beneath him and how foolish they had been, and how selfish for the baby. It was very upsetting and F was furious, especially at having to ask charity from the AVF: it was humiliating. He said bitterly: '*Do people think we are just fighting machines and have no feelings at all?*' He said Henri's heart was not in his job after he got married. On the tram, I put my head on his shoulder, saying: 'I could stay like that forever' and he replied: '*Why don't you stay like that forever then?*' It is so difficult! Then went to Gran's with Patsy. F was very quiet; even Gran noticed. F and I wrote to his mother. Then he told me: '*You are not a baby: you are my* petite femme,' which pleased me very much.

French Without Tears: a film directed by Anthony Asquith (1940). *Petite femme*: darling wife.

Saturday 16

We went to meet Feriolo for lunch; F and he were very noisy. They told me I had chosen the table because the waitress was ugly! Then Maurice showed us photos of his wife, Anna, who is very pretty, and their lovely baby, Chantal. He asked me to tell Mummy how beautiful the baby is. Then we all went to see *Double Indemnity* with Barbara Stanwyck. Some Frenchmen sometimes call me '*Barbara Stan Week*': they find it funny! F was telling me that once, in North Africa, he pretended to be ill and went out in civilian clothes; as a punishment the Air Force cut all his hair off: the French are cruel! Went and had rather a sad tea at the *British*. Feriolo gave me his address before leaving. He left his wallet with his precious photos in it. So I gave it to Patrick, the receptionist; hope he gets it. F still very bitter about the AVF. Said nationality should make no difference; I said that it did and he said: '*Do you love me or not?*' It's all so complicated and so upsetting. He called me '*petite femme*' and I liked it, but it made me sad too. Daddy and Mummy went out after having said goodbye to F and Patsy went to bed. I was afraid and he told me: '*An airman's* petite femme *must be brave.*' We kept looking at the clock all the time: I hate it. He cried in the dining room: his eyes were red; he even looked quite noble as his face had changed. He said I shouldn't go to the tram with him, but I did. Walked so sadly to Penny Lane.

What a leave you had, my poor *Bébé*, you who need so much tenderness!

Double Indemnity: a film directed by Billy Wilder (1944).

Sunday 17

Feel completely numb; no feeling whatsoever. Everything reminds me of Cis. The house is very quiet. Yesterday he said there is a point at which everyone cracks. I wrote to him a miserable little letter. He rang up and sounded very low. I was not too cheerful either. He slept all the journey long and only woke up at York. Jacques, who was returning from London, came in late, as usual. He didn't wake up at York but at Darlington. Luckily nobody noticed, then the famous '*Doublepatte et Patachon*' were seen together again in the mess. Pat is better.

Darlington: some fifty-six miles north of York.
Doublepatte et Patachon: Doublepatte (tall) and Patachon (small), the inseparable,

burlesque heroes of a series of silent films, *Pat & Patachon* (*Long & Short*), shot by Danish director Lau Lauritzen; the films were very popular in the twenties.

Monday 18

Saw a Halifax so close that I could see the pilot. Cis rang: should have gone out but the weather was too bad. He sounded more cheerful. He said, when we were going to St Helens, how lovely it was to be going on a journey with me, knowing that we would be coming back together. What are we going to do?

Tuesday 19

Got a letter. '*Darling, the sky is clear now and the shining stars light up its dark blue hue. I'm not too sad, but everything just seems a little unreal. I can only think of yesterday when I was still in your arms, and of the long, long interval until they are round me again. My only thought is that I love you and we are far apart. I'm thinking of your beautiful eyes that were so sad and full of tears when I left you. Don't worry too much. [...] I so much wish that your love for me didn't cause so much pain. I'd give anything, even my life if necessary, to see you smile, but as usual these are only words, pathetic words which can do nothing. [...] I love you darling, and nothing evil can result from a love like mine. Sleep well, darling; forget the dark side of the world, and tonight let's walk together along the enchanted paths that only love can conjure up. Go to sleep, petite femme, and lay down your weary head. You can't rest it on my shoulder, but my heart's with you. Good night, darling, I must leave you, for it's very late. I love you, I love you, I'm madly in love with you and kiss your dear face, in tears, which both eludes me and haunts me in turns. Goodbye Bébé. Best regards to Riri, Mummy, Patsy, Gran and Mrs Dick. Make a face at Mrs Watson if you see her. My respects to Joan and Sheila. Please stroke Globule for me, and I send you kisses again but very tender ones, because I'm afraid I might wake you up. A thousand words of love to you. I do love you, Barbiche. Frankie, Duke Elvington, or Sheikh of Scunthorpe.*'

Duke Elvington: a pun about the name of the famous American jazz composer, pianist, and big band leader, Duke Ellington, and the name of the village of Elvington. Sheikh of Scunthorpe: *The Sheik* was a 1921 silent film by George

Melford starring Rudolph Valentino). Scunthorpe: a city in North Lincolnshire, fifty miles from York. Francis found the name funny and referred to a girl from that city whom he had met and told Barbara about.

Wednesday 20

Feriolo telephoned: he is very grateful about the wallet, and has again received news of his family. Said: 'I hope that all your wishes come true.' He's sailing tomorrow. I hope he will be safe and finally get to see his wife and the baby. He is nice; kept telling me to give his love to my parents. F rang. The weather was too bad to go out yesterday. He was teasing me and seemed fairly happy. He said once: '*I sometimes feel like carrying you off.*' On Saturday night we were sitting in the kitchen and quite suddenly he kissed the hem of my frock; it was a lovely gesture. He told us about the escape of François' crew's air gunner and how he had parachuted into a tree. He buried the parachute, as they all must, and walked seven nights across Germany in flying kit. Once, crossing a bridge, a German sentry shone his torch; so he merely crossed to the other side of the road. He finally reached the American lines and got back to Elvington ten days after the crash.

Sergent Soury-Lavergne: a rear gunner in the crew of *lieutenant* Condé (346 'Guyenne' Squadron), shot down on 2 November 1944. Five men killed.

Thursday 21

His letter of 19th is as sad as the one I wrote to him. '*My adored one, I received your little letter this morning; how melancholy it seemed. I myself feel quite indifferent to everything around me, and nature once again seems to be in harmony with my feelings: thick fog has shrouded everything around us since yesterday evening; and with the fog clouding our minds, everything is so blurry and confused, I can't even read. […] But let's not be too sad, we've now got to pay for the few fine days that we enjoyed. You'll smile again, darling, and again I'll take you in my arms, I'll touch your long hair and kiss each of your fingers. […] No, life is not too harsh because you love me, and why should I care as long as I know that your little heart is beating for me wherever I may be. […] Oh darling, we don't belong here; time is not on our side, and a thousand*

and one nights is such a short time for lovers. One year has gone by like brush-fire, and I'm now in love with you as I've never been before. [...] Listen to the breeze which says: 'I love you'. Each breath of wind is like a kiss from my eager lips. Good night, darling, I love you, I love you, you're my soul, my heart, my love, my everything. Good night, petite femme. *I love you. Francis.'*

Heard *Music! Maestro Please,* which he often sings in French. Must be out tonight. Poor sweetheart!

'*Time is not on our side*': referring to the poem *Les Yeux d'Elsa,* from *Cantique à Elsa,* by Aragon (1942).
Music! Maestro Please: sung in French by Léo Marjane.

Friday 22
Bought a record by Lucienne Boyer: *Je t'aime.*

Saturday 23
Cis rang. Had been out on Thursday and hadn't returned to Elvington when they landed near Scarborough: sounds like flak. Thank Heaven they are ok! He has received his Christmas present, has bought and sent mine off. Jacques was pleased with my card. Cis said: '*You are my* petite femme, *especially in shops.*' He thinks I am frugal. He asked me if I had '*a target for tonight*'; I don't know what he meant. Such a pity that he can't come for Christmas! Heard *Tristesse* on Radio Andorra.

Target For Tonight: title of an RAF documentary film directed by Harry Watt (1941).
21 December: Cologne marshalling yards. On the way back, '*G for George*' landed at RAF Carnaby emergency airfield, near Bridlington (some nineteen miles from Scarborough) in East Yorkshire.

Sunday 24
Christmas Eve. F did not ring up: am very worried about him. Had an air-raid warning last night; bombs somewhere, but we did not get up to go to the shelter.

Monday 25

Christmas Day. Couldn't sleep: too worried about F. He gave me a wonderful green-coloured powder compact, in real leather: it must have cost the earth and it really is a beauty. Bless him! I shall always treasure it. He enclosed a little note: '*With all my heart, my love and best wishes. Francis.*' Heard the King on the wireless, and also the bells of *Notre-Dame*. Thought of Cis, whom we would all have liked to be here. Thankfully he rang up; spoke to Pat who sounded fairly cheerful and to Jacques who does speak with an Oxford accent. He is nice; I thanked him for being so kind to F. Seemed to be glad that I had sent him a Christmas card. F quite cheerful. Had been out last night and had to land on another airfield again, because of the fog this time. Had a good Christmas dinner on the station later in the evening. Said how much he wished he were here with us and asked me to give his best wishes to all the family. Jacques gave him *The Oxford Book of French Verse* for Christmas. It's Pat who chose the powder compact.

A quiet Christmas, but much happier for us than for some poor souls. Poor Pat, how she must miss Henri!

24 December: Mulheim-Essen airfield in the Ruhr. '*G for George*' hit by flak. Only one French crew went missing: that of *Lieutenant* Leroy's (347 'Tunisie' Squadron) shot down after having completed the mission. Five men killed. The two survivors, *sergent-chef* Guédez, mid upper gunner (Geneviève Monneris' father) and *sergent-chef* Duran, flight engineer, met again in a German jail on Christmas Day.

RAF Carnaby emergency airfield was equipped with FIDO (Fog Investigation and Dispersal Operation).

The Oxford Book of French Verse, 13th–19th century, by St John Lucas.

Tuesday 26

Bombing of Rundstedt's lines. Cis must have been out.

Field Marshal Von Rundstedt's offensive in the Ardennes, the Battle of the Bulge.

Wednesday 27

Bomb on Manchester last night. Heard *Venez donc chez moi*.

Chez moi: sung by Lucienne Boyer.

Thursday 28

Cis did not ring. Am so worried about him.

Friday 29

I wish he would let me know his news; everyone is getting very anxious. It's nearly a fortnight since I had a letter. What can have happened to him?

29 December: Coblenz.

Saturday 30

Cis rang up at 6.15 pm, thank Heaven! He is very busy and rather tired. His squadron has been decorated and he has the right to wear another ribbon (an *étoile* perhaps?) His lighter is still working. Said he had recently earned his pay, and he had missed telephoning me very much. I am so relieved to have heard him. Pat is much better. They're going to a ballet on Monday. I also got his letter of 27th. '*You know, it's been the same old story all over again, just the way it was before my last leave: we were bored every day, and in spite of that I've only 'been to town' twice since I came back. Nevertheless Christmas Day wasn't too bad for me. But you know I went to town on Sunday and on the way back we couldn't make it to Elvington because the fog was too thick. And if you'd seen how we came back in a lorry, it was a real nightmare: we were approximately thirty miles from our station, it was Christmas Eve and we'd landed on an airfield where there was nothing, not even a canteen. To top it all off, they sent lorries to fetch us, but the one Jacques and I got in was driven by an English lad who didn't even know the way back. So after starting off in the fog and wandering like ghosts along country roads, it was midnight when we reached Elvington. I thought of you darling, with all my heart and soul, and so much wished that you were with me. Please forgive me for not writing sooner, but I simply couldn't. I imagine you must have felt concerned and this is why I feel so guilty. But I couldn't even send a telegram. Well, I hope I can do better on New Year's Day. [...] I'll write a proper letter tomorrow. Good night darling, 'see you' tomorrow, and also at 9. I love you darling, good night. Regards and best wishes to all. Your Francis, who's thinking of Barbiche, his petite femme, more than ever. Sealed with a thousand kisses.'*

I received a very nice note from Jacques as well, in perfect English, to thank me for my Christmas card and wish me a happy New Year 1945. He hopes to see me soon. He says that I must never talk about gratitude about what he may have done for Francis, that they naturally get on well and are happy, just thinking they can rely on each other, whatever happens.

Sunday 31

I am writing this at 11.50 pm and it feels a bit melancholy. It's been a lovely year, in many ways, and I'm sorry it's all over. Cis probably out. What a way to spend New Year's Eve! Poor sweetheart, I wish him the best of the world, and to all the poor foreigners that I met, I wish them back home soon.

1945

January

Monday 1

New Year's Day. The postman chatted about F! Saw *Carnet de bal*: it was wonderful! Louis Jouvet quoted: '*Dans le vieux parc solitaire et glacé, deux formes ont tout à l'heure passé*' exactly as F does. I could hardly restrain my tears. Shots of Paris with barricades and de Gaulle in the newsreels. Hope F got to the ballet. He didn't ring up. A year today since I met him: it seems like centuries. Dear little Cis, my sweetheart, my little bear, let's hope he will be safe this year again! I don't know what we must expect.

Un Carnet de bal: a film directed by Julien Duvivier (1937).
'*Dans le vieux parc...*': quotation of the first two verses from *Colloque sentimental*, a poem from *Fêtes galantes*, by Paul Verlaine (1869).

Tuesday 2

At the canteen, Helen let me read a letter from her French correspondent in Le Havre: there have been four thousand dead. I saw two *sergents* from Elvington. A year today since Cis came home; he looked so small and shy, but seemed rather on his best behaviour.

Wednesday 3

Cis probably went to Ludwigshafen last night: there was a report in the newspaper. He did not ring up. I hate this silence. He must be so busy and tired. Poor little soul! Sheila heard that a terrible accident at Elvington caused the death of fourteen soldiers. They were killed at bomb loading on the station. It's awful!

28 December 1944: whilst loading bombs into a Halifax, one exploded, killing eight men and injuring five others among the French members of ground crew, and killing six British personnel.

Thursday 4

About half past 10 am a telegram came saying Francis was missing: '*Regret to inform you that your friend Francis Usai is missing as the result of air operations on night of 2nd January. Any further information received will be immediately communicated to you.*'

We were all horrified, although we knew that it would happen sooner or later. I don't know what to say. I feel so empty, so lonely. I spent most of the day in bed, crying. Poor Pat, what will she do now, with no support left? I rang her up but they said she wouldn't be available for a fortnight: perhaps she has come home. I told Sheila who was most upset. Mrs Dick came round in the evening; she was nice and said that, at least, I had given him all the happiness he had known in England. It's awful, such a good boy! And tall kind Jacques whom his fiancée is waiting for! And poor Morel and *Chérubin*, and all the others! I looked at the clock at 9 pm because it seems impossible that he is missing. Poor darling, I can hear his voice, I can see him asleep in the armchair, with poor Henri at the *British*, kissing my hand, saying to me '*courage!*' on the train, walking on the sand at Kirkby Thore, or on the bridge at Appleby. I knew it would only last a year. '*Je ne suis qu'au printemps, je veux voir la moisson.*' I feel numb, I don't know what to do anymore. There is no-one now to call me '*petite femme*' or '*Barbiche*' or '*Bébé Rose*'. We were so happy together, we did wonderful things. I don't think there is hope, but if so, he will manage. It all seems to me unreal. I keep thinking that he will telephone perhaps or that I will hear something at least, but 'the rest is silence!' It's the end of the day. Oh! Cis, you were perfect:

there was no-one like you, and I love you and you loved me. Oh! Cis in the huge plane, in the cold night! He wanted to go back home so much, and see his mother and his friends again. Poor *Mme* Uzay who loved him so much. Goodbye darling, I give you a kiss.

2 January 1945: Halifax '*G for George*' of *lieutenant* Cottard (347 'Tunisie' Squadron) was shot down by mistake by American flak, on the way to a mission on Ludwigshafen, and crashed in the area of Metz, in Lorraine. It was the only loss that day, among the 389 aircraft taking part in the mission.

Chérubin: nickname of *lieutenant* Cottard the captain.

'*Je ne suis qu'au printemps...*': 'I'm only in the spring; I want to see the harvest': verse from *La Jeune Captive*, by André Chénier (late 18th century).

'The rest is silence': the last words of Prince Hamlet in Shakespeare's play *Hamlet*.

Friday 5

I feel awful, so empty, very unreal. The last fortnight has been terrible. Sent telegram to *M*. Uzay and Maurice Feriolo.

Saturday 6

Went to Mr Frank's. He was extremely sweet about F; I expect he knows what it's like, as his son is a paratrooper. Joan came home. She was extremely sweet too; she said she had burst into tears on hearing the news, and that I had given Cis so much happiness and we loved each other, that was all.

Mr Frank: the dentist.

Sunday 7

I was writing a difficult letter to *Mme* Uzay when Pat phoned me in the middle of it. She did not know and I had to tell her the news; she took it marvellously. She turned up from St Helens an hour later. She looked awful, so white and poorly. Poor Pat, she doesn't want to stay in York now. She's so sweet and wonderfully brave. She seems still convinced that Henri is still alive. She said he had completely lost his nerve, as was plain to see, and they had awful rows as she never thought he might get shot down. Jacques was losing his nerve too, which is why F stressed that he had confidence in him. She talked about F being sweet to her landlady's children, playing games with them at Christmas. The girl she's staying with, one Mary Mason, is a charming girl. Pat and F had been to the ballet on New Year's Day; he had made her promise to come to see me saying: '*Tell her that I love her, that I always will, and that I keep dreaming of her beautiful eyes.*' How lovely! Pat said: 'You think he's dead, don't you?' and I said: 'Yes!' She is so sweet. Wish I had half her courage. She insisted on accompanying me to the tram stop. Went to see the Dicks who were very sweet.

Monday 8

While we were having supper, another telegram arrived from Elvington, saying Francis was injured in a French hospital: '*Further to telegram 4 Jan. No10935, Sgt. Usai now known to be injured and admitted to hospital in France. Stop. Degree of injury not known, you will be informed of any further news.*'

It's marvellous to hear something definite at last and to know he is alive, but the telegram says the extent of his injuries is not known. I expect it's serious: probably the plane crashed or maybe F parachuted. Poor darling, he's never been in hospital in his life. Hope to heaven it's not an amputation, or burns, or that he isn't blinded. I suppose it's too much to expect that it is not serious. Thank God, I know that kind people are looking after him and doing all they can to help him. Let him live, let him live! Telegraphed Pat; I only wish she could hear of Henri. Oh! Cis, my little baby, you were wearing the medallion and you had Nostradamus. He will have the will to live, I'm sure. Maybe he will be all right; I dare not to think about it, my little Cis! Went to see about his suit this morning. They were horrid: they said I had to pay; most sordid! Wrote to Antoine Morel's father.

Tuesday 9

Joan, Mary Owen and Beatrice were so moved hearing about F being safe: their eyes filled with tears. Mummy told Mr Frank who was very pleased. I am so worried about Cis. I wish I knew how he is, but maybe the longer I don't hear the better. Pat sent a telegram: she's ill in bed but glad for F. God bless my darling, my little bear!

Wednesday 10
Got a sweet letter from Roger Bordelais, written on Sunday when there was no news yet.

Thursday 11
Wrote to Roger. I hope Cis is safe. I wish I could hear more about him. Maybe he'll write; he would if he could. It's so worrying. I love him.

Friday 12
Had my studio portrait taken for F at Bacon's. My Cis, write to me! I wonder all the time how you are. Heard Jean Sablon singing *Ces petites choses*.

Saturday 13
Roger wrote me another very sweet letter. He says F is rather seriously wounded in one leg. I hope he is not trying to hide anything from me. He's really glad about F being safe and calls him '*our* Francis'. Maurice Bordier also wrote; he hopes to see me and says how fond he is of Cis. Wonder if exile makes these boys stick together. Sheila heard that five of the crew had baled out in American lines, but no-one knew of Jacques and Cis. Hope poor Jacques is ok. F probably stayed in the plane; I do hope he hasn't to have his leg off. I think a lot about Jacques and him. How kind of Roger: he hopes to meet me next Friday; hope he can.

Sunday 14
Pat and Mary came to see us. Poor Pat, she does look ill. She is very glad about F. She seems definitely to be going to Algiers, and I think it would be a good thing. Henri's parents seem very nice. Jean Dahnen had been to see them before she married him. They are very aristocratic. His father should have come to the wedding. Henri was crippled as a little boy; his mother went to Lourdes, and he was cured. Pat seems only to be living for the baby. Poor, poor Pat, she has done nothing to deserve this. Uncle Max can help her about clothing coupons.

Monday 15

Met Pat who had been sick twice before coming. Went to Cook's. They seemed very doubtful about her passage, which they said must be a priority, which upset her very much. Pat told me about F. He was practically engaged to a Spanish girl in North Africa, but now she does not write. When he first met me, he only wanted a friend, but then he really began to love me, of which Pat and I are convinced. She also said that he wanted to marry me, that he had enough will to wait and even to do that hated job of accountancy. One day, she heard Henri saying to F: 'Behave properly with Barbara, otherwise I will wring your neck!' Dear Henri, he need not have bothered. I suspect Pat thinks that I don't love F enough to marry him. Poor Cis, he even suggested opening a night-club to earn enough money for me! It's just like him, my dear angel. I didn't want to leave Pat alone as she was upset. So I hurried up to the university and came back and had lunch with her; then she told me all about Henri. Poor soul, she misses him so much. She cried; it was awful. We then bought a trunk and went again about F's suit. Pat sent a cable to *Mme* Martin. She said she had really enjoyed herself.

Tuesday 16

At the canteen, a horrid soldier showed me a pipe for which an old Frenchwoman had asked 150 francs, but he had just taken it without paying. What a bad opinion she would have of English soldiers! Wish F would write. Our 9 o'clock rendezvous is our only contact. Jacques told Pat he was a bit upset as F never confided in him. F is very discreet when he wants to be.

Wednesday 17

Dinner: still no potatoes. Lots of Halifaxes out yesterday. Hope poor Roger and Maurice were ok. Oh! Cis, just write me a little note! This wait is awful.

Bombing of Magdeburg in Germany: two Halifaxes of 347 'Tunisie' Squadron missing, those of *capitaines* Bresson and Marin. Six men killed.

Thursday 18

Got a letter from Dr Smart about Pat's baby-clothes. F once said to Pat about me: '*Poor little thing, she's so good.*' Perhaps he is being moved or suffering from shock. I do want to write to him.

Dr Smart: the family's woman doctor.

Friday 19

Met Pat and Mrs Pattimore; went to the English-Speaking Union about baby-clothes. Mrs Britten was very kind, and so were Mrs Freeman and Barbara. But Mrs Pattimore was hopeless and very disdainful, only wanting 'dainty' things; I felt ashamed for her. Mrs Britten's daughter brought me a letter which Mummy had entrusted to her. It was a tiny little note from Francis dated 5th January and written very shakily on American Red Cross paper. '*My darling, I'm going to try and write these few lines as I imagine that for some days now you must have been terribly upset. Jacques and the rest of the crew must be back by now and they probably think I'm dead; I can't give you details but Jacques will explain it all. At any rate I was quite seriously wounded in the plane but after crawling a bit I managed to bale out. Don't worry darling, I'm better now, but unfortunately I'm stuck here for three months at least. This is an American hospital and I'm rather well looked after. I've got to leave you here darling because I'm not supposed to write, I'll write a longer letter when I receive one from you. Please tell them at the station that I've written to you. I love you, I love you more than ever. Goodbye* petite femme. *Your Francis.*' He seems fairly cheerful although he isn't supposed to write. I am so pleased; that pathetic little note means more to me than any other letter he's written.

Saw Sheila who was pleased about F, and Pat was glad to hear about him too. Mrs Pattimore rather got on my nerves: so extravagant and not adaptable. Pat has written to Ministry of War Transport about her passage to Algiers. Went to the *British* and met Roger Bordelais, as nice as usual. His fiancée, Irene Owen, was there too. He says Jacques is still missing, which will be a big blow to F, and that the plane had a wing and an engine on fire. F was hit before anyone; the others all baled out together, then F jumped, and Jacques was alone on board, with five tons of bombs still in the plane. Poor boy, I'm afraid he hadn't much chance, I'm so sorry. Everyone speaks so well of him. Roger said he was '*magnifique*'. F seems to think he is ok. Morel has gone back to France. When the five landed, *Chérubin* went to reconnoitre, thinking it was Germany. He said, if he wasn't back in five minutes, they were to make their own way. Roger told me to write to his squadron leader, *capitaine* Stanislas. He was kind and spoke so nicely of F. He said he had thought of writing to me when he saw that I had already been notified. Wrote to F: lovely to write to him again! Poor Jacques, I am so sorry. Wish Pat could hear from Henri.

English-Speaking Union: English–American organization which delivered parcels sent by Americans.

Mrs Britten and Mrs Freeman: friends of Barbara's family. Mrs Britten was also a neighbour.

Barbara: a former schoolfellow.

Saturday 20

Rang up Mrs Britten to apologize for Mrs Pattimore's behaviour; she was impossible. Wrote to *capitaine* Stanislas and sent Maurice Bordier's letter to F. Mrs Orford asked after F. Her son, who was also in the RAF, was killed. Joan rang up; Mrs Manson had told her that I had heard from F. Dear Cis, I can hardly believe that you wrote to me. Oh darling, three long months before you come back. Get better soon! I hope you will soon be healed.

Sunday 21

Listened to Jean Sablon on Radio Paris. Also heard General Valin telling about a raid by the 'Lorraine' Squadron. Wrote to *Mme* Uzay and read F's letters again; he really is most fluent and intelligent.

'Lorraine' Squadron: FAFL bomber squadron, created by General Valin in July 1941, integrated into the RAF as '342 Squadron' in April 1943.

Monday 22

20th birthday. My best present is that little note from F I got on Friday. Today got a telegram from him which must have been very long in coming so much delayed: '*Am wounded. All's fine. Tell the crew. Letter follows. Kisses.*' Has address of 36th American Hospital in Dijon. Big surprise: also got a very nice letter from the Uzays, dated 8ᵗʰ January. Poor souls, they are most worried, they only had got my first telegram. Jeanne is in hospital with appendicitis. Rose is 18 and seems very nice. She says she could understand my French and Cis seems fatter and more manly to her; he must have sent them a photo of him; I think he is thin. She enclosed photos. She is very dark, very like Cis. Jeanne is lighter and more buxom. Papa looks tough and rather strict. I am glad to have this letter. Met Sheila and we wandered round, choosing books for Cis. Wore my *hibou*, Francis' badge, which Uncle Max kindly has made into a brooch for me. I also thought of this time, last year, with F doing his imitations, talking about '*Macaronis*', or him sitting reading English by the fire. Do hope he isn't in great pain; he must feel lost in an American hospital. I do wish I could do something.

Hibou: owl on 347 'Tunisie' Squadron's badge.

Tuesday 23
Posted Cis' parcel: books and cigarettes. Saw *Heart of a Nation* with Raimu, Louis Jouvet, Michèle Morgan and Suzy Prim. Heard it was the last copy left; it had been buried by the roadside in France, then dug up, and then smuggled to America.

The Heart of a Nation (French title: Untel père et fils): a film directed by Julien Duvivier. Filming started in late 1939 but was interrupted by the war. It was released in the USA in 1943.

Wednesday 24
Roger Bordelais went back. Hope he had a good leave. Heard *I'll See You Again*. Poor Cis, I hope someone is taking adequate care of him, and that he's happy and comfortable.

Thursday 25
Bitterly cold. Wrote to him. Hope he is feeling better. I do miss all his regular letters and phone calls. Hope so much he gets my mail, or he will worry.

Friday 26

News at last! Had a longish letter from him coming from Dijon, dated 13th January. '*Hello darling petite femme. At last I can write a few lines to you, I suppose you've already received the short note I sent you via the American Red Cross. I wanted to send a telegram but haven't been able to so far. How worried you must have been my poor darling, especially since the rest of the crew probably don't believe I'm still alive. I suppose Jacques must have written or explained the whole thing to you, at least until the moment when he jumped out. At any rate, in spite of my wounds, I managed to get out of my turret and bale out moments before the plane crashed to the ground. Some American soldiers and a French gendarme found me an hour later. The poor gendarme was so moved at seeing a French airman that he burst into tears and hugged me. They took me to an American hospital – that was the one where I wrote you my first letter. Five days later I was put on board a hospital train and taken to this place. And now it's only a matter of being patient: a piece of shrapnel went right through my right thigh and the bone is shattered. Well I'll wait, we'll wait, but I can see that I'll be feeling very lonely for I've got nothing here that belongs to you, darling, except for your bracelet and your little medallion. Listen darling, do send me one of your photos if you can, this is what I'd most like to have. Well, I was very lucky and I think I must thank Providence. The only problem is that I'm far away from you, my poor darling, and wish so much that you could be by my side. However at least I can write to you and that's some consolation, but I'm going to stop here darling because I also have two pieces of shrapnel in my right arm and it's a little difficult for me to write for long. Goodbye and go to sleep petite femme, I leave you thinking of the day when we are re-united. My warmest regards to your family and 'The Three Graces'. I love you Bébé, more and better each day. Your Francis.*' He seems so gay and brave despite his injuries, just his own self! He should have come on leave today. Hope he doesn't remember it.

'The Three Graces': Sheila Smith, Joan Hughes and Pat Moore.

Saturday 27

Went to see Kathleen Orford about getting a letter to Cis through the American Red Cross; she was so kind. I will take it to her tomorrow. In the newsreel, I saw a short film: *The War in a French Village*. One could see berets, bicycles, the crowd getting out of Mass on a Sunday, French policemen (God bless the one who found Cis!) the village square and the city-hall. The village was called Pagny-sur-Moselle.

Kathleen Orford: daughter of Mr and Mrs Orford, the Rigbys' neighbours.
Pagny-sur-Moselle: a city in Meurthe-et-Moselle, in Lorraine.

Sunday 28

Wrote to him. I wonder how he feels on French soil. And if he didn't come back here? At least, I know he won't fly for a few months. I can't seem to see his face; I only see a vague shape, a shape with a sweater (with a hole!), a raincoat or his peaked cap with its bright gold band. My little treasure, my dear bear, I love you so.

Monday 29

Lunch with Beatrice and Olga. I gave them my reasons for not marrying Cis. Beatrice agreed. Sheila heard Elvington is snowed up. I wonder if Jacques might be alive. Met Mrs Dick who was very interested in Cis. I can't stop talking about him to everybody. They will end up finding me really boring.

Tuesday 30

Nice letter from Flying Officer Haworth who, strange to say, knows nothing of F, where he is, or what is wrong with him. Anyway I wrote and told him myself! Wish F could get some of my letters. One from him arrived today, dated 19th, just like his old letters, very sweet indeed. '*My darling, please forgive me for such a long interval between my two letters but my right arm has been operated on and up till now it wasn't very good. I've got some information, Bébé, and it'll be some nine weeks before I'm sent back to England. That's a long time but after all it's necessary if I want to be able to walk again as I want to. But you mustn't let this new ordeal throw you into despair. Out of sight, out of mind, as the saying goes, but I don't believe it's true. My heart's never been closer to you than it is now and never do I miss our little rendezvous every evening. Be patient darling, and above all don't allow this to disrupt your studies. Just tell yourself that after all I'm not that unhappy, because I know that in England there's a little heart which beats for me, and above all I'm now in my own country whereas all the fellows suffering here are thousands of miles away from theirs. [...] How is Pat? Poor little sister, she must feel very lonely now. It's a good job Jacques probably goes to see her from time to time. Telephone her sometimes if you can, darling, that'll make a nice change for her. As for me, you see, I'm not feeling too bad; my leg is in a device that reminds me of a bicycle. [...] By the way what have you done about my uniform? Just ask Jacques to send you the rest of the money and take it if you haven't already done so. In any case I'm going to write and explain this to him. [...] Do tell yourself that I love you more than ever, as much as I possibly can. I tenderly kiss your two little hands, and yes, I'll even dare to kiss your lips. I'll think of you at 9 Bébé! With a thousand kisses from your Francis who's more than ever yours.'* The men next to him in bed are Americans; the nurses are American too and very nice; some French girls brought him books. He thinks Jacques is back at Elvington. Poor little boy, I know he is in pain but he never complains. I do so wish to see him.

Flying Officer Haworth: RAF liaison officer.

Wednesday 31

What a long month! I thought it was never going to end. Letter from Pat: one can't send Red Cross parcels. Proofs of photos from Bacon's very nice; will send one to F.

February

Thursday 1

Joan's still annoyed with me 'because I won't sacrifice myself' and marry F. Sacrificing myself would be a disaster. Cis really needs a domesticated

and charming wife: not me! Russians ten miles from Berlin; if this
continues, I'll never see him again, though that's a very selfish thought.
Sent him two hundred cigarettes. Saw a Swedish hospital repatriation
ship at Pier Head, the *Drottningholm*: she was white and all floodlit.

Friday 2

Poor F, I do hope he's got one of my letters; he'll worry otherwise.

Saturday 3

Saw in *France Magazine* an article on the *Groupe Tunisie* of the FAF.
Went to AVF. *Mlle* Foog, of the FFI, spoke, and *Mme* da Horta sang!
Got another letter from Cis, dated 22nd January. He still thinks Jacques
is fine and he's going to write to him. '*My little darling, another short
note tonight because whenever I write to you I'm happy, nothing else
matters then, and it seems that you are here, that I can speak to you,
touch your hair, and kiss your oh so beautiful eyes. Why do I have to
be far away from you and remain so still? I only need to be reminded
of you by something or other, and then my heart beats faster. Darling, it
hurts me to be far away from you, I wish you could be right here by my
side to murmur some sweet, silly words once more. But it's stupid of me
to complain, because this is my own country; I'm now receiving letters
from my family almost every day, and I'm looked after like a child – but
happiness without you is meaningless. [...] But I'm selfish not to think
of you, my poor darling who was in tears last time I saw you. I was so
afraid for you at the beginning, and once again I blamed myself when I
considered that if you wept, it was because of me. Do please write soon
so I can hold something that you have touched, and that may have kept
some of your perfume. But don't be too miserable, my love! No matter
how far away I may be, I'm always at your side and I'm sure you can
sense this presence around you. Listen to the wind, darling: it whispers
words of love. Look at the sky, and you will see the star that we've so
often gazed at together, which is as bright as ever. Whatever you touch
or look at must surely remind you of my love.*'

He thanked me for the two telegrams I sent to his family and says his
little brother Dédé already likes me and dreams of getting to know me.
They're having two film showings a week.

Sunday 4

Read F's old letters. He talks so much of Jacques.

Monday 5

Letter to F returned because I had enclosed a photo. How stupid of me!
Letter from Pat Moore to say that Maurice Miodon, her paratrooper
boy-friend, was killed on 1st June 1944 in Finistère. She is most upset.
Oh! Cis I so wish to see you.

Censorship forbade sending photos to other countries. Finistère: a department
of France in the extreme west of Brittany.

Tuesday 6

Extremely nice letter from *capitaine* Stanislas who was very pleased to
hear F was safe. Went to see *Saludos Amigos*; wish F could have seen it:
it's just his sort of film. Walked to Pier Head; lovely night. Feel very sad
and wish so much for Cis to be here with me.

Saludos Amigos: an animated feature package film directed by Norman Ferguson
and produced by Walt Disney (1942).

Thursday 8

Wrote to John, asking him to write to F, saying that I am writing too, as
his letters seem so quick. I hope he can: it would reassure him.

John: a soldier friend who was in Germany.

Friday 9

Went to the *British* to pay my AVF subscription. *M.* da Horta is being
promoted to be *chargé d'affaires* in India. *Mme* da Horta asked about
F and seemed upset to hear what had happened. She said I looked Slav!
Met Mary Mason; Pat is going to London to live with the Singletons (I
don't know them). Have volunteered to knit for French soldiers on the
Vosges front; much laughter at home as I'm not so good at knitting!
Made up small parcel for F. Feel very sad; I miss him so much. Do hope
he has heard from me. Why hasn't he written?

Saturday 10

Letter from Rose. They hear regularly from F. Enclosed photo of Dédé who looks sweet, frank and jolly.

Monday 12

At last a letter! Cis gave it to an American soldier who was going to England. '*It was your name that I uttered after I'd slept the sleep of the dead for two whole days. It is your face that I see when I shut my eyes; it is your voice that I hear when I fall asleep. No, darling, nothing can separate me from you, you're just another part of me. When you are far away, I'm like a body without a soul. [...] When will I be happy again and feel your sweet, young arms round my neck? When shall I be able to cover your face again with mad kisses? How I long to see you again, darling, how I yearn to hear your voice and hear you say I love you.*' I am so proud that he mentioned my name first; no-one could ask for more. He says he's been in that American hospital in Dijon for two weeks, that he will have to stay another two months there and that the nurses are looking after him well; his leg is held in an appliance as his thigh bone is broken. I do hope he has had one of my letters.

Tuesday 13

Canadian, at canteen, said he would take a letter to Cis as he is stationed near Antwerp. Was in Bayeux when General de Gaulle was there.

Wednesday 14

I do wish Cis would write. Hope it's only the post and that he has not had a relapse because of Jacques.

Thursday 15

About *Polyeucte* I got an acid comment that my spoken French was much better than written! Packed up parcel for Cis.

Polyeucte: a French tragedy by Corneille (1641).

Saturday 17

When will you come back? I'm longing to put my arms round you so much.

Monday 19

Daddy bought two jigsaw puzzles for F. Oh! Cis, write to me! I'm longing to see you or even hear from you, my sweet little owl.

Wednesday 21

Letter from Pat who is going to London on Wednesday. She was rather hurtful about me telling F Jacques was missing. French mail very bad.

Friday 23

Dr Hanna asked me was there anything wrong. So I told her the whole tale about F, though Heaven knows why! She was very sweet and said I was still young, did I go out with any other men, and that women always had to wait and that I ought to get my degree to help F. I am surprised how understanding she was. Oh! Cis, write to me, darling. I love you so much and want you near me.

Dr Hanna Schuma: German lecturer.

Saturday 24

Letter at last from F, dated 31st January. He has had no letter from me: it's heartbreaking. '*My darling* petite femme, *I'm not feeling too well tonight. It may be due to fever, and I've just got to write to you, I simply must; I always feel better when I talk to you. [...] Why have I got such dark thoughts even though you love me – for you do love me, don't you? Haven't you given me proof enough? You've given me something wonderful, the most a woman can give a man. [...] What I'm afraid of is not that you might forget me or not love me; no, but you might think that because I'm far away from you and in my own country at last, I'm drifting away from you. This thought has been gnawing away at me and haunting me ever since I've been here. How can I explain this without upsetting you? In my first letters I tried to sound as gentle as I could, but did I manage to convince you? I do so wish I could have a letter from you, but know the mail between France and England is very slow. Why didn't you answer my telegram? But I don't want to have you worrying; I've already given you enough trouble so far, so I'm going to put an end to this tirade of sadness. I just want you to know*

that I now love you even more than in the days when we were together.
Good night, now, darling! It's 9 o'clock and I'm thinking of you. As
usual, with all my kindest regards to your family and our friends. Sweet
dreams, darling, I'm going to try and get some sleep. A thousand kisses
from your Francis who adores you.' On the back of the envelope, he
wrote: *'con todo mi amor.'* I do hope he's heard from me now. Anyway
I feel so much better.

Went to Alder Hey Rehabilitation Hospital. The patients do gym,
woodwork and handicrafts. They all seemed very cheerful and
surprisingly not bored. An instructor showed us the exercises they do
for muscles.

Heard *La Chanson des rues*. Wrote to Cis. God bless him! Dear Cis,
when shall I see you again? I can't wait to put my arms round you. I
don't know what the end will be.

'Con todo mi amor': 'With all my love'.
La Chanson des rues: sung by Jean Sablon.

Monday 26

Letter of 22nd January to F returned with the words 'no record': it's too
bad! Must be the right address because Rose gave me the same one
and her letters got there. I'm so upset because he'll be wondering why I
don't write. Poor F, we seem fated not to be able to correspond. Wrote
to the officer in charge A.P.O. 554 and to Rose too.

A.P.O.: Army Post Office.

Tuesday 27

Sheila and I set off to the American Red Cross where a very nice woman
told me I had got the address wrong: it is A.P.O. 380. She thought 'USAI'
was his rank! Anyway I do know now what the address is. Wrote to Cis.
I do hope he gets that one at least. How much I miss you!

Wednesday 28

Nice letter from Antoine Morel. Mine arrived at his parents' when he
was there. He told me what happened on 2nd January. They were shot

down at Metz at about 6.15 pm. Guy, the flight engineer, parachuted with F to whom they gave a blood transfusion immediately; he must have been very badly wounded. They're waiting for a new pilot. Poor Jacques! Antoine has sent cigarettes to F. Went to Mrs Dover's for some French books.

Mrs Dover: a neighbour who had lived in France.

March

Thursday 1

His letters of 18th and 19th February arrived at the same time. He got my first parcel, at last! '*If you knew how happy I am, I want to jump for joy and dance in spite of my wounded leg. Yesterday I received my first parcel, the first thing I've received from you since I was wounded: it was your cockerel. If you could have seen me, I kissed it again and again. I never tire of reading your short note again and again, either. The chap who's in the bed next to mine could tell you how I trembled with joy. When they brought me that parcel I let out a cry and sounded both like an elephant trumpeting and a Sioux on the warpath, so much so that the frightened nurses came, believing something terrible had happened. […] I don't feel as lonely as I did two days ago now that I've got something from you, something that you touched and retains some of your perfume. I love you darling. This little gift made my day more than anything else in the world and now I know that I'll recover more quickly.*' He says he's going to write to Pat and Jacques. He got my first letter only the day after, and that's when he knew about Jacques. He is frightfully upset and says it is all his fault. '*Jacques – what a terrible shock it was to learn about him, and that he failed to return. Up to now I was quite certain that I was the last one to abandon the plane. But now a terrible doubt is worrying me sick. If he was aware that I'd been wounded, didn't he possibly stay in the plane so he could try to help me out of it? No, that's impossible, some of his remains would have been found in the wreckage. Anyway I'll tell you exactly how we were*

*shot down. It happened right at the moment when the navigator was
informing us that we were flying over the front line. I suddenly felt a
sharp twinge at the back of my right thigh, just as if a whip had struck it,
and a slight pain in my right arm; Jacques then turned the plane round
and the two port engines were hit and were suddenly ablaze. At that
moment* Chérubin *ordered us to bale out. I told him I was wounded
and he sent Guy the flight engineer to help me out of the plane. Guy
helped me with my parachute but he couldn't extricate me altogether. I
urged him to jump, and said that I'd get out somehow. The last words
that I heard from Jacques were: 'What about Francis?' Then without
knowing how or why, I found myself right at the lower end of my turret,
so I crawled to the emergency door and baled out. Some thirty seconds
after my parachute had opened I saw the plane crash to the ground.
Send me some information as soon as you can, for I cannot bear the
idea that Jacques may be* [a word is missing here] *for trying to save my
life, but I do hope just the same that he jumped before and landed in
our lines, but let's stop here with this topic because it's too painful.'* F
is the only Frenchman in the ward. He has had letters from Pat, from
Mrs Singleton and her children, Marguerite and David, and also from
Mrs Dick, which delighted him so much. He asks about his uniform
and doesn't want to raise false hopes about his return. *'Don't worry too
much about my coming back, and keep smiling; I don't want to sound
too optimistic; after such misfortunes one becomes superstitious in the
end. […] Your letter did more for my good health than any doctor in the
world.'* He is wonderful!

The little cockerel which Barbara had bought at the British Council charity sale
on 4 November 1944.

Friday 2

Went to the *British* to see *Mme* da Horta. And there, *Mme* Kléber
told me Roger Bordelais was missing: I was most upset; such a sweet
kind boy. And Maurice Bordier is too; he had a wife and children in
Algiers. It really is too ghastly! I don't know anyone now at Elvington,
except Antoine Morel; they have all gone. Poor dear Roger, poor
Maurice!

A letter from Rose: there are British soldiers in Berre. Broke *Fleur bleue*.

7 February 1945: on the way back from a mission on Goch (Germany) *capitaine* Stanislas' Halifax was shot down by a night-fighter above Asten, in the Netherlands. Six men killed. *Capitaine* Stanislas was the only survivor. *Lieutenant* Pelliot's crew, also from 347 'Tunisie' Squadron, were shot down on the way to Goch on the same mission. Three men killed.

Fleur bleue: sung by Charles Trenet.

Saturday 3

Mrs Dick had an extremely funny letter from F, in English, saying he was very jealous. Went to AVF. Irene was there, naturally most upset: Roger and she were to be married on 8th March. She showed us a photo of the crew and old '*G for George*'. Roger was from Toulon and 23. Apparently *capitaine* Stanislas has come back safe.

Sunday 4

Reception at the AVF in honour of the consul, M. Triat, who looks rather nice and quite funny. *Mme* da Horta spoke an excruciating English, which was rather sweet. Then we sang *La Madelon*, *Auprès de ma blonde*, *Madame la Marquise* and *J'attendrai*. I met M. Duvergne who lives in La Ciotat and is going to Marseilles; I think he's in the Merchant Navy. He's thrilled to be going home. I gave him F's address and some toys for his own son and Dédé. We asked an Elvington airman about Roger but he knew nothing. Heard someone singing *Je suis seule ce soir*. Alas! Will F ever come back?

M. Triat: the French consul.

Monday 5

Two lovely letters from F, with enclosed notes for Mummy and Mrs Watson. His arm has quite healed; he says it's just one more scar. Still asks about Jacques. '*I often have the impression that I'm going to wake up in my room at Y. and hear poor Jacques say: 'We've missed breakfast again; up with you, we must go to the Squadron H.Q.' Quite frankly*

I haven't realized it yet, but the hardest thing for me is to look back on my accident. It all happened so fast that I wonder if it really did take place. [...] I know absolutely nothing about the crew, I didn't even know that they were on leave; at any rate they're lucky. By the way if you hear anything about Jacques, even the slightest thing, please send me a telegram.' Oh! dear Cis, my heart is light. Wrote him a short note. How much I love him! However I think he will never come back.

Mrs Watson: a Belgian lady at the canteen.
'Y.': York, but Francis meant Elvington station.

Tuesday 6

Saw *Circonstances atténuantes* with Michel Simon and Arletty who sang *Comme de bien entendu*. It was most indecorous in places and very amusing; reminded me of Cis. Beryl Wood engaged. Oh! Cis, I will never be engaged to you, and yesterday he wrote: '*I love you like no man has ever loved a woman.*' I feel so cruel as I cause him so much grief and what he wants will never be. God! I so want to see him. He says: '*I only live for the day of my return.*' That's the same for me: what shall I do if I don't see him again? I love only you. We're trapped.

Circonstances atténuantes: a film directed by Jean Boyer (1939).

Wednesday 7

Three letters from Cis! I really have a marvellous week with letters. Mine take ten days to reach him. He says that he doesn't suffer from his injuries, only from my absence. '*Without you even the brightest days are sad; everything becomes gloomy, nothing else matters, life doesn't mean anything to me, everything becomes tiresome and boring. [...] When you look at yourself in your mirror, Bébé, just imagine that I'm looking over your shoulder. I'm thinking of you, when you are sweetly sleeping in your room where the moon is your only visitor, and my thoughts tenderly inspire your dreams. I'm not sending you my love from the bottom of my heart, for you already own my heart, and it'll never be big enough for all the love that I feel for you.*' Everybody is very kind to him. He can have as many cigarettes as he wants. He smokes about thirty a day. He says he likes to watch the smoke blowing away, that he has nothing else to do, and that it helps him to dream. '*If you meet a girl with big blue eyes whose name starts with a B, tell her that I love her, that I always will, that I spend my nights dreaming of her, that she's my heart and soul, my guiding light, my pleasure, my everything. Tell her that my whole being, all my heart and soul, all my thoughts and kisses go lovingly towards her.*' His letter of 1st March filled me with joy; he was tremendously happy as he had got three letters from me and the photo with my black dress. '*I saw you again, darling, and I wept for joy. You look so pretty in that photo, and it is exactly you. When I wake up every morning just looking at it makes me start to talk to you and kiss you like the idiot that I am. If I have dark thoughts I look at you and smile. When I received it I shouted my war cry. It was so dreadful that the windows shook. All the Yanks covered their heads with their blankets as they believed this was the end of the world. Even the birds stopped twittering for they didn't understand it was a cry of joy.*' He still agonizes over Jacques. '*What could have happened to him? I don't know, I just don't know and it's driving me mad. He was the only friend I had left. To him alone I could reveal my innermost thoughts, for only he and poor Henry could understand me. Our points of view were so very much alike. With him I would have been able to do anything. Why did I have to lose the two best friends I had in the world? You know, he wasn't at all like the others. And he remained so cheerful in spite of everything, so witty. But I'd better stop talking about him, it makes me* [a word is missing here] *but if the Boche killed him, once again I can assure you that I'll avenge him.*' He told me what happened when he found himself on the ground. '*No, Bébé, in spite of the snow I wasn't too cold when I'd landed, because I covered myself with my parachute: silk can keep you warm. How many times I cried out for both my mother and you, in that awful moment. [...] No! Bébé, life is not always squalid; it all depends which way you take it, and life's simply how we want to see it, for it's up to us to decide what to make it.*'

His injuries are healed up now but he sometimes suffers from nerves. He asks me to thank Roger Bordelais for what he did for me. How will he react when hearing that he is missing and Maurice too? It'll be another terrible shock for him again. Poor Roger should have been married tomorrow.

Had tea with Joan who said she had learnt a lot from me and that I was right about marrying foreigners.

'Without you even the brightest days are sad': referring to *Dis-moi pourquoi*, sung by Lys Gauty.

Friday 9

Sheila was told Jacques had probably been wounded and it was his duty to stay in the plane. Just hope he was killed outright.

Saturday 10

A letter from Cis. He had got two of mine on the same day. They all come through the Red Cross now, he's even overwhelmed with mail and parcels. He's given a lot of milk to drink and many meals. In the afternoon, some ladies from Dijon or Red Cross girls visit him.

I suppose that I should decide that awful question about him. I really don't know what I must do. Come back quickly my beloved!

Monday 12

Letter from Dédé, phrasing just like F. Had a long and serious discussion with Mrs Dick who says I can't make any decision yet, as perhaps the need will not even arise. I'm sure F will stay in France, I do dread it.

Thursday 15

Letter from Pat. She's in London and mentions the flying bombs which terrify people. She seems to be going to Algiers about the beginning of April.

Most interesting letter from Rose. They have had a dreadful winter: no clothes, no food; she is now wearing shoes with wooden soles, like we are. The Germans took over the airport near Berre; Sheila said how kind F was.

Friday 16
Heard Rina Ketty (F's idol) singing *J'attendrai*.

Saturday 17
Two very sweet letters from Feriolo who says he is coming back soon.
He heard that F was safe via his wife, Anna. He is a nice man. I feel so
sad and lonely.

Monday 19
Mrs Rowe, who has just had a baby, rang up about Pat's maternity
dress but she didn't mention coats. Oh! Cis, I'm longing for your return.

Tuesday 20
Three letters to F returned. I don't know what to do. Poor soul, he will
be so upset.

Thursday 22
Two letters from him. Still very upset about Jacques and feeling guilty.
'No, no, no! Guy never baled out when I did; I was still under my turret
while he was already standing near the escape hatch. He only harnessed
my parachute and I do remember, actually I'm absolutely certain that
Jacques said to the navigator: 'What about Francis?' and this just before
my intercom was disconnected. That's why I suspect he remained on
board for me, and I want to clarify this point when I get back to the
station and the navigator can provide the information, for Jacques
probably baled out last. Please try to understand, darling. We were even
closer friends than I was to Henry because we'd gone through quite a
lot of danger together. I'm sure he tried to do something for me, and I
must know. He has a mother, a fiancée, and if something happened to
him because of me, I want them to know about it, and forgive me if they
can. I know it's not my fault, but I caused it just the same.'

After nine weeks, his leg, at last, is out of that awful traction
appliance; he's in plaster. Says that he worried more about me than
about himself. 'No, don't be afraid, the only week when I was worried
was just after I'd been shot down, when I thought that you believed me
dead and I could imagine your grief, and that's why I sent the telegram.'

René, a friend from where he lives, visited him with his fiancée: says he was even happier than when he met Maurice again in Liverpool! René promised to take his father to him as soon as he would have enough petrol. A Red Cross girl brought him a little bunch of wild violets; he enclosed three of them for me in the envelope on which he wrote: '*A kiss for you in this corner.*' He reads Shakespeare's comedies in English and asks me to send him *Le Crève-cœur*, as it seems they don't know Louis Aragon in Dijon! Dear Cis, when will you come back?

I knitted and finished three gloves: they look awful!

Friday 23

Went for his *Crève-cœur*. Bought two records: *Le Fiacre* by Jean Sablon, and *Biguine à Bango* by Charles Trenet. At the AVF, I played with Dominique, the consul's daughter. *Mme* da Horta, very nice, said she would pray that F and I would be reunited.

Saturday 24

At 3.30 pm the postman came with a letter from F: he is somewhere in England! '*21.03.45, don't know where. Hey there, my darling, guess where I am? In England! [...] I flew again this morning, the first time since Jan. 2nd, but I wasn't in my good old Halifax 'G'. [...] I'm in an American hospital in the middle of nowhere, but this letter will travel fast, much faster than the previous ones. Don't write here because I think I'm due to leave tomorrow for an English hospital; I'll send the new address as soon as I can. Today is springtime and our own spring starts today, too. I can't tell you any more because I'm too happy to know what to say. 'I love you.' Regards to everyone, and a million kisses to you, petite femme. I simply want to tell you in every possible way and in every possible language that 'I love you.' Francis.*' I just can't believe that he is breathing the same air as I am. How lucky I am! But what a blow for the Uzays! They'll have to wait ages before seeing him.

Sunday 25

Oh! Cis, it's amazing that you're back again! I think I am so lucky. I must never complain again. I do so hope that I may go and see him.

Monday 26

Letter from F. He was handed over to a Canadian hospital near Winchester. He tells me about his return to England. '*I left Dijon at 7 on Saturday evening – an awful journey, and on Sunday morning I found myself … in Nancy. Right! I stayed there a day. On Monday morning, another departure; this time I landed in Paris. I thought I'd be able to get some rest, but couldn't. On Tuesday evening, just as I was falling asleep, someone shook me, gave me my identity papers and I was abruptly told: 'You're flying back to England.' We were taken to the aerodrome where we spent the night. On Wednesday morning we took off at about 10 and two hours later, I was back in dear old Blighty. But it wasn't over yet: when I got off the plane, I was taken to an American hospital (by the way, you must have received my first letter and heard from that American soldier on the telephone)* (I've received no phone call at all!) *and stayed there until midday today. At noon, I was again carried into an ambulance and here I am in this place where, hopefully, I shall now stay. My right leg, the lower part of my stomach and half my left leg are now in plaster, but I'm happy, I feel well, I'm in a wonderful mood, because I know that you probably are, too. […] I don't quite know what to write about, I'm a little surprised as I wasn't expecting to return to England so quickly. Yet I can send you a big, a huge kiss and tell you 'I love you.' Yes, it's true, I love you, why say anything else, I think it's the most wonderful thing I can tell you. […] It's almost 9 and you know that I have a rendezvous. Sleep well darling* petite femme, *the sea's no longer between us.*'

Tuesday 27

His letter of 23rd. He's now in an RAF hospital at Wroughton, near Swindon, in Wiltshire. I'll never get to see him, it's so far! '*Here we go again! I've changed hospitals; I wonder if all this travelling is going to stop one day or if this continual wandering will go on for the rest of my life.*' He seems to be fine and doesn't complain. He'll have to have an operation to repair his leg's nerve which was severed. His right foot is dead: he can't move it. Poor darling, he didn't want to let me know how bad he was, not to worry me. He's pleased to have a Belgian in the bed next to him as he is the only Frenchman. '*To think that four days ago I was still in Paris! Just the same it feels great to be in the same country as you; I hope I'll soon get well and will be able to go and see you.'* Oh! Cis.

Wednesday 28

Everybody seems to think that the Germans can't hold out much longer and that the end is near. I wonder how Cis feels now that Duisburg and Ludwigshafen are captured.

Thursday 29

How lovely it is to get his letters so quickly now! Mine only took two days to reach him as well, although the last one had taken twenty-four to France. He thinks that he'll be going to another hospital specializing in nerves. He feels he has come home and seems glad to be under the RAF again. *'You know, when I left Paris I felt sad at leaving France but was just as happy at the thought of seeing England again, even without taking into account my feelings for you. I think I'm fond of old Albion, somehow this is a sort of second country to me.'*

Sent him a Cross of Lorraine. Feriolo is going home to Marseilles.

Cross of Lorraine: symbol of the Free French Forces.

Saturday 31

Daddy had a very funny letter from Cis, saying he gets nothing but cabbage and potatoes. Letter from Rose who complains of the Americans' behaviour. Their father was about to get a ticket for Dijon when he heard F had gone to Paris: bad luck!

I posted him a parcel with a building set, newspapers and a little duck.

April

Sunday 1

Feel so lonely.

Top: 1. Francis and Barbara. Liverpool, 25 October 1944. *Middle left*: 2. The British Council, Liverpool. *Middle right*: 3. Pier Head and Merseyside, Liverpool. *Bottom left*: 4. The French tricolour flies over RAF Elvington, 1944–5. *Bottom right*: 5. French airman, Elvington village, 1944.

Left: 6. Francis. Evanton, February 1944. *Below*: 7. Barbara, late 1943. *Above*: 8. Text written on the back of the photograph (image 6) from Francis to Barbara.

Opposite page, clockwise from top left: 9. Patricia Rigby. 10. Barbara in her black dress. Liverpool, 12 January 1945. 11. Henri and Pat Martin's wedding. St Helens, Lancashire, 16 September 1944. 12. Mr and Mrs Rigby, Barbara's parents.

roupe 1/25. 1ère Escadlle. Nº9. Equipage. Lᵗ COTTARD

13. *Lieutenant* Cottard's crew (Francis Usai's crew), 347 'Tunisie' Squadron. Top, from left to right: *Sergent-chef* Antoine Morel (wireless operator). *Sergent* Guy Dufaure (flight engineer). *Sergent* Francis Usai (mid upper gunner). Bottom, from left to right: *Sergent* Jacques Leclercq (pilot). *Lieutenant* Daniel Cottard (navigator and captain). *Adjudant* Antoine Adaoust (bomb aimer). *Sergent-chef* Henri Aubiet (rear gunner).

14. From left to right: *Sergent* Jacques Leclercq. *Sergent* Henri Martin. Pat Martin. *Sergent* Francis Usai. York, 3 October 1944.

15. *Lieutenant* Hyenne's crew (Henri Martin's crew), 346 'Guyenne' Squadron. *Adjudant-chef* Jean Chabroud, bomb aimer (first from left). *Lieutenant* Auguste Hyenne, navigator and captain (fourth from left). *Sergent* Henri Martin, mid upper gunner (second from right). The other crew members on the photo remain unidentified and include *Sergent* Guy Roca, pilot. *Sergent-chef* Louis Maxerat, wireless operator. *Sergent-chef* Jean Laherrere, flight engineer. *Sergent* Jean Reynal, rear gunner. All killed on 4 November 1944.

16. *Capitaine* Stanislas' crew (Maurice Bordier and Roger Bordelais' crew), 347 'Tunisie' Squadron. From left to right: *sergent* Roger Bordelais, rear gunner. *Sergent* Maurice Bordier, mid upper gunner. *Sergent-chef* Henri Berdeaux, wireless operator. *Capitaine* Stanislas, navigator and captain. *Sous-lieutenant* Corentin Rognant, bomb aimer. *Adjudant-chef* Jean Aulen, pilot. *Sergent-chef* Raymond Patry, flight engineer. All killed on 7 February 1945, except *capitaine* Stanislas.

Above left: 17. *Sergent* Francis Usai. *Above right:* 18. The first and only French military memorial in an English Cathedral. Inaugurated on 20 October 2011, York Minster – the 66th anniversary of the French Squadrons returning to France. *Below left:* 19. *Sergent* Jaques Leclercq, pilot in the crew of *lieutenent* Cottard, 347 Tunisie Squadron. Killed on 2 January 1945, at the age of 20. *Below right:* 20. Henri Martin, on his wedding day.

Opposite page, top to bottom: 21. Handley Page Halifax, 347 'Tunisie' Squadron, RAF Elvington 1944. 22. Halifax 'Friday 13th' in 346 'Guyenne' Squadron colours at the Yorkshire Air Museum. 23. The Yorkshire Air Museum, Elvington, York, in the present day – just as it was when Francis was stationed there.

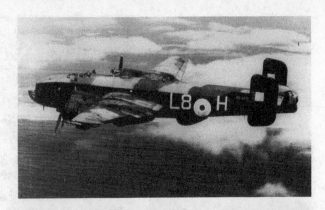

Above left: 24 & 25. Telegrams sent by RAF Elvington to Mr Rigby, chosen by Francis as his 'next of kin', 4 and 8 January 1945. *Above right:* 26. Telegram envelopes. *Left:* 27. Telegram sent by Francis to Barbara from 36th American Hospital, Dijon, January 1944. *Below:* 28. Insignias of 346 'Guyenne' and 347 'Tunisie' Squadrons, and the Insignia of the RAF Bomber Command.

Monday 2

A letter from F, very funny and cheerful. '*The Belgian fellow next to me is very funny; he has such a strong accent that every time he speaks, I burst out laughing. Oh! And this morning, we were both lying on our bellies – every morning we are turned over like pancakes in order to relieve our backs – well, we were in that position, looking like two toads trying to swim, and it was impossible to see what was going on behind us. So he'd just cracked an even funnier joke than usual and we were convulsed with laughter. Bang in the middle of it, we hear a big voice boom: 'Stop that racket, will you!' We turn our heads and see the medic – a captain – and the nurse pursing her lips more than ever and glaring at us. It seemed so funny that instead of stopping us, there we were shaking with laughter again and two minutes later, everyone in the ward, including the captain, was rolling about, convulsed with Homeric laughter. These Frenchmen are just impossible!*' If only I could see you! I will have to be patient. He did understand that the hospital is too far for me. '*I'm thinking about those blessed days in KT when the wind caressed your hair, and the wonderful moment when we said we loved each other; our love has sailed so far under a fair wind, and above it our star still shines and will soon bring us together.*' He seems to be worrying a lot, but I suppose he has nothing else to do. I wish I could help.

KT: Kirkby Thore.

'*Our love has sailed so far under a fair wind*': referring to Bercé par la houle, sung by Reda Caire.

Tuesday 3

Three letters today. Another one which made me laugh. '*Your words are quite insufficient to describe the enthusiastic crowd that welcomed me when I got off the plane. Some people had arrived on the previous day and slept on the aerodrome to be in the best places. A delegation of young girls, fifteen in all, greeted me with flowers and I gave each of them a kiss, a brotherly kiss, as I always do. The Lord Mayor presented the keys of the city and even my old friend Jojo was there, but I really was too busy to pay much attention to him. But I forbade the newspapers to mention the event and that's why you couldn't read about any of the details of my arrival.*' He says he only saw a little bit of sky and *Gare de l'Est* in Paris. He wears my Cross of Lorraine around his neck. He apologized for not having thought of my birthday; poor darling, he was in hospital in France. His nerve hurts him sometimes but he keeps his spirits up regardless. '*About my leg, that piece of shrapnel went exactly through the middle of my thigh, half-way between the knee and the pelvis. [...] My nerve! It's bothering me today because it's rainy weather. But if it's raining down on the city, it's no longer raining in my heart. It's now springtime, we're 20, the sky is blue, everything is cheerful, and we should celebrate. Come on,* Bébé! *Let's get away, I know places where we can dream, so come and dream of love with me – tonight I'm rich, rich with love, and your eyes will be my pearls and your smile my diamonds.*' He has called the new WAAF '*Bécassine*' and says the one on night duty is as beautiful as a movie actress, but '*thick as a plank*'! Bought a book on Marie-Antoinette for him.

'*The sky is blue*': beginning of *Au bal de l'amour,* sung by Tino Rossi. *Bécassine*: a Breton charlady, heroine of a comic strip, whose name refers to a naïve, simple-minded girl ('Snipe' in English).

Wednesday 4

His letter of 2nd. Pat wrote to him. She went to say farewell to her mother in St Helens; she was able to get a seat on a plane and is going to Algiers in about a fortnight's time. He was pleased with my parcel. He seems to be having good fun with the Belgian: he says that '*he's a real good sort*'.

Thursday 5

Got a letter. I think he is so sorry that he didn't have a chance to see his father again whilst in Dijon. '*Poor Papa, I realize he did all he could to come all that way to try to see me, and just as he was about to succeed, I had gone. You know, it's incredible how he has changed since I joined the Air Force. When I was at school, he never used to bother with me, except to tell me off because I'd come home too late. The moment I was an airman, I could sense how much he loved me for he did all he could for me. He even honoured me by taking me to his club.*' I don't know how I would have reacted if F had had more serious injuries, but

I didn't mean that I wouldn't have loved him any longer. '*Darling I'm pretty certain that you denigrate yourself when you say that it would have been impossible for you to bear serious wounds; yes I'm absolutely certain of it, for otherwise this would mean that if I'd been disfigured, you would have stopped loving me. But my darling girl, think of all those poor people without hope in life; think of the wonderful happiness they must feel when looking at a woman with a genuine smile on her face and not a trace of disgust for their own mutilated face. But I believe that as far as you are concerned, you are over-sensitive, and I hope that it's not because you are hard-hearted but on the contrary you are tender-hearted.*' The Sister took him for a Scotsman! '*Oh! How horrid! How revolting!*'

Friday 6

Mummy bought a pair of shoes for me and two summer dresses, seven coupons each: we were lucky. Had an interview with flabby chap at the tailor's about F's suit, for which he has not yet got the cloth. What a nasty man!

Saturday 7

His letter of 5th. Antoine Morel went to see him on Wednesday; F was delighted. He brought him Turkish cigarettes and gave him news from the crew and Elvington. '*He talked a lot about the station and sad to say, nearly all the old hands are now gone. All my friends have now bought it; they're either dead or reported missing. Pierrot, Maurice, poor Aristide, all of them with no exception! They're all new recruits now. Well! That's life, or rather the opposite.*' Perhaps in six months, he'll have three stripes as he has been nominated to the superior rank. He has been awarded the palm and silver star to his Croix de guerre. I wondered if he would get it. How lovely! But then he deserves it. And all the crew were 'Mentioned in Despatches'. He will also get the Caterpillar like all the airmen who parachuted. How wonderful if Jacques could come back! Went to the Post Office and sent him a congratulatory telegram. Met Pat Britten who said F would be a long time in hospital. At the AVF, we had a farewell concert for *Mme* da Horta to whom we presented an illuminated address. She made a highly emotional speech of thanks and seemed genuinely touched. She told me to greet F for her. Talked to a Breton from Quimper and a Norman from Le Havre who had been interrogated by the Gestapo, hung up by his arms; he also had had frost-bite in the Maginot Line.

Came home and found another letter from Cis. This time, his mind seems at rest. *'I think I can put my mind at rest a bit about Jacques. Without going into details, Antoine has told me what happened: Jacques certainly baled out, but his parachute failed to open or maybe he lost it, because sometimes he didn't fasten his safety harness. If you don't fully strap the parachute harness, only your arms are secured and when it opens with a jerk you just go through it, just as if you were putting on a hat that's too big and with a gaping hole. I'm sorry I upset you because of my somewhat obsessive insistence; I've stopped worrying now, and 'only' feel an immense grief at losing such a dear friend, almost a brother, even if there's still some hope left because his body hasn't been recovered.'* I wonder what he meant about his return to England. *'I realize that a simple 'sarge' like me doesn't count for much in the French Forces, but when I tell you why I've come back to England, then you may change your mind, however I can't tell you about that in a letter.'* He talks about himself and his father. Says that one day he came home at 6 am on the day before an exam, and his poor father was enraged. Calls himself a libertine, which I think is exaggerated. *'My father was right: I was a very bad boy when I was younger; I could never obey an order, or even listen to advice, and I was argumentative. [...] Yes indeed, I was a libertine, and I think I still am a little. Do you know why I was so cool with you when we first met? Do you remember the first evening when you walked to the tram to see me off? I suggested I should take your arm and you answered: 'Yes, if it's proper.' I was piqued and said to myself: I'll show this young lady that a Frenchman can be more than extremely well-behaved. At that time I didn't want to become attached to anybody for fear I should lose the proud independence I enjoyed. But you were so different from other girls that all my tactics were useless, and naturally I found myself beaten and defenceless – I was in love. For once I'd come across a girl worthy of interest, but unfortunately she wasn't in love with me, or at any rate she said she wasn't. At that time I bared my soul. For a time I believed that you could never love me, but it didn't last. But the time when I really despaired was the first time I kissed you. You seemed so cold, and yet I could feel that we were forming bonds between us. You know the rest as well as I do. But I'm writing all this to prove to you that the term 'libertine' was far more appropriate than you thought and that you really are different from others since you broke down all my defences, and for all the others Henry never said anything to me. But since you love me I'm happy, aren't I? [...] I hope I'm not boring you with all my secrets but every day we must learn to know each other a little more. I do so wish that you could read my mind like an open book.'*

My brave little chap! I wrote to him and sent him the photograph of both of us.

Tuesday 10

Letter from F. He's now in Church Village, near Pontypridd in Wales: as far away as ever! Sounds very low and out of sorts. *'I'm yet in another hospital! I left Wroughton the day before yesterday; the journey took five hours and on arriving here I was half-dead. Moreover the young lady at the wheel was crazy and drove the ambulance round the bends at breakneck speed. Well, you can imagine what kind of journey it was. We stopped twice on our way, and guess what it was for? [...] Yes, tea breaks, ugh! Enough to make me sick!'* They put him in a ward dedicated to nerve-injured patients where he is the only Frenchman once again. Luckily, he seems to like the place. *'The hospital is quite alright, and very modern, but the nurses are like all others and the Waafs aren't even good-looking. Ah! Where's beautiful Helen? To think that she was already calling me by my name, to think that my efforts with her were all in vain – it breaks my heart! You know the hospital is perched on the side of a hill facing south, so the sun shines on us all day long. Through the window I can see the whole plain nestling at our feet and in the morning it is beautiful. Imagine a sort of purple mist covering the whole valley, with red, orange and golden hues as the sun gleams over all this. I really do wish you could see all this.'* Mummy sent him a box of spring flowers.

Wednesday 11

Fortunately, he felt much better the day after. He wrote me a very nice letter. *'I felt depressed yesterday but it is all over now, but if yesterday*

*I could sing the beauties of the sunny, mist-shrouded valley, today it's
raining. But the rain has its own appeal, too, and I like it, especially at
night. Have you ever listened to the music made by the raindrops? It gives
me a healing and soothing melancholy. It seems the rain is singing for
my heart, and across the countryside I imagine I can see big mushrooms
growing while in the hills the wind sounds like a violin. Sometimes, too,
the rain seems to sing a mocking song. On such occasions, as if in an
infernal sarabande, can't you see all the stray cats singing and dancing
in defiance of the deluge pouring down from the sky? Tonight, however,
the rain that soothes our fever will have left for somewhere far away,
the countryside will look joyful again, the trees will seem to be shaking
themselves dry, and the birds will not complain about this refreshing
downpour. And thanks to the sun that's shining anew in a clear blue sky,
I shall be able to see the reflection of our love, purer and brighter than
ever before.'* He says that a very sweet WAAF looks only after him and
another boy also in bed. All the others are convalescents.

Francis refers to *Il pleut dans ma chambre*, sung by Charles Trenet.

Thursday 12
Letter from Antoine Morel, saying that F cannot move his ankle.
Wonder if he has had an operation. I feel very worried.

Friday 13
His letter of 11th. He was overjoyed with the flowers. *'First I want to kiss
you for it's the only way I have to prove how happy I am. This morning
I received some flowers, a gift from the Rigby family, and I was so happy
– even happier than if I'd received all the gold in the world. But you must
also kiss Mummy, Patsy and Riri for me. Actually I'm a little embarrassed
and somewhat overwhelmed by everything that you've all been doing for
me, because actually I haven't done anything to deserve it. I also received
your telegram and the nurse asked me if I was an American Frenchman
because the address was: Sgt. Francis U.S.A. – surely an absent-minded
lady at the Post Office again! […] Thanks, too, for the little flower. As for
the whole bunch, it has pride of place on my bedside table next to your
photo.'* He seems to get on well with his English companions. *'There's*

*only three flying personnel here among thirty men [...] but just the same
there is this rather elderly English gentleman to make up for all the rest,
for his sense of propriety is exquisite and very English. I really enjoy
talking with him for I understand every word that he says. As for the
fellow next to me, he is irretrievably, stupidly English! I cannot, even
once, protest against his chauvinism without his lashing out at France
and her inhabitants with a torrent of abuse. But what amazes him most
is that he makes me roar with laughter, and the more I laugh the angrier
he gets and vice-versa.'* It must be hard for him to stay in bed thinking of
his comrades back at the station. I wonder if they've gone on operations
again. *'Of course the whole crew get their two stars and palm but I did
nothing more than they did; on the contrary they can still serve their
country, while I am in bed, pampered and taken care of like a baby.'*
Can't wait to see him again, but I wonder how our reunion will go; we
may remain speechless that day. *'You're right, I shall be totally unable
to speak when I see you again for the first time, but isn't silence more
eloquent than any words? When I can express my love for you in silence,
then I shall be happy. [...] I'd like to whisper to you tenderly all the
words of love that one murmurs on one's knees. How I wish I could
see your bright, smiling eyes, which to me are a reflection of heaven.
How my heart beats when I think of that – I love you without fear
either of regrets or for the future. I'd like to soothe you with infinitely
tender words, words that happiness turns into magic, and hear the sweet
confession of your love from your heart. Good night, darling, may you
dream sweet dreams; I want night to be gentle to my loved one. Regards
and thanks to Mummy, Riri and Patsy. Kind thoughts to Gran and Uncle
Max. A brotherly kiss on the velvet cheeks of the Three Graces. Hello to
Nelly, a friendly pat on Globule's back. Good night darling, see you at 9,
in five minutes, I love you.'*

Saturday 14

Letter from Rose, very interesting. Says the Germans are the Devil's
machines. She danced till 5 am at Easter! She sent me her photograph:
she is the image of F, but prettier of course! Looks very chic and nice.
Newsreels at cinema showing devastation of Münster and de Gaulle
presenting colours to French regiments.

Sunday 15

Heard Ravel's *Pavane*. Morel sent huge parcel of F's clothes for me to send on.

Monday 16

Letter from F. 'No, *the crew is still grounded, they're still awaiting reinforcements and somewhat it saddens me to think they'll complete their tour without me. What do you think of all these losses in the squadron? What a difference three months can make, but I hope that this is only a bad patch. I'll feel like a stranger if I go back to the station.*' At the moment, he doesn't feel like having some occupational therapy at the hospital, anyway certainly not the one of the man next to him! '*It drives me mad when I see the other fellow at work over his needlepoint like an old woman. No, I'll throw everything up in the air two minutes after having started if ever I'm given something to do.*' He hasn't had an operation; he'll have his plaster changed soon and sounds rather miserable. '*Thank you for the photograph, but I can see that I've lost at least 50% of weight.*' The end of his letter is very nice. '*Do you know what I'm thinking of right now? I'm thinking of the first time I settled in front of your fireplace at home, and how happy I was that evening. The fire reminded me of some postilion wearing a powdered wig, spurring on his white steed between his blue-clad thighs and whipping him on just like a cheery wind and tearing off three green leaves from a budding branch. Light as air, these flames fluttered about and danced the way Marie-Antoinette and all those ladies would dance in their golden dresses only yesterday. I wished that fire would never die out, for it stood for the Hearth par excellence. [...] Regards to Riri, Mummy, Patsy, Gran and Max. Hello to dames Dick and Watson. Hello to Nelly. Give Globule a kiss on each ear. Good bye, my Loved One, may every breeze bring a kiss from my ardent lips. I love you, and all my tender thoughts flow softly towards you with immense love. I love you. A thousand kisses and more.*' Looks as if I won't see him till June at least; it's so sad.

Found Maurice Feriolo quite lost near home. Has a moustache now and looks like Ronald Colman! He is going on the 11.45 pm train, will cross the Channel, and then go across France by train. He was so upset about F. As we were having lunch, he said rather wistfully: 'It would be perfect if Francis were here, too.' Seemed afraid that F would limp and wanted to know when he would be cured. He told me that F loves me so much, that he will never forget me, and also that all Frenchmen are jealous! He will go to see the Uzays to tell them what a nice family F has found. He was very gay and made Mummy and Nelly laugh. Patsy fell completely! Hasn't told Anna he is coming. I gave him some little bits for her and Chantal. Hope he has a lovely leave. I was so happy to see him because he reminds me of Cis. I wrote to him and sent him oranges and crosswords. Heard *Valse grise*.

'*The fire reminded me...*': referring to *Joli feu de bois*, sung by Charles Trenet.
Ronald Colman: a British actor.
Valse grise: music by Maurice Jaubert in the film *Un carnet de bal* (1937).

Tuesday 17

For his birthday, bought *Britain in the Air* and a book of Spanish fairy stories on which I wrote a little dedication: 'For him who lives in the country of the fairies, each beat of my heart. Your Barbara.' Mrs Watson gave me a note for him. Two airmen from the 'Guyenne' came into the canteen: *adjudant* Auriol, a bomb aimer from Perpignan, and *sergent-chef* Jaffeux, a wireless operator from Paris. They were going home, having finished their tour of operations. They knew Jacques and Antoine, and had heard of F. They knew Henri as well. They were so nice and amusing. They asked me to send their best wishes for a good recovery to F. A bit later, another Elvington man came in, an Alsatian from Colmar, who knew F and Jacques quite well. He worked in the operations room and had had lots of discussions with F. He is a *caporal*. He escaped in 1943 and was held in Miranda. His father was killed by an American shell, his mother is dead and his two brothers are prisoners in Germany. Speaks excellent German, wears thick glasses and was a law student. Said he did not want to go back to France and that F had told him the same. Wrote to Cis.

Heard concentration camp liberated by our troops at Bergen-Belsen on 15th April. Thousand of Jews and Soviet prisoners found dead in horrific circumstances.

Adjudant Auriol, a bomb aimer, and *sergent-chef* Jaffeux, a wireless operator in
   the crew of *lieutenant* Flesch (346 'Guyenne' Squadron).

The camp in Miranda: many Frenchmen tried to reach Britain via Gibraltar
   or North Africa but were arrested in Spain after secretly crossing the
   Pyrenees. They were sent to Miranda de Ebro, the location of one of Franco's
   concentration camps, where they were held with prisoners of the Spanish
   Civil War. A relatively large number of flying personnel and ground crew at
   Elvington had been held in Miranda.

Bergen-Belsen: Nazi concentration camp in Lower-Saxony, where Anne Frank
   died.

Thursday 19

Letter from F: out of plaster since Saturday, at last! He couldn't write
earlier as he wasn't very well the last few days. '*About every two minutes
I could feel pins and needles all down my leg, burning sensations and
a searing, even blinding pain. [...] The pain has subsided now. [...] The
leg wound is totally healed, only the scars can be seen and the thigh is
constricted where the piece of shrapnel cut through. As for the nerve
there's still no operation planned and I suppose it'll be the last to heal.
Honestly, I think I'm in for it for much longer than I had bargained for.
But my leg is no longer in plaster. [...] It's in a kind of splint, but it's only
to keep it perfectly straight. I must practise and flex the muscles and
nerves that were not severed, and I can assure you that it's a pleasure to
see them move.*' Poor little soul, what he goes through! He was pleased
to get my oranges and also a French Red Cross parcel with two hundred
cigarettes, chocolate bars and note paper. Says he eats like a horse but
it'll take six months for him to recover what he lost in a fortnight's time.
It's he who asked Morel, when visiting him, to send his clothes on to us:
it's his washing which he had left at the laundry just before being shot
down. He wrote to me from the terrace where they had put him in the
sunshine. '*If only you could see me right now – I'm literally roasting.
I've taken my pyjama top off and put it over my head, and Olive says I
look just like Gandhi! I can see the whole valley below and some girls
riding their bicycles along the road. I feel well, delightfully well, so well
that I've suddenly lost all wish to be poetic, and given half the chance
I'd start dreaming of cigars and comfortable armchairs! Why am I so*

far away from you, little darling, why am I in this place if you're not here, why can't I enjoy the view and the sunshine with you, why can't we enjoy anything and everything to the full? The day may not be far when I can hold you in my arms, when my lips again say 'I love you'; I'll say it again and kiss that dear face, and on that day I'll be on top of the world!' I do so want to see him but sadly can't see any chance till June.

Olive: the young WAAF looking after Francis.

Friday 20

Letter from Morel. He is having leave again and will come to see me; *adjudant* Auriol did give him my regards. Went again to the tailor's who doesn't have material yet. Letter from Cis: he was glad to hear that they think about him at Elvington. '*I'd never have thought that everyone knew me back at the station, for after all, apart from my small circle of friends, I hardly spoke to anyone. Well I'd like to say 'thank you' to all these boys, and if I don't get better with all their 'get well' wishes I might as well become the Emperor of China! Yes, I do remember the boy in the ops room, he used to hand out the flying rations, you know, the chewing-gum, chocolate and sweets. I only knew him by sight but he seemed to be rather a nice fellow, even if he was a pen-pusher.*' Says he misses his good laughs with the Belgian. He has been moved to another ward; the men next to his bed are a warrant officer, very sweet and shy, who was knocked down by a car when getting back from a dance, and an Australian '*giant of a man, but tremendously kind*', called Jack. He devoured all the French books in a week, so that now he has to read English books; he had asked for easy books to read to a young girl: she brought him books for babies! Pat wrote to him. '*She says she's very busy because of the papers she needs, she's been spending whole days running between the French Embassy, the consulate, etc. She says she thinks she'll be leaving on the 20th. Yet another friend who'll be going away, for I do like Pat, she's been so marvellous to me. She very much wants me to be her child's godfather, and so do I if it can be done by proxy.*'

So she has gone today. I do admire her. What a decision! Packed Cis' birthday parcel.

Saturday 21

Mrs Dick is sending him chocolates for his birthday. It is very kind of her.

Sunday 22

No more black-out, except on the coast. Russians in Berlin.

Monday 23

Letter from F. Seems to like the place where the hospital is very much. *'It's on the side of a small hill. To the right, a small green wood, for lovers; facing it and a little lower, a large meadow that's even greener; in the small valley there is a winding, uphill road that passes right outside the hospital. It's a lovely, narrow lane, very quiet and yet quite busy. To the left, Church Village, with a few houses looking as if they were hanging over the roadside – there's only one thing missing, and that's a small church and its steeple – and in the background, round, purple hills.'* I wonder if he will have the operation. He says that I must not worry and that all the wounded who can walk have sick leaves. *'I believe that I, too, can obtain sick leave, unless you're afraid of being seen with a chap who limps. No, I'm just being nasty; you have permission to give me a slap for that bit, provided you give me a kiss afterwards. Oh darling, if you knew how happy I am to be loved by you. Sometimes I wonder if I deserve such happiness. I'd like to shout for joy and tell nature, the sun, the moon, the flowers and the trees. Right there on the roadside there's a tall birch tree which I'm sure would understand me. [...] It also seems to me that I could face up to any ordeal, as long as I have you, my darling* petite femme.'

Mummy received a very nice wallet which F made with his own hands; she wrote to thank him. I wrote to him too. Jeanne sent me a photograph of her and Jo: she looks rather consequential, but very smart. Russians have captured sixteen suburbs of Berlin.

Tuesday 24

Cis' birthday. Wonder what this year has for him. What a good thing we cannot see the future! His letter of Saturday: he'll be having electrotherapy to stimulate his foot now that his thigh bone is stronger. *'My bone is now perfectly alright, it's totally set and my right leg is as long as the left. I didn't remain for two and a half months with 40 kilos hanging from my foot for nothing!'* When he was in Dijon, he heard dreadful things about the Germans. *'Concerning all those German atrocities, I didn't believe in them much before going back to France, but over there people who can be trusted told me about them and all those stories are most probably true, I'm afraid. You see, old music- and art-loving Germany is gone forever. They're only a gang of bullies now; but the Germans were deliberately brought to this point; little by little their sensibilities were totally dulled so that now they are just sadistic brutes.'* However there were some good ones too; I think one must not condemn all a people. All that fuss about his uniform begins to annoy me seriously, and him too. *'I'm sure the tailor is having a laugh at our expense – and have you noticed that something seems to prevent me from getting that new uniform? The first time, Pat was supposed to fetch it. […] Then on the morning of Jan. 2nd I intended to send you the £8 and just as I was about to go to the post office I was called to briefing. Those £8 are still with Intelligence in the little bag in which we emptied our pockets before each mission. I don't think Morel can send it, because each time there's an 'accident' all the missing airman's belongings are collected and left at the RAF Depository, so only the rightful owner can get them back. If he's not back within six months, I'm not sure; maybe they're sent to his next of kin.'* Chérubin sent him a very sweet letter. *'I'd never have thought he would do so; he says he may be able to come to see me.'* I wrote to him.

Wednesday 25

His letter of 23rd. He's started the electric massages with a pretty brown-haired WAAF who is a sergeant. *'It tickles at first, then it hurts a little, but not much; it feels as if I'm being pricked, but for the first time in three months I saw my little toe move; it was marvellous, and now I can also bend my knee a bit – fantastic, isn't it?'* All the staff are women, even the doctor. He already misses Olive who has just gone on leave. In the ward, they seem to help one another quite well. *'Well, I've just knotted the tie and laced the shoes of the poor W.O. who got hurt at the dance. It's fantastic how we can complement each other with our disabled limbs.'* Poor Cis, he must be fed up with bed!

W.O.: Warrant Officer.

Thursday 26

Ecstatic letter: seems thrilled with all the parcels and letters he received for his birthday. '*You know, this morning rather reminded me of the Christmas mornings I knew when I was young. My bed was literally swamped with letters and parcels because I opened them all at the same time. They made such a heap over my tummy and I had stuck the small flag on top and proclaimed the whole lot 'French territory'. I just didn't know how to cope with all this. Oh! darling give a kiss and a big hug to Mummy*, Riri, *Patsy and Mrs Dick and tell them that through this I'm trying to express my warmest thanks; not for the gifts they sent – these matter as well, of course – but for their kind gesture. As for you, my dearest darling, my* petite femme, *I'll try to love you even more than I have so far. [...] There's nothing more you can do to make me happy, you've done all you could and I'm fully happy, and the only cloud that remains is that I cannot see you.*' Says how kind we all are to him; it's not difficult when he is so sweet. '*I must tell you once more how happy I am today. You see, I can feel that people who are no relatives of mine are fond of me, I can positively feel it and, believe me, this is very pleasant. Now let's give each other a fond kiss for the beginning of my 23rd year – I love you darling, I love you and all I can say is nothing compared to what I feel.*'

The letters I sent in February to him in Dijon eventually reached him after having gone through Wroughton. Got a letter from M. Duvergne who seems upset about Toulon which is in a fearful mess. Says the little boy liked the toys. He wrote to the Uzays and enclosed a letter from Jeanne.

Friday 27

Antoine came home. Seems to have brightened up a lot but speaks very broken English. Told us that the plane crashed on the way to Ludwigshafen about 6 in the evening. He parachuted and landed in a carrot field. He then walked for fourteen miles until 2 am and then fell asleep on a haystack where a farmer found him. He thinks Jacques fell down a shell hole and was too hurt to move. Poor boy, he was only 20!

Said F, whom he visited at hospital, looks quite ok and will come soon on leave, about June. Letter from Rose; they have only had one from F since he came back to England.

Saturday 28

Letter from Cis. His foot is still insensible at the moment. He received a birthday card from his mummy which he was overjoyed with, the first one for so long. I offered to make up a parcel for his family. He's glad of that and will send me some money and two coupons for the soap; it is what they most lack. I will buy tobacco for his father for the ration in France is only four packets a month. He can save up, as he doesn't go out, and even sent a postal money order to Daddy to put his money at the bank. He spoke about the Germans again. '*My darling, I'm not saying that the whole German people is rotten to the core; you know that I have no personal hatred towards them, but a whole generation is indeed and the germs will have to be eliminated. It'll take a long time as you say; moreover in the future we mustn't give them the opportunity to become too powerful again for in the German psyche there is a primitive, immeasurable hubris, and they have to learn that might is not always right, for this is something they have forgotten.*'

Monday 30

Letter from Cis, with a rather good drawing of a Scots terrier which looks like Rufus so much. Says he has always liked drawing and feels like starting to do it again. He seems indeed rather gifted. The wallet was in fact intended for Daddy: he mistook 'Mrs' for 'Mr' when he wrote the name on the envelope! '*Of course she must have been surprised because a wallet is not exactly a gift for a woman – but you can expect me to do such a silly thing!*' So he's going to make something else for Daddy.

Germans' surrender rumours everywhere. Read *Gil Blas* which is most amusing.

Gil Blas de Santillane: an 18th-century picaresque novel by Alain-René Lesage.

May

Tuesday 1

At 8.30 pm a flash on the radio to say Hitler was dead; Americans in Munich and Dachau. Mummy afraid I might be in town at the declaration of peace.

Hitler committed suicide in Berlin on 30 April 1945.

Wednesday 2

Armistice signed in Italy; can't be long now. Admiral Dönitz is the new Führer. Got two letters from Cis. His only pleasure, on Sunday, was a fried egg at breakfast! He doesn't do anything else but sleep, read and eat, as there is neither treatment nor activities on Sundays. He wrote to his family each week and doesn't understand why they've received only one letter from him since he came back to England. He was horrified to hear that Jeanne and Rose go out without chaperons, but he isn't for me! Was pleased that Antoine came to see me. '*Did he tell you that the fat rear gunner landed in a stream and could only get out with difficulty because of his weight? Honestly I don't exactly know where I landed; I only know that it was approximately fifty kilometres from Dieuze, the village where was the hospital where I was taken.*' The W.O. and the glider pilot, who can walk, regularly come to chat by his bed, to the nurse's great displeasure, as the three of them leave tons of ashes in the ashtray. They seem to get on well. '*They do everything they can for me, and on the other hand I dress them every morning; I mean, I help them with their ties, I tighten the belt on their trousers, etc. because they're both wounded in the right arm. [...] Do you know that I can now raise my right leg like a dancer? I did it this afternoon when the 'glamorous Waaf' came for my daily dose of electric treatment.*' On Saturday night, he had read a very exciting book, full of adventure and gunshots, and the day after he teased the Sister. '*When the Sister came with her trolley, I pinched her talcum powder dispenser – it looks exactly like a submachine gun. I started singing or rather bawling the tune from 'Light Brigade' and then sprayed the other fellow with talcum powder, amid much shouting and banging. The poor nurse nearly choked and called me a 'bad boy'. But I don't think I am; I only wanted to have some fun. In order to pacify her, I offered her one of Dad's sweets a little later, and this time she ran her hands through my hair (naughty, naughty!) and said I should grow up.'* He made a little donkey, which he intends to send me for the crèche's children and he put my photo between his legs. He also would like to make a bag for me, like the W.O. did for his girl-friend. I don't think I will be able to go to see our Cis; I am sorry, but let's still hope! Tried to do the essay on Pascal, which was awful!

Pascal: a 17th-century French philosopher.

Thursday 3

Berlin gave in to the Russians yesterday. We have linked up with them, and also captured Hamburg and Rangoon in Burma. Atmosphere already victorious. Did Pascal essay.

Friday 4

Went to AVF and saw *Mme* da Horta who kissed me again. Letter from F. He also heard on the radio, on Wednesday, the German army's surrender in Italy; he was overjoyed. He receives lots of mail and spends most of his time in replying to it. Joan wrote to him and told him about her unhappy love affair with Honoré.

Saturday 5

Huge surrender of Nazis to British. Denmark and Holland free. Our work done, after all this time. Went to AVF. Played *La Madelon*, *J'attendrai* and *Boum*. Then I saw *Le jour se lève*, with Jules Berry, Arletty and Jean Gabin: it was very sordid but much more true to life than American or British films.

Letter from Cis. He's making a case for his razor and will be starting my bag soon. At the beginning, he said it was not for him and now I can see he is pleased to make something with his hands. He heard from Robert, a boy from the Leclerc Division who was with him in hospital in Dijon. That poor boy is really unfortunate: he was just out of plaster when, two days later, he fell off a stretcher and broke his leg again! And in addition, his fiancée told him they were through. Cis called her '*Miss Honoré*'!

Le jour se lève (Daybreak): a film directed by Marcel Carné (1939). *Boum*: sung by Charles Trenet.

Sunday 6

Everyone on edge about the news.

Monday 7

Armistice signed at 3 am. Russians are to occupy the east of Berlin, the Americans the south and south-west, the French the north-west, and the British the west. Germans are going to be used to clear up the destruction they have caused. It seems so queer to think that now is *after the war*. However we must not forget that it is not over in the Far East and all is not so nice for those who lost their beloved ones, or are desperately waiting for news, like Nelly, whose brother is a prisoner, like Gran's chauffeur's son, and also the soldiers in India and Burma. Went down for some errands for F's family. Bought some lilies of the valley for Mummy. Lots of Allied flags on the buildings. Red, white, blue ribbons on sale everywhere. Went across the river and saw the *Johann Van Oldenbarnevelt*, a troopship, and all the men cheered. Letter from F of Friday: he is going to get up in a bit, but before that, he'll be spending his Victory Day in bed, poor boy! '*Last night the W.O. and the glider pilot were slightly tipsy, and caused mayhem in the ward. The civilians in Pontypridd are standing drinks to all the convalescents they see in the blue uniforms with red ties. So Good Heavens! What will it be like when Germany capitulates!*'

Tuesday 8

VE Day. No incoming or outgoing posts. Daddy went to the office as the government still wants food distributed. General Jodl signed the armistice for the Germans, but the ceasefire has already been given. Met Mrs Dick; Mummy said I might go to the canteen with her. She was so upset that her son Colin, who is in the RAF in Canada, wasn't home. It was pouring with rain. The usual canteen helpers were there; we were extremely busy. At 3 pm Churchill spoke, but although it was relayed on loud-speakers, we couldn't hear a word. He merely announced the cessation of hostilities. We went down to the office and had a look at St Georges' plateau, which was jammed with people. I had never seen so many, mostly young women with families. They wore very gay turbans. Lord Sefton spoke, and they played *God Save the King* (F always calls it '*the Godsave*') and other tunes as well. Then we went back to work. Hundreds of men came in, some a bit drunk, but none objectionable. A few wanted to kiss me. An extremely handsome commando of Special Forces hugged me. Some Frenchmen came in, one of whom was going back to France. Some of the men were playing a guitar and singing. In celebration, the superintendent gave us tinned pineapples and cream. I am very glad that I went: I feel I *did* something. All the men seemed very jolly, except for two mournful sailors who were not allowed out tonight! We came away early and walked through town: there was a great deal of bunting up. Nobody was drunk. Hordes of people drifted aimlessly about: it all seemed rather flat. The Dicks came over, which was very nice. Patsy opened the famous tin of condensed milk, which she had been promised at the end of the war! Listened to the King's speech, quite touching, and heard German broadcasts from London, descriptions of Liverpool, and ones of Paris from Pierre Lefèvre and Jacques Duchesne, and also General de Gaulle. No-one seems to have been very rowdy. We drank a toast to Colin and Francis. Poor Cis! I hope he had some sort of celebration; it must have been horrid for him. I thought about him such a lot; I decorated his photo with red ribbon and a tricolour and wrote a little card to him. I also thought of all the others I know, wherever they are. It will take a long time for things to get back to anything like order.

The office of the YMCA which ran the canteen.

Lord Sefton: Lord Mayor of Liverpool.

Pierre Lefèvre and Jacques Duchesne: presenters of *Les Français parlent aux Français*, on BBC Radio London.

Wednesday 9

Holiday again. Hundreds of flags everywhere. Went to flicks; the news was excellent, with a short review of Hitler's career. All the kids were yelling. Russians celebrated victory: they deserve it. No letters. Wrote to Cis. Wonder what he is doing.

Thursday 10

Everyone seems to have had a quiet time, except Joan who was at the *British* both last nights and had to walk home through packed streets. Submarines and battleships surrendering. Channel Islands ours, once more. Dunkirk freed. Think the *Felix Roussel* has gone to Belfast. Oh! Cis.

Friday 11

Bought soap for Cis and things for parcel for the Uzays, tea and tobacco for his father's pipe. Do hope F does not come before exams.

Saturday 12

Got two letters of 10th. It's exactly what I expected: he was rather sad at the armistice. 'Et voila! *But I can't feel any joy or anything; I haven't the impression the war's over, and in any case it's not. Millions of people have stopped suffering, and this makes me happy, but I can't feel enthusiastic; it seems to me I ought to have shouted for joy, or burst into song, but I only wept for a moment when the armistice was announced. It's true that I hadn't dreamt of spending V-Day in hospital. Since the war began, I'd dreamt of flying over the* Arc de Triomphe *on such a day. But I have to remember that the poor soldiers in the Far East are in a much worse situation than mine. Some died yesterday and the day before. They'll never return to their own country, while I still have that hope. But I confess I felt rather melancholy when I saw the village all lit up and heard the singing and the shouting. I ought to have been happy, since everyone else was. You, too, must have been very happy, but I couldn't help it; the ward was so quiet, so empty, there were only three of us, the rest were in town, and it wasn't envy, darling, but rather despair. I wished you'd been by my side, and then I might have cried, but it would have done me good. I just can't begin to explain and analyze all the strange, complex and paradoxical feelings that troubled my mind during those two days. It was some sort of astonishment mixed with joy, but above all this a kind of melancholy.'* Chérubin wrote to him: he nominated him for the DFM, which can take six months. He's going to send him his golden Caterpillar badge. Another Frenchman arrived in his hospital: he was able to go to see him in a wheelchair to help him as an interpreter. He also was visited by a Frenchwoman, married to a Welshman, and her two daughters; he was very pleased to be able to speak French with them. I know he misses me, as I miss him too. Time goes by so slowly for him. *'It's getting dark, darling, and I'm thinking of you even more. Night is bringing a fresh breeze to the plain. I'm thinking of our evenings together, and the times we spend together at dusk, I'm thinking of our loving kisses with such exquisite delight. I'm thinking of the shining stars which come out and lend us their light so that we can kiss each other, those kisses which blossom like flowers which we desire, and that we want to last forever. But we'll share again more of such moments; I shall hear your heart beat again, read your inner thoughts in your eyes, and hear from your lips the words that give me such happiness. Meanwhile I can only love you from a distance, and write the words I wish that I could whisper in your ear.'*

Sent him a sprig of lily of the valley. Did my hair à la Victorian. Everyone fed up about the wonderful treatment given to Göring.

DFM: Distinguished Flying Medal.

'*Those kisses which blossom*': inspired by *Les baisers dans le soir*, sung by Rina Ketty.

Sunday 13

Churchill spoke rather well; was extremely cutting about de Valera.

Oh, Cis! He asks about seeing each other again after he has gone. I don't know what to do.

De Valera: the Irish president who was neutral but refused his ports to the Royal Navy against the German U-boats.

Monday 14

His letter of 11th. He was thrilled with my card for Armistice. '*Where was I when the war was declared? Well, I was still in Civvy Street and maybe I was dancing. But I'd never have dreamed of finding myself in England for the Armistice.'* He thinks that what he did during the war is quite natural. *'Frankly I feel rather embarrassed when you thank me; I never thought of that. I only thought that we had to get rid of the Germans, and that, since England was lucky enough to have been saved from invasion, we had to prevent her from ever knowing such a fate. But I've no right to your gratitude, because what was uppermost in my mind was to avenge France and liberate her, although towards the end I felt I had become somewhat English (sic).'* He received fifteen letters on Friday, among them seven from me, all coming from Dijon, including one of 22nd January, the one I wrote on my birthday. He wishes me good luck with the tailor; he particularly wants him to put a beautiful 'AG' on his uniform. I went back to the shop on Saturday, and they said that his measurements would certainly have changed since his accident! All that fuss drives me mad. Got two books from Cis: one, *English Traits*, and the other on legends of Naples. He tells me not to send accounts for the money because it smacks of the grocer! Wrote him a short note. Starting to think I will never see him again.

English Traits: by Emerson (1856).

Tuesday 15

Letter from Dédé, written on 4th May. Says F used to try to talk English, even in France. Feriolo went to see them two days after he got home, which seems to have pleased them no end. It reminded them all of Cis. He talked a lot about us. I am glad he went. In German class, Miss Schuma talked about world politics. I told her about Cis being in England; she said that she hadn't liked to ask for fear of making me unhappy. Seemed really pleased. The man at the canteen gave me two bars of chocolate for Cis.

Wednesday 16

His letter of 14th. I'm so happy for him: he has stood upright for the first time in five months! *'Yesterday I was anaesthetized so they could take off the remaining splint, and now my leg is totally free. Hurrah! I stood up on my bed a while ago; can you imagine this? Standing up straight, the first time in almost five months! But I soon sat down, for I felt dizzy and the whole ward was spinning in my head.'* He hopes to be fit enough to get a leave in June. He's mad with rage against the tailor. *'First a volley of polite abuse addressed to the tailor! Listen, tell him this, word for word: I want that uniform made to the former measurements; I haven't lost any weight at all, and sooner or later I'm going to lose my temper, take a Halifax and drop a whole load of bombs on his shop if he doesn't make that uniform. I'm furious because first and foremost I was wearing my uniform when I was shot down. Then the Yanks first cut it off and burned it, and I don't want to pay a fine because I was found walking along the streets in my pyjamas.'* I know he is longing to see me again too; already six months since his last leave, and we still have to wait. *'Do you know that every morning when I'd got back from leave, each time, I would tell poor Jacques: 'Only forty-four days left and we'll be going on leave.' He thought that I was overdoing things, but I wasn't. No sooner have you and I parted than I am dying to see you again and it gets more pressing with each day that I spend away from you.'* Seems pleased about the parcel to his family, which unfortunately was returned as I had no permit; I doubt that I'll get one. Wrote to the censor. Saw a child with an SS cap on, green and rather smart: no-one was taking any notice!

Thursday 17

Letter from Cis on women's education: I think he's cracked! He sounds much better anyway. He kissed the lily of the valley because my hands had touched it. As soon as he'll be allowed to go out, he will go to the village to ring me up. *'I dream only of one thing: seeing you again. Please God, it'll soon happen!'*

Friday 18

Letter from F. He heard from Pat just before she left to Algiers. *'Yes, Pat sent me a letter, just before leaving, a very short letter in which she asked me to convey her apologies for not writing to you, but she'd been terribly busy during the week before her departure. She left by air and I haven't heard from her since. I think that was the day before V-Day. I hope she finds the solace she needs in North Africa. I was so sorry*

I couldn't see her before she left, for I'm very fond of her, and she's Henry's wife. Poor Henry, I think there isn't much hope left now. The end of the war was so close, it's awful. How happy he would have been to be there for the armistice. Our poor team ran out of luck; of the three of us, Henry, Jacques and me, no-one has been able to take part in the celebrations. Well, that's how it goes, and I'm the luckiest of the three. But let's forget about this; I don't want to make you sad, but I can't help thinking of those who were my two best friends and would have been so happy to see the war's end. Jacques and I even intended to work together after the war. We had envisaged all sorts of plans, as gangsters, night-club owners, settlers, spies – you know, daft, even crazy stuff. That was why I got on so well with Jacques; he could behave so much like a child, while being so serious at the same time, and often Henry couldn't understand us when we burst out laughing for no special reason. Everything made us laugh, and woe betide the butt of our jokes.'

Met Mummy in town and we went to Reid's. The man was insolent and refuses to make the suit without coupons! Hope the RAF will give Cis some. I am upset again.

Reid: the tailor.

Saturday 19

Two letters from him. Unfortunately, the doctor said he should stay in bed still some time, as his thigh bone is not strong enough and his muscles are too weak: '*I can wait; I'm used to it now.*' He thanked me for the books and the chocolate. Says I should have kept one bar at least; at the hospital he's given two a week. He's delighted to get news from his family regularly: Dédé, Rose, Jeanne, all write to him. It sounds as if, three days after the victory, they were still dancing on the village square at Berre! Even his father wrote a letter to him, which he was thrilled with. '*My Papa, ah! This is the first time he has ever written to me, wonderful, isn't it? He says that for three years he didn't know whether I was dead or alive, that he's happy everything has turned out well, and what pleases me most, he says he is proud of me – my Papa is proud of me! That's something I had never dared to imagine. Poor Papa, he says: 'Come back soon and we'll have a party for a whole week.' I've never realized all that*

I owe to him as much as I do now. You know, when we were younger, the four of us I mean, we weren't very rich, but I never heard him complain to Maman. He made it possible for my brother and sisters and myself to study only through his hard work. To me he is a sort of self-made man.' His father can be proud of him indeed. Time goes by slowly at Church Village. *'Nothing new here. The days go by and each is much the same as the preceding one; nothing changes, it's rather monotonous, but everything's all right really since I love you. All of this will be forgotten when I can hold you in my arms again; nothing will matter but your heart next to mine. When will I hear again this very short poem I found so enchanting? When will I hear you say again 'I love you'? Very soon, won't I, Bébé? Do tell me it won't be long! When the birds go to sleep, and when the trees are but grey ghosts, I know that over there in the distance there's a shining light; it's my favourite star, it's the fire of our love.'*

Letter from Rose who says milk is short. She seems potty about English!

'When the birds go to sleep': beginning of *La Maison sur la colline*, sung by Rina Ketty.

Sunday 20
Met Colin at the Dicks': he's back from Canada and has brought home hundreds of silk stockings!

Monday 21
Whit Monday. Letter from censor, telling me to write to the French Red Cross, which I did. Wrote to Cis. He was on leave last Whit Monday. Feel so lonely.

Wednesday 23
Letter from F, enclosing a rather nice one from *Chérubin*. The crew are going back to France. *'I've received a letter from Morel; he says the rest of the crew will probably leave for France at the end of the month. It's all over, the 'Gs' no longer exist, the crew has disbanded; I'm sorry it has, and rather sad, for although those seven men were so dissimilar, I really believe, without flattery or vanity, that we made up a very fine team. I'm enclosing the latest letter from Chérubin, so you can tell me*

what you think of him. I feel slightly guilty for I think we somewhat misjudged him.' It sounds as if the flying personnel treated in Church Village are sent for convalescence to Hoylake: it would be too good to be true! Poor sweetheart, when will he eventually be able to leave his bed? '*It's now almost five months since I've been lying in bed, and my back must be as flat as the board on which Maman makes her cakes.*'

Letter from Ardenne: they're making plans to go back to Guernsey.

Hoylake: a small seaside town near Liverpool at the north western corner of the Wirral Peninsula.

Ardenne: a friend of Barbara's.

Thursday 24

Letter from F: he had already given coupons to the tailor. '*Now listen to me as I roar with fury, but don't be afraid for I don't bite! Tell that tailor he's dishonest for I gave him those twenty-four clothing coupons the first time I saw him about my uniform and he never gave them back. Remember, I had obtained a hundred of them on the previous day. If he won't understand, don't insist, I don't want to cause you trouble, you've already had enough so far. I'll see to this when I'm on leave.*' I would not like to be in the place of the tailor that day! The doctor asked for his size of shoes: it's rather a good sign. '*You know, I'll have to walk with a special shoe, with some kind of springy sole, for my foot will take time to recover, but I'll be able to walk like anybody else.*' He ended his letter so tenderly. '*I have sworn to love you always, as in the love songs that the accordion played so well at the dance, do you remember? You never promised anything, but your eyes seemed so tender that I understood at once that this was love.*'

Wrote to him. Seems years since I saw him. Churchill resigned. I wonder what will happen now.

'*I have sworn to love you always*': *J'ai juré de t'aimer toujours,* sung by Lys Gauty.

Friday 25

Letter from Cis. He can now bend his leg at 130 degrees. He's gaining about 5 degrees each week and will be having an X-ray in ten days' time; then perhaps, he'll be able to get up, at last. He's looking forward to being able to ring me up. I haven't heard his voice this year. '*Listen to the song the leaves make, darling. Aren't they saying 'I love you'? Yes, I'm sure they are, they really are, for if the world is against us, Nature is on our side. I know that you can see the sun set at the same moment as I do, that the air that I breathe is yours, too, and that the breeze I can feel has also stroked your hair. Maybe you looked at that star so high up in the sky? Never mind the world, its woes, or the foggy winter days: for me, the beautiful blue sky of my love is in your eyes. Well, darling, I'll leave you here. Tonight at 9 I'll be with you again. Good bye, darling, goodbye – remember that I'm happy since your heart beats for me.*'

Saturday 26

Went to see the Matron at the Ministry of Pensions Hospital, where I am to work for national service during the holidays. Am afraid Cis may come on leave while I am there. Got a letter. He says that, if there was a dance for wounded soldiers in his hospital, he would go and would dance on his hands! He wishes me good luck for my exams. I want to see him so much.

Ministry of Pensions Hospital, Woolton.

Sunday 27

Worked a bit on *Gil Blas*, then wrote to Cis. Pat Moore came; we talked about Maurice, her French boy-friend who was in the SOE: he was betrayed by another Frenchman.

Monday 28

The handbag F made for me came: it is really lovely, very well-made and of good leather.

Tuesday 29

A year today since he came on leave and we stood in the park, under the tree, in the thunder: it seems ages ago. His letter of 27th. Says he bit the new nurse's finger because she had called him 'Frenchy'! One morning, he wouldn't let her wash his back as he was engrossed in reading *Le Crève-cœur*. He also walked round his bed, when the Sister wasn't looking. As for his suit, I am ordered to stop the whole thing: '*Unconditional surrender until I'm back.*' He made a tobacco pouch for Daddy's pipe in only one day. Guy, his flight-engineer, is going to see him. The French lady visited him again; she works at the YMCA once a week, like me. She brought him sweets, cakes and cigarettes. Each evening, he's having cocoa, which he calls '*cow-cow*'! '*Our corner of the ward here is now an international settlement. Yesterday a Czech arrived, together with an Indian from British Guiana, and it is now extremely confusing because the Indian's name is 'François', the Czech's is 'Francizek', the English fellow behind me is 'Frank', and my name's 'Francis'! For the English there's only 'Frank'. So each time somebody calls out that name, four heads turn around! Each of us will need to be given a number.*'

Thursday 31
Got a letter. He asks me to thank Daddy for the chequebook which he sent to him: he now calls him 'his banker'! He's sending Adaoust to see his parents when he gets to France. He hasn't yet heard from Pat since she's gone to Algiers. Real trouble in Syria: French firing.

Adjudant Adaoust: the bomb aimer in Francis' crew.

June

Friday 1
Cis got a letter from Pat at last, rather alarming. '*I won't be writing a long letter, for I'm rather upset: I've received a letter from Pat, and guess where from? London. Yes, she's back but I don't know why. She only wrote a short note, just an hour after arriving. I'm concerned about her, darling. She says she spent a terrible month in Algiers and thought she'd go mad. She's also received some information about poor Henry, and no, we'll never see him again. I knew that it was bound to happen, but absurd though it may seem, I was still hoping. But this is now definite;*

his child will not know or rather will <u>never</u> know its father. But I'll do my best to replace him. I have the impression that something bad happened in Algiers; it is my duty to look after this child – I must, don't you agree, darling? Poor Pat, she didn't deserve that; no, it's unfair, and it makes me mad when I think of it. This is so disheartening. I'll be sending more details as soon as I can. Now I want to think things over; will you forgive me if I leave you so soon? Goodbye, darling, I'll think of you tonight; I need you more than ever.' I wonder if it is the Algerian food riots or problems with the Martins. Wrote to him. He seemed so upset. Trouble better in Syria: armistice. De Gaulle is so obstinate.

Saturday 2

His letter of Thursday. The rain makes him melancholy: '*Il pleure dans mon cœur comme il pleut sur la ville.*' He told me about Verlaine's friendship and fascination with Rimbaud at some length. Went to AVF meeting. Saw Pat Moore who was very interested in F's explanation. She met an old flame, Roland, from Algiers, who knew F and also Jacques. Said her Maurice got the *Croix de guerre* for blowing up a train of German workers. He dropped behind the lines on D-Day. It was a Belgian, not a Frenchman, who betrayed him. *Mme* da Horta put in her positively last appearance. Funny, a bit of my life going. Saw Miriam who lectured me on 'finding a suitable husband'!

Miriam: Barbara's relative.

Sunday 3

Our first kiss, a year ago. Wrote to him.

Monday 4

Letter from Cis; seems very bored. He tried to walk again. '*Oh! I got up again this morning but the Sister arrived and I had to run on one leg to get back to bed. I tried to stand on both legs and 'my bad leg' seems steady, but it's a strange sensation when you stand on a foot which you can't feel.*' He's still waiting for his flight engineer to visit him. He burnt letters which overfilled his cardboard box and apologized for having burnt some of mine. Wrote to him.

Tuesday 5

Useless instructions from French Red Cross. Mr Frank took out a tooth. His son, Tim, was on the attack on Rangoon. Wrote to Cis. I wonder if his leg is all right; I am a bit worried.

Wednesday 6

Anniversary of D-Day. It doesn't seem a year ago, and yet so much has happened! F and I had such a good time that day. Letter from him. He was very busy at making a little rabbit, red colour with a yellow tummy. He will send it with the tobacco pouch for Daddy. Was amused at my dancing the Rumba; not surprising! He always says: '*Tu danses comme un clou!*' He hasn't heard from Pat again. '*The poor girl must get some rest. She needs it. Her first letter was only a short note and she didn't give any details. Yes, she's staying at Mrs Singleton's; at any rate that's where she wrote from. These people are so wonderfully kind and if or when I'm on leave I'll have to pay them a visit. It's not a question of feeling responsible for her, for I realize that her parents did not really look after her after Henry went missing; it's a question of what I think and feel I must do. I know that what I'm saying is rather mean, for Mrs Pattimore has been more than kind to me, but they seem to think that Pat can manage things by herself now, but she can't. It's impossible, you understand darling, especially in her situation.*' Wrote to him. Peter Davison wanted to give me twelve clothing coupons for F, but I made him take 5 shillings for them.

'*Tu danses comme un clou*': 'You dance with two left feet!' Peter Davison: Sheila's friend in the Merchant Navy.

Thursday 7

Letter from Cis. He's making a small pink elephant for me, and another big blue one for Patsy. More about Verlaine and Rimbaud. Every day he's having physiotherapy. '*Don't talk to me about 'exercise time'! I sweat blood; I'm told to bend my leg, raise it up, etc. This is 'deadly'!*' However he does not show any signs of getting up soon. Anyway, he is in good spirits and does his best to cheer me up, although it should be the contrary. '*Come on now, Bébé, don't brood. The world is rotten to the core, but there is still some beauty left in it somewhere: in the setting sun, in the rain; beauty exists everywhere you want to see it, and it makes up a little for all the dark aspects of the present day. [...] Come on, darling, smile for me, we've got our love to help us fight and this gives me strength.'* He quoted this lovely verse from his *Crève-cœur*: *'Au biseau des baisers, les ans passent trop vite.'* and added: *'But it seems like ages when you're not by my side.'* Packed up a parcel for him.

'Au biseau des baisers...': excerpt from *Elsa, je t'aime*, a poem from *Le Crève-cœur*.

Friday 8

Letter from F. Pat wrote to him and told him why she had to come back from Algiers, but she told him not to tell me. *'I've received a letter from Pat; she explains what happened to her, but, darling, I can't tell you anything because she asks me not to say anything to anyone, 'not even Barbara', she wrote. All I can say is that coming back here was the only possible solution for her and that more than ever she needs affection. She's so marvellous: in spite of all her worries, she nevertheless managed to spare a thought for me and tell the helper to send me some books. I may be able to go to her child's baptism, after all. I think I'll grow very fond of this child, perhaps even more than if it were my own. But that's too much, darling, much too much; didn't she suffer enough before? Has tragedy no end once it has begun? But I won't go on like this, it makes me furious when I think of it. I'm going to answer her letter right away.'* He'll be finishing the little elephant soon. He was told that the English can see pink elephants when they're drunk, but there is no special double-meaning from him! The silly female at the Post Office would not register the parcel. Wrote to Cis.

Saturday 9

£25 arrived from F to put at the bank: he had just been paid and says he had never been so rich! Saw *Le Chapeau de paille d'Italie*: very funny.

Un Chapeau de paille d'Italie (The Italian Straw Hat): a silent film directed by René Clair (1928).

Monday 11

Interesting letter from Dédé, and two from Cis. Good news: they have given him shoes. He thinks Pat won't return to Jersey; she intends to look for a job in London after the baby is born. A friend of her, the helper looking after soldiers in London, sent him a huge parcel of books: Alexandre Dumas, Alfred de Vigny, Gustave Flaubert, *Les Pensées* by Pascal, and also lots of others. He thanked me for my parcel too and was pleased with the coupons. Wrote to him.

Tuesday 12

Letter from Ardenne. She talks about her house in Guernsey which had been turned into a fortress by the Germans and stripped. Bought *Golden Treasury* for Cis.

Palgrave's *Golden Treasury*: anthology of poetry (1861).

Wednesday 13

He sent a parcel with the tobacco pouch for Daddy, *Jeannot Lapin* for the crèche's children, and a sweet little pink elephant for me with a blue howdah. They are beautifully made: he is so clever. He's been transferred to Ward 2 and now is in a room with two beds. Seems well and happy. He tried his shoes on. He doesn't seem to have kept a very romantic memory of our first kiss! '*Oh, no! Don't try to deny it, these are the very words you said on June 3rd 1944: 'Francis, you're not a man!' and I answered: 'Not a man, eh?' Then I kissed you, a little roughly I think. And what do you mean by: 'I was just teasing you in order to make your leave more pleasant'? Honestly, when you answered: 'Yes, if it's proper' on the evening when I offered you my arm, I was piqued.*' These exams are not going well. Wrote a long letter to Cis.

Jeannot Lapin: Benjamin Bunny.

Friday 15

Thank heaven, exams are over! Beryl came and asked me out for tomorrow.

Saturday 16

Letter from Cis. He seems to like his new room and laughs a lot with the Belgian next to him: it reminds him of 'the good life' at Wroughton. He can go round in a wheelchair now. Says that he eats a lot but doesn't put on weight. The hospital has written to Elvington about his uniform. The Belgian went to the cinema; F hopes to be able to go soon too. '*Good night, darling; a field of stars for a village, four houses huddled together with their shadows dancing in the dark – that's where I'll take you off to. If there is a quiet place anywhere in the world, I'll find it and carry you off there. Francis the kidnapper.*'

Beryl, Bert and Lovat came for me. Went to the Adelphi for dinner.

'*A field of stars*': beginning of *Mon village au clair de lune*, sung by Jean Sablon.
Bert: Beryl's fiancé. Lovat: Beryl's Scottish cousin; he was an officer in the Merchant Navy.

Monday 18

Made parcel up for F. Went to Beryl's; saw Lovat.

Tuesday 19

Long, cheerful letter from F. He was allowed to go out at last: they took him in his wheelchair to see a show at the NAAFI, outside the camp. '*I could feel the wind and even touch the grass.*' The morning after, he went out on his own to the terrace to play cards and Monopoly with the Belgian and an Englishman. The three daughters of Mrs Jones, the French lady, visited him. Hilda, the oldest one, pushed him at top speed in the corridor, and everybody had to move out of the way! He seemed so happy that day, but when the evening came he became melancholy. '*You probably went to Gran's this evening and I wasn't there. I couldn't drink Uncle Max's beer, and when you left you didn't tell me: 'You smell of beer!' with that slight grimace of dislike that suits you so well. We didn't stumble in the dark on our way home; we didn't stop at the door. When, oh when shall I see all this again? Sweet or unpleasant memories, painful or comforting memories, I want to live this again. I was happy this afternoon and now it makes me think of you. How lovely it would have been to spend the afternoon with you. I wish I could have taken my first steps while I leant on your shoulder, I want to feel like a little child and snuggle up close to you; I need your tenderness. But let's be a little more patient; I need to be because the goal is now within reach.'*

I do hope that he will come soon. Wrote to him.

Wednesday 20

Another cheerful letter. He is thrilled with the wheelchair; in the morning, he can't wait to get up and '*go haunting the corridors*'! He can go to his electrotherapy sessions on his own and see his friends whenever he wants. He always thinks of me tenderly every night. '*It's already 10 but you'd think it was 7, it's just as light as day. I wish I could be on the terrace for the night breeze is as sweet as honey. Has Merlin ceased to exist? I'm sure he wouldn't turn down my wish to see you brought here in a silver chariot pulled by eight white deer. I'd be like one of the Wise Men awaiting the appearance of the Star, because you'd be my star. Don't say no, because isn't a star the glimmer that suddenly appears in a dark sky? Isn't it the light our eyes are drawn to whether we want to look at it or not? The light that comforts us just by looking at it? Haven't you been all this for my soul? [...] Merlin isn't here but this can't prevent me from coming back to you. If my kisses could be birds, then your room is an aviary full of them.*' Went out for a bike ride with Lovat by the Mersey. Everyone I meet never seems to measure up to Cis. Such long months since I saw you, my brave little chap.

Thursday 21

Set off early to Threshfield. Felt so quéer to be in a car again on the roads. Saw German and Italian prisoners working in the fields. Wrote to Cis and enclosed a little rose in the envelope. If only he were here, how perfect it would be!

Threshfield: small village in the north of Yorkshire, near Ripon.

Friday 22

Nothing from Cis. Wrote to him.

Saturday 23

No letter: I suppose he has lost the address I had given to him. Wrote
to him again. Saw lots of Italian prisoners, many like Cis, and also a
German; I would like to have spoken to him, but this is not allowed,
naturally. A year this week since Cis turned up at an unearthly hour of
the night: it won't happen this time.

Monday 25

Back home. Went through St Helens and saw Lowe House where Pat
and Henri were married. What a tragic wedding! Letter from Cis: he's
going to walk, officially. Says that he must wear a strange device to
strengthen his knee's muscles which have remained motionless for so
long. Wrote to him.

Tuesday 26

Dr Fletcher said: 'You have the taste and the talent for French!' Sent Cis
my French test to see what he thinks about.

Dr Fletcher: French lecturer.

Wednesday 27

Had two letters, one forwarded on from Threshfield. He seems very
cheerful. He went to the cinema, which he was thrilled with, although
the film was not interesting; at least, he had a chance to enjoy himself a
bit. Mrs Jones came to see him again with a huge bunch of roses, as he
had told her that he is fond of flowers. He dare not say anything now
as she spoils him so much; she brought him coffee because he doesn't
like tea and her daughters will bring him beer next time. He began to
put some weight on his right foot which gets blue when he puts it on
the floor. He's very glad that he can wash himself in a bath now. He also
has a new wheelchair which goes on the road, with three wheels, two
brakes, a light and a speed gearbox! He worries that he hasn't heard
from Pat again and is going to write to her. He enclosed rose petals
which he kissed for me. Wonder if he will get leave while we are away,
am afraid so.

Thursday 28

Two letters from F again, one forwarded on. Says his bone is quite strong now and he can stand on his two legs. He stayed in the bath for an hour: '*It was a wonderful feeling!*'

Spent all my money today! Bought *Vous qui passez sans me voir, La Chanson des rues, Le Soleil et la lune,* and *Les Enfants s'ennuient le dimanche.* Phoned the Matron at hospital about my uniform.

Vous qui passez sans me voir and *La Chanson des rues:* sung by Jean Sablon.
   Le Soleil et la lune and *Les Enfants s'ennuient le dimanche:* sung by Charles
   Trenet.

Friday 29

Letter from Cis. I think he isn't as jealous as before. Anyway, he says that I don't need to justify myself each time I'm going out, and, if once he behaved like an idiot, it is no reason to do it again! '*Please tell yourself that as long as I know that you're happy and that you can smile and forget about your worries, then I'm happy too, and will only begin to doubt your love when you tell me you don't love me anymore, and even then – maybe!*' He will have two or three weeks' leave. I replied to him. I wish he would come soon, before we go away.

Saturday 30

At last, he has got up! He's on crutches, '*Read this carefully: done it, this time! At last I can get up and stand on my two legs – and this is OFFICIAL! [...] I feel like a man again now that I can – and if you could see how I can use my crutches. [...] I've waited so long for the day when I can get up, walk again, with almost as much impatience as for the day when I can see you again. Let's be happy tonight, darling: soon we'll be together, I love you (3 x). I'm glad you're not here tonight, for you would already be dead, smothered by my kisses. Good night, darling, my beloved Bébé, my love, my blue angel, good night, but beware of my kisses tonight for the roof of your bedroom is going to collapse. I love you.*' Of course, he has done too much and has tired himself out! He must keep on wearing that appliance which helps his knee. He received his Caterpillar member card with the badge, a little golden caterpillar with two red eyes: the nurses have found out, at last, that he was flying personnel!

July

Sunday 1

Went to the hospital and was received by the Matron: was given two beautiful starched aprons, ordered to wear stockings (in summer!) and put my hair up! Men are a very rough type but amazingly cheerful and gay. I am in an amputation ward. It is heartrending to see some of the men. Most of them were wounded during the invasion. Hours: 9.30–12.30 am. It's a new kind of work, quite agreeable. I have to make the beds, wash the wounded, wash the bandages, help with dressings, go for some errands, and also prepare the '*cow-cow*'.

Got two letters from Cis. He was able to take his first steps in the corridor, which seemed to him ten kilometres long, and the day after he already walked with only one crutch. He thinks he will be able to go around the hospital for a while within two or three days. Hope he does ring up. Dédé passed his *certificat d'études* and is expecting the results of his other exams. It's odd as I have the same feeling as Cis when I try to see his face: it's something quite elusive. '*Your face? I still can't see it when I'd like to; it comes and goes and I can only catch a fleeting glimpse in my mind's eye, without ever being able to control these visions.*'

Certificat d'études: School Certificate.

Tuesday 3

At hospital, a wounded man who has only one eye left said to me: 'I'm watching you!' He has a glass eye in the place of the other one. Wrote to Cis. Wonder if he will ring up tomorrow.

Wednesday 4

Fierce political argument in ward about crisis of housing and communism. When I see those wounded men, I can imagine what Cis has been through. Expected that he would ring, but still nothing. Sheila rang to say we both passed our second-year exams!

Thursday 5

Letter from Cis. Pat had her baby: it's a boy! I thought it would be. '*On Sunday afternoon I received a telegram, and wondered who could have sent it; it was the Singletons – the baby has arrived, darling; it's a boy and Pat is quite alright. I'm very happy because she'll be much better now and she'll be able to work.*' Poor Henri, he would have been so happy to have a son. Cis seems to make progress very quickly. '*Just another couple of days and I'll send my crutches flying; I'm beginning to walk faster now. Yesterday evening, I went to the cinema without a wheelchair. [...] I'm feeling alright but the muscles in my calf are a bit sore for I haven't exercised them for a long time. [...] My leg is already stronger than it was five days ago.*'

At hospital, talked to Pilot Officer Geoffrey France who was shot down over Duisburg and prisoner for five and a half months. He lost a leg. He's from Bolton, near Manchester. Germans were good to him, especially the doctors, but they couldn't save his leg. Wants to go on flying, like Cis. Wrote to him. Wish he'd hurry and come.

General election. Wonder who will win: it will make a difference to our lives.

Friday 6

He still hasn't rung up. Got a letter with a flower coming from his *tante* Rosalie's garden. Mrs Jones brought him another lovely bunch of red roses. All is perfectly fine. It's really been a new life for him since he started to walk again. '*In my view, I'm living the life of Riley: I get up at 10 or 11, have a bath, put on the appliance which I call my leg, and go and smoke a cigarette; then it's time for lunch; afterwards I have a short walk; have a snooze; tea-time, then I read; time to have supper, then I go to see the illustrious Germain, go back to my room, drink my 'cow-cow' and write to you – as you can see even a millionaire couldn't lead a better life.*'

At hospital, they trimmed Douglas' stump; he spoke with a Scottish accent under anaesthetic. Taffy started to walk with his new legs: he was so proud. Called Pilot Officer France '*Prune*'. Asked him home tomorrow.

Tante: aunt.

Pilot Officer Percy Prune: a wartime cartoon character, created by Bill Hooper and Anthony Armstrong, in a comic strip narrating the adventures of an RAF pilot officer, as a way of instructing pilots what not to do if they wanted to save their lives and their aircraft.

Saturday 7

Letter from Cis. He couldn't phone on Wednesday, as the doctor came to see him. Everything's all right, except he caught a cold. The doctor said to him he had made great progress. So the long lie-ins are over! Now that he can walk, he must get up early to go and have breakfast at the mess at 8 am like everybody. The advantage is that he can have more food and it is better. He now has two Belgian friends, Léon and Roger, with whom he can speak French. Says they are hilarious. They were wounded by a mortar shell during training. Cis would like me to find them female penfriends, as they don't know anyone in England. Wish he had phoned.

Prune came to tea with the Orfords. At AVF, met *lieutenant* Ruitier, from Paymaster Headquarters of the FAF, who is from Bordeaux. We had a long and interesting talk about Syria, about which he is most upset.

Monday 9

Eclipse. The sun looked like a moon with a thunder sickle. *Prune* says he has nightmares: he dreamt that he was falling again. Stanley arrived in the ward; both legs were amputated: he suffers from shock. The men were most agitated: the atmosphere was sultry and they couldn't go out. Two letters from Cis. He congratulated me for my exams. Couldn't phone from hospital, as the long-distance calls are not allowed (he was furious), but he is going into village on Wednesday. '*You never know whether love will be sad or happy, but I want mine to end with me. The dream we have together is rather a crazy one, but let's hope that it may give us the happiness of loving each other for the rest of our lives.*

Promises, promises – these can be said very lightly indeed, but not when you feel driven on by some force that you confusedly feel is capable of changing the world.' Says he cannot wear uniform: the wounded must wear a kind of sky blue suit, with white shirt and red tie, not very well made. Has had no pay. Wrote to him.

Tuesday 10

Cis rang up: he sounded so happy! First time I have heard him this year. I'd forgotten his voice. Neither of us knew what to say. He has no idea when his leave will be. Had long talk with the telephone operator in Cardiff who said: 'There's a call for you from South Wales, a Frenchman too: I'm surprised at you!' Went dancing with Beryl, Bert and Graham. They played *I'll See You Again*. See you soon! Oh! Cis, at last I heard you.

Marsden was in a very bad way today, crying and cursing; I was most upset.

Wednesday 11

His letter of 9th. He also had the same thought. '*We will meet again very soon, my* petite femme, *and when this day comes, Old England is going to have a shock (earthquake).*' Pat wrote to him. '*I had a letter from Pat today; she seems well and only talks about her baby. She says he weighed 6 pounds 14 ½ ounces when he was born. She's in a maternity hospital and very pleased with it. She sees her baby only five times a day, when a nurse brings him. But all the same she's still tired. She says: 'For me life is over; I must begin another with the sole duty of bringing up my child and making him happy.' She really is a real woman now and I think things will improve from now on. But she doesn't want to think that it's definitely all over now with Henry; she clings to anything and everything and I find her obstinacy a little frightening. She must get used to the idea that he's dead and it's awfully difficult for me to broach the subject. Anyway I have a little godson now, a big chubby-cheeked boy, and I feel very proud; I wish I could see that marvellous boy, but maybe I'll scare him with my nose; he can nevertheless play with me, and this is some consolation.*' He's invited to tea at the Jones' today. The Wing Co comes every Thursday; he's the one who will decide if F can go on leave.

Lovat came for breakfast. Met *Prune* at the gate of the hospital and pushed him home in his wheelchair. He has got the DFC. Lovat came and we all went in the park, then we pushed *Prune* back. Sister was glad that we took an interest in *Prune*.

Wing Co: Wing Commander.
DFC: Distinguished Flying Cross.

Thursday 12

Letter from Cis. He can't remember what he told me on the phone! Says he was so moved, so was I. '*I must have sounded stupid, but as soon as I heard you, I couldn't think of anything at all to say. But it was so wonderful, my darling, so marvellous: it was you in person, you again after such a long time. You haven't changed, you know; in the telephone booth I had the impression that I was in York and I was going to take off after speaking to you.*' He doesn't wear his appliance any more, but only a spring-loaded shoe. His foot, which hasn't moved for so long, and his ankle are swollen. He's tired in the evening but feels twice as light without that terrible load. Went to see *The Hard Way* at the cinema with the two Belgians and the other Frenchman.

The Hard Way: a film directed by Vincent Sherman (1943).

Saturday 14

Sent him a telegram to wish him a happy 14th July. We celebrated it at AVF.

Monday 16

He rang up last night when I was out, and said he would be coming on leave. His letter of 13th. He was surprised that I didn't recognize him straight away on the phone last Tuesday. When he said: '*Good evening, darling!*' and I said: 'Sorry?' he thought that he had mistaken the phone number! He was also annoyed that the call was interrupted several times. He is having a marvellous time now, visiting. '*I hope you're not cross with me, darling. I bet you think I'm forgetting you and I would rather have those little pleasures, but I'm dying to do and see again all those things I've been deprived of; they*' *once seemed so trivial and they are now so important to me.*' He went to the pub in Pontypridd with François on Wednesday; he drank three beers and started to feel drunk. Then he took the trolley to go to the Jones'. He found their home quite French. Hilda lent him a book of poems by Milton. He went to a show in the evening. Pat wrote to him. She's called her baby 'Paul', and not 'Henri', as she thought she would do. It's certainly better like that.

Letter from Jeanne, who expects F in two or three months' time.

Tuesday 17
Poor kid in the Navy has had a double amputation and has lost one kidney: he takes it very badly. Wrote to Cis. He rang up: sounded very happy.

Wednesday 18
Letter from F. He called Mummy '*darling*' when she answered the phone on Sunday. He says it doesn't matter as she is his 'maman *number two*'. He had a very nice 14th July. Mrs Jones brought them a bottle of wine and a big cake which she had decorated with a big pink sugar Cross of Lorraine and little French flags. He was asked to tea. He met Mr Jones who had visited Marseilles before the war. He was thrilled to talk with him about the little places which he's fond of. He enclosed a little tricolour from Mrs Jones' cake and also a postal order from Lillywhites for the bank, which is the overpayment for the peaked cap and stripes he ordered in London.

At hospital, Matron said: 'We'll make a nurse of you!' Navy boy very low; he's on fluid diet. Sheila, Lovat and James came.

James: Lovat's friend, also an officer in the Merchant Navy.

Thursday 19
Douglas said no-one would marry a man with an artificial leg. Cis rang. The poor little soul has got to go back to bed again, after his brief taste of freedom, because his foot is still insensible: it is heartbreaking for him. I feel so upset. Poor Cis, he has the most appalling luck. Wrote to him.

Friday 20

Went to ask Matron if I could stay another week, and she said: 'Yes, it's good work you are doing!' Poor Jim Latimer: he had an operation and wasn't too good; he had to have morphia. He clung to my hand and said: 'I never did any harm to anyone. Why should this happen to me?' I never heard Cis talking like that, anyway not with me.

Saturday 21

His letter of Thursday. He had a test to check his nerve's sensitivity. '*The Wing Co examined me and said my knee needs manipulating. It's nothing, just to help me bend my knee a little more. It'll mean staying in bed a week or so, but afterwards I may have an operation if my leg is strong enough. If I do, there are two solutions: either they'll make only a slight incision in the nerve, and in two weeks' time I can be up and about; or it'll be completely severed, and then I'll have to stay in bed with a plaster for two months.*' He doesn't seem too depressed though. He thinks the operation is for his good, even if it may delay his leave. He spent the afternoon at Mrs Jones' who had made pancakes for tea. She asked him to shell the peas, as he told her that he always helped at our house! He even danced the jitterbug with Edith '*with the grace of a three-hundred-year-old elephant!*'

Went to cinema with Lovat. He's hoping to emigrate to New Zealand.

Sunday 22

James came. We talked about Pascal. Walked in the park, and then found *Prune* at home: he had pushed himself on his wheelchair. They got on quite well and teased me a lot.

Monday 23

Prune flirting like mad with nurses! Wrote to Cis.

Tuesday 24

Met Lovat and James at Reece's for dinner, and then dancing.

Wednesday 25

Letter from Cis. It's he who is confined to bed, once again, and who should complain, and he does his best to cheer me up. '*On no account must you worry about me, and above all you mustn't feel like crying; in any case I'm quite all right in bed, and if you think about it for a minute, I no longer need to get up at 7 now. [...] At 9 or so on Saturday morning, I was taken to the operating room. There I saw my old friend the Wing Co. A girl with flaming red hair gently inserted a needle into my arm, and I just had time to say 'au revoir' before I was in dreamland. When I came round, my knee was very painful and much swollen. What is quite funny is that it seems, or so Germain told me, that I babbled incoherently while I was asleep; I was hot and kept saying something was ablaze. I also kept asking for my parachute, and begged Jacques to bale out. And then the next minute I was cold and could see snow everywhere. But I can't remember anything; it's very strange and I suppose the crash has left a lasting impression on my brain, more so than I imagined. Well today I feel a little better; my knee hardly hurts and it's only slightly swollen. [...] As for the operation, if it has to be done, I'd like this to be as soon as possible. You see, the sooner I'm operated on, the sooner I can leave the hospital. You're not to worry at all because all this is for my own good. How I long to see you, too, only God knows how much I do; just one look from your eyes, your lovely eyes, and I'll be willing to put up with any kind of trial. [...] I'm going to tell Dédé to light a candle in* Notre Dame de la Garde *so I may soon see you again.*' He already found a way to tease a new nurse: it's rather a good sign! '*This morning I made a recently arrived Sister yell; I don't like her at all. She's a fat, ginger-haired, matronly woman, who has openly said she doesn't like the French! This morning she brought a bowl of water so I could wash. No sooner had she left than I leapt into the bathroom. When she came back, she saw the water in the bowl was clean, and no patient in the bed. At that moment I emerged from the bathroom, as fresh as a daisy, having just had a bath. She nearly had a fit and didn't say a word to me for the rest of the day, which, between you and me, really made my day. I know you're going to blame me and say all the Sisters are doing everything they can for us. It's true, but that one really needed to be*

*taught a lesson; now I'm ready to smile at her and to be as gentle as
a lamb. Don't lecture me for that, darling: I only wanted to be a bit
cheeky.'*

Spilt boiling water over my hand: my own fault. Matron saw it and I
had to go to the doctor's who sent me home.

Thursday 26

Letter from Dédé, enclosing photo of himself: just like F, a bit less dark
perhaps. Wrote to Rose and Cis. Went to Reece's with Sheila, James and
Lovat. They played *Chez moi* and *J'attendrai*.

Labour government in power with majority of two hundred seats:
huge defeat for Churchill.

Saturday 28

Went to concert of Philharmonic Hall with Lovat: *Piano Concerto*
by Tchaikovsky, *L'Après-midi d'un faune*, which I didn't like, and the
Overture to Tannhäuser, which I did.

Prélude à l'après-midi d'un faune (Prelude to the Afternoon of a Faun): by Claude
Debussy. *Overture to Tannhäuser*: opera by Wagner.

Sunday 29

Wrote to Cis. *Prune* arrived, looking well, and stood up. Gave me some
advice about F: to love him until his departure, but not to marry him!
Pushed him back up to hospital.

Monday 30

Letter from F. He fell on Thursday and hurt his leg: nothing serious
luckily! *'Yesterday morning as I was leaving the bathroom, the
swing door hit me in the back and I fell to the floor squealing like a
slaughtered pig, but worse still was the fact that I fell on my right leg
and bent it; I heard a ghastly crack (later I realized it was my shoe)
and told myself: that's it, sonny, you're in for another six months in
hospital! The Sister on night duty, the one who's very kind and always
smells so nice came to pick me up; she examined me and never have
I been so scared as during those few minutes. At last she said that no*

harm had been done, but as it was very painful, probably due to the impact, I stayed on my bed all day. Today, however, the pain has totally gone and I can walk again. What's most astounding is the result of all this: in a way I did myself a second manipulation so I can now bend my leg nearly 80 degrees. Hurrah! Hurrah for falling in corridors, and what's more it proves my bone is solid enough.' He got a letter from Pat who is back home and fine. Mrs Jones had cooked macaroni specially for him on Wednesday.

Went to concert with Lovat: *Eine Kleine Nacht Music, The Enigma Variations* and a Rachmaninov concerto.

Eine Kleine Nachtmusik (A Little Night Music): by Mozart. *Enigma Variations:* by Edward Elgar.

Tuesday 31

Prune came. He told us more about being shot down. Wheeled him back. Listened to Radio Paris. Someone sang *Au clair de la lune* and *Vous qui passez sans me voir.*

Au Clair de la lune: a famous 18th-century French folk song and lullaby.

August

Wednesday 1

Wrote to Cis. Concert with Lovat: *Barber of Seville*, a Bach concerto and the *Siegfried Idyll* which I enjoyed most. Cis rang up whilst I was at the concert. Said he was at the Leas, at Hoylake. I can't believe it!

The Barber of Seville: comic opera by Rossini. *Siegfried Idyll:* by Wagner.
The Leas: a former school for boys, located in a big manor house surrounded by beautiful gardens, converted into an RAF convalescence centre during the war.

Thursday 2

Heard the telephone: it was F. Said he was coming on four days' leave. He came up, looking so frail and worn. He walks very slowly with two sticks and has a short calliper on his foot. He's wearing RAF battle-dress. He seems so pleased to be here; he even cried a bit. He went round the house, saying 'hello' to everything, greeting the furniture as if they were his friends. It felt as if he had never been away; it's queer because it's such ages ago. And he seems so thin. We sat in the garden, in the sun, and talked. He brought his escape map which is printed on silk; I shall wear it as a scarf. Played our records. F is so tired but seems just the same: talks a lot and pretends to be a wounded hero! Says he has no pain but he can't kiss me passionately because of his wound when he stands up. I am so sorry for him.

Friday 3

F and I went at a very slow pace to shops. Took him to have his hair cut; he looked much better. Came back on tram where people were so kind to him. James came. He also was very kind to F who said, if he were to have an English friend, he would like him. His father is a minister; we had a discussion on religion. Then went to concert with James and Lovat: *Meistersingers, Don Giovanni* and Beethoven's *5th Symphony*. James got a taxi. Francis has a new act: a flea called Norman!

Die Meistersinger von Nürnberg (The Master-Singers of Nuremberg): opera by
    Wagner. *Don Giovanni:* opera by Mozart.

Saturday 4

Cis got up late. I cleaned his shoes! We went slowly to town to Sunderlands about the suit. They were very obliging: black-market clothing coupons! We went by back streets, to avoid the crowds, to go to Reece's where we had a good tête-à-tête lunch. Poor F was so happy. He looks so pinched. Saw a film on demobilization. He had to keep getting up. Then we went to the *British*, which seemed like old times. We met Sheila. Cis was so delighted. We stayed there quite a long time. Poor Cis, what he has been through! Showed me his scar which is neat and well-done. He finds the Leas lovely. He then became very sad because of the old subject of marriage.

Sunday 5

F very tired and quiet: sat and read. He can't do much actually. His shoulders are so thin. We sat out in the garden and he went to sleep in the deck-chair uneasily, like in December last year: he shivered and tossed. *Prune* turned up. He says I must not use the scarf yet because it is still secret. Cis was telling us he was going to have a night-club! It was very funny. They got together about bombing raids. Pushed *Prune* back.

Monday 6

F much better in spirits. We went to see Mrs Dick. Then we played records. It was just like old times: he was so tender and so sweet. I shan't have to worry when he goes back now. Poor F, he does need someone to look after him.

Tuesday 7

F lay on the floor: it is more comfortable for him because of his calliper on his foot, but he seems quite content just to sit. Went to Lloyds bank. The manager, Mr Stewart, was very charming and explained to him all about his account. We had lunch at Reece's with Sheila. F bought a bottle of wine for 40 shillings! He did enjoy it, as did Sheila. He was telling us more about his night-club activities, which was most amusing. Sheila left us and we went to the *British*, where we sat and talked. F said how fond he was of Jacques, how he missed him, more than Henri, and he had complete confidence in him. He asked to see the photo yesterday. Said how the fact that someone loved him had helped him no end, and he also felt he had never been away. He thought his leg would have to be amputated. He really seemed to enjoy himself but we had to set off for Hoylake, to the Leas. The place looks marvellous and well-kept. There are hundreds of airmen but nobody looks as ill as F. I had to leave almost immediately. Poor Cis, he looked so fed-up and lonely. Oh! Cis, my poor little baby.

Barbara refers to the photo taken in York on 3 October 1944.

Wednesday 8

Cis rang up: arranged a meeting-place. Bought him a collar stud. Got to Hoylake station. We went to a rather dingy café but where everyone was very kind. Cis looked better and was very gay. Walked down to the shore, which was very pleasant. Then went to cinema where again everyone kind. Cis thoroughly enjoyed himself; he said it was like old times and he seemed so happy, poor sweet. We walked slowly up to the station. He is so grateful. He looks so old and shrunken.

Thursday 9

Cis rang up: he is having the day off tomorrow. Seemed very happy.

Friday 10

Got the train for Hoylake and met Cis who looked much better and seemed in good spirits. We walked slowly to the Green Lodge Hotel where we had lunch. Cis was thrilled. A waitress yelled to us that Japan had accepted unconditional surrender. Cis had a drink on the strength of it. Went and sat on the promenade in the sun. F said he would like to swim. He also said he wanted so much to see me, when he was in France, that now that he was back he couldn't bear to leave me. When his return home was indefinite, it was all right, but now that he knows it will be in about five months, he feels very bad about it. We sat in a field and he put his arms round me, saying that I could never measure his love. Talked of Henri and Jacques, and said he wanted to see Pat. Said also he will come to see us while we are away. I may not see him now until his last leave in England.

Saturday 11

Went on holiday with my family to Dolgelley. Met Uncle Billy and Aunt Marjorie. Wrote to F in the gloaming. Poor sweetheart!

Dolgelley: in North Wales.
Uncle Billy and Aunt Marjorie: friends of the family.

Sunday 12

Wrote to Cis. He rang up: he seemed happy and said he felt ok, but he didn't know anything about a '*perme*' yet. I do feel so miserable about him, poor little soul!

'*Perme*': informal French for 'permission' (leave of absence).

Tuesday 14

No news. Wrote to him.

Wednesday 15

VJ Day. Church bells rang for the total end of the war. All seems a bit incomprehensible: no-one knows what the peace terms are. F telephoned to say that he was coming today! Mummy and I went down into town for accommodation for him, which we found with a motherly old soul, Mrs Felton. Children had made a huge bonfire and there were more on the hills. When I got back, I found a letter from Hoylake. '*Even now I can't believe that you are gone – it was so much more usual for me to leave you! It seems that each time I take the train, it is to be with you again, and each time my heart misses a beat and tells me you're no longer here. Do I need to tell you that life seems empty without you? It's only three days since you left, but they seem like ages. Should I confess that I was a coward last Friday and didn't have the heart to go back to the Leas? I was afraid of the prospect of having to face my own thoughts, which, for a man, is the worst thing that can happen. And so, laden with this heavy burden, I went to the British, where there was a dance, and stayed till the end. I saw Mary Owen, who seemed surprised to see Francis without Barbara. But she didn't see that Francis himself was absent, too; I was miles away from the dancers whom I was listlessly staring at. I may have been with you, but I don't think so. Just like each time we are apart, my mind felt as if it were drowned in a sort of gloom and hopelessness, something like a fog hanging heavily over both my spirit and my heart. The few – so precious few – days we spent together went by oh so quickly, and I can understand the line by Lamartine and react exactly the way he does. Was it all a dream or did I really hold your hand and kiss your lips? I don't know, I don't know*

*anything at all, except that you're no longer here. [...] On Saturday
morning, I walked back to the bench where we were sitting on Friday
afternoon, and stared at the sea. I watched the water that one day will
separate us for ever.*' Luckily, Mr Pearson took good care of him; he
drove him to visit the old city of Chester which he liked very much. F
slept at his house. He was very sad when he got back to the Leas on
Sunday night.

At last, he's here now! His train arrived very late. He seems better and
walks with only one stick. Went to a farm where we had lovely tea, with
eggs and milk. How queer that the war has finished today and that Cis
should come the same day!

Francis refers to: 'Just one person is missing, and your world is a desert', a verse
from the poem *L'Isolement* in *Méditations poétiques*, by Alphonse de Lamartine
(1820).
Mr Pearson: director of the British Council.

Thursday 16
Went for Cis in Uncle Billy's car. He had had a good night and the old
lady had been very kind to him. Came back via the little bridge, which
Cis managed quite well. Played draughts.

Friday 17
Went to meet F who was struggling along the road. Saw many German
prisoners in *Feldgrau,* in the fields. Had to queue for lunch, which
worried me because of F. He was in good spirits but I was sad and
wept. Poor Cis, he said: '*We have such a short time.*' Also said he never
thought he would be on holiday with us again. He talked to various
children. Whilst the family was at the cinema, we sat outside and
watched it gradually getting darker and the lights coming on: it was
lovely. Poor Cis, he was so happy. Then we played draughts and Daddy
took F back in the car. He hopes to go to France on three weeks' leave.
He is so good!

Feldgrau: (field grey colour) field uniform of the German army.

Saturday 18

Went for Cis, then we went to the village where he bought a silver mug for Paul. Went for a walk and sat on a log. F seemed very happy. Had tea outside and discussed. He bought some sweet peas for Mrs Felton. He shouted '*ladrone*' to an Italian POW who grinned back. Went to cinema to see *It's a Wonderful Life* which amused F, which is the main thing. But in the middle, a man went berserk and started screaming. I was terrified in case it started a fight. It would have been so difficult to get F out, but he was marvellous: he was quite calm and collected. Half the audience left, the man was removed and it was all ok. Took him home. Lovely night. My dear little soul!

Ladrone: thief, in Italian.
It's a Wonderful Life: a film directed by Frank Capra (1946).

Sunday 19

Cis' last day. I am not upset as I used to be, as there is no danger now. Cis talked to more Italians. At tea, he ate nearly a plateful of bread and butter, which I was glad to see. Daddy took him home in the car.

Monday 20

Dreamt poor Jacques was still alive and had rung me up to look for Cis. Went to get him. We went into the Catholic church where I was chased out by the priest for having no hat! Cis quite cheerful. He put his arms round me and kissed me on the sofa, as he did eight months ago. Explained, about his injury, that perhaps he will be only a fortnight in bed. Was talking about flying; he may go as an instructor to South America. Took him to the station and saw him off on a through train. Thank goodness, he wasn't sad. So much better this time than last year. Oh! Cis.

Tuesday 21

Wrote to him.

Wednesday 22

Cis rang: he was at the *British* with Sheila. He had had a good journey. A lady, whom he had met on the train, took him back to the Leas in her car. Thinks he will be there till next week. Dear Cis!

Thursday 23

Letter from F, quite gay. Joan came to see him as a surprise, on Tuesday evening, and took him to the *British*. She even played the piano for him, in the interval of the dance. F says she applied for studying at Montpellier University. Wrote to Cis.

Montpellier: a large city in the south of France.

Friday 24

Met Mrs Felton who asked kindly after F. Said he was a perfect gentleman! He rang: was at the *British* with Sheila.

Saturday 25

Letter from F, full of love but rather melancholy. '*My darling, listen to my sad song this evening, for the rain is falling monotonously, both arousing and soothing my senses at the same time. The leaves of the trees along the path are rustling in the wind, and there's even a slight chill in the air. The evening is filled with a kind of mild, almost supernatural desolation. It is humid tonight, and the darkness seems so immense. I listen to the rain beating down on the roof and I feel happy to hear it singing down the gutters. [...] Darling, I think of you, of the two of us, and it makes me sad, I'm afraid. But even in the throes of grief man can still dream of some sort of joy. These poor little thoughts keep rolling through my mind like pebbles in the sea. I listen to their lengthy tales, all about the poor stars lost in the sky and separated by the endless exile of eternity. Lost in thought, I gaze at the raindrops and the unfathomable silvery darkness. I think of the beautiful flowers that all seem to say: 'I love you'. Love is forever. But all of a sudden a gust of wind blows, destroying all these frail flowers, these trembling things that evoked the love of the wind. Then they seem to be saying: why, o why crush my illusions? Where does infinite love exist? The infinite doesn't belong to anyone, not even to flowers; it lies in nothingness, it will be there again for these flowers next springtime, but nobody can claim it as their own. The night is trembling with a silent emotion, interrupted only by the song of the raindrops. I wish I could find words that might bear you away with me to a world of infinite sensations.*'

Went home.

Sunday 26

F came early bringing some silk stockings! He was very gay and did his acts. Played records and lay about in the sun. Went to Gran's where Uncle Max gave him a box of cigarettes. Had supper and took him to the tram early.

Everyone indignant about the stoppage of Lend-Lease food of the United States who claim, in exchange, military installations in British possessions. Most people think that it is because the Americans dislike a Labour government.

Lend-Lease food: enacted by Congress in 1941, the Lend-Lease Act empowered the President to sell, transfer, lend, or lease war supplies – such as equipment, food, and weapons – to America's allies during World War II. In exchange for the valuable assistance provided under the Lend-Lease Act, the Allies were to comply with the terms set by the President for repayment.

Monday 27

Letter from Rose. Went to library and got out *Flight to Arras* by Saint Exupéry. Went to Hoylake. Very hot. Met Cis and we had tea. Nice cakes: F ate all the chocolate ones! Said the men, at the Leas, drink and gamble so that they have no money to go out. We went and sat on the sand, which was very pleasant. F was rather sad: he said he had no aim and lived only to be unhappy. We went up to the station after looking at the sea. He wanted to come to Liverpool with me.

Flight to Arras (French title: *Pilote de guerre*): by Antoine de Saint Exupéry (first published in the USA in 1942).

Tuesday 28

Went to the *British*, then to Reece's for dinner. F was very happy. He keeps wishing he could dance. Sheila and I took him to the station. He was very proud of his new mac. Sheila said F had asked her if she thought he could make me happy.

Wednesday 29

Prune came. He manoeuvred his crutches quite well. He had had a good VJ Day, although saddened by the thought of his crew, as they were all killed. He has unfortunately fallen for a married WAAF! Francis turned up. He is leaving on Monday. Next time I see him, it'll be the last.

Friday 31

Went to meet F at Hoylake. He was very spick-and-span. We sat on the bench in the sun and watched the sea. How charming he is! We talked about French and Russian films. Small boy asked him for any badges. Went to cinema: *The Thin Man Goes Home*. They showed pictures of the atom bomb at which I didn't look. I don't want Cis to go away.

The Thin Man Goes Home: a film directed by Richard Thorpe (1945).

September

Saturday 1

Met Cis who looked very well turned out. Went to the *British* at AVF meeting: F was the only Frenchman on leave there. *Mme* Kléber very sweet. Met a friend of F's (from Nîmes) in the FAF, with his girl-friend. We all sat and talked. F drank beer which they serve at the canteen. Sheila came with us for dinner to the Adelphi. F came home quite easily, pretending to be merry.

Sunday 2

F fairly cheerful. Showed him a poem I wrote about him: he was very amused. Mrs Dick asked us round for coffee. Mr Dick was talking about Paraguay and Argentina where they lived. He was a representative of a British paint company in Buenos Aires. Had lunch at home and F helped wash up. Said a nerve in his leg was hurting. Went in the park and sat in the field where F nearly went to sleep. He is going back to Church Village tomorrow. Would not go to get a new suit: he has become superstitious about it now. Poor Cis, his life has been broken, I think. Says the English are wrong to hide their feelings. Went home and had tea. Then we lay out in the garden and played draughts: as usual, F won. He was very sweet and tender like before. He was sad also because of us parting soon. He said: '*I feel you really love me.*' I have a feeling that he won't come back any more. Poor F, my heart is full of pity for him. His wound never seems to annoy him. He doesn't realize what a care he is. I feel a bit like a grandmother, saying that! His eyes change colour: they go almost black when he's upset, and they are quite golden when he is happy. I am so sorry to see him go; he seems part of family life now. Queer how he adapted himself. We have had a lovely month. Made up the parcel for Pat.

Monday 3

Six years since the war broke out. Patsy got her School Certificate: quite a good one. Letter from Dédé who has passed first in all his exams. He is going into Air France. Phone rang: it was F who had missed the train! He said: '*What about having lunch with me?*' Met him outside the *British*. Sent off Pat's parcel and a telegram to Patsy. F was so gay, like a child with a new toy, and almost dancing with joy at having cheated the RAF. We walked slowly along to the second-hand bookshop. F bought a book of legends and *Servitude et grandeur militaires*, by Alfred de Vigny. Had good lunch at the Royal. F was so happy. I was glad he wasn't melancholy: the extra day helped! Walked up to Lime Street station. F sat on his case: looked like a small child, holding my hand. Queue, but I bribed a porter as the train was very full. Neither of us felt a bit sad, I don't know why. F very sweet: he is a darling. I love him, in spite of myself. Hope he got back ok. Oh! Cis, you who are part of my life! Heard *Liebesträume* tonight.

Liebesträume (Dreams of Love): by Frantz Liszt.

Servitude et grandeur militaires: by Alfred de Vigny (1835). While travelling in the train, Francis signed it for Barbara, adding a quote from *Histoire amoureuse des Gaules*, by Bussy-Rabutin (1665): "*Absence is to love what wind is to fire. It puts out the feeble, and kindles the great.*' Remember that! Francis. 3rd September 1945.'

Tuesday 4

Canteen: acted as interpreter for four or five pathetic Frenchmen trying to find their room at the hostel. Two very amusing *caporaux-chefs* from Elvington, who came from Madagascar, called me 'Barbara Sandwich'! Wrote to Cis and made him a parcel. Feel very lonely.

Caporaux-chefs: corporals.

Wednesday 5

F rang up. He has been to see Mrs Jones by trolley this afternoon. As she wasn't home yet, he had to wait at one of her neighbours' who showed him a postcard from Marseilles which her husband had just sent her. The doctor said one wouldn't know his leg for the same one! No sign of the operation yet. F seemed quite happy. I do miss him. Listened to Bach-Handel programme: *Brandenburg Concertos 3 and 5*. I liked the latter and *Let the Bright Seraphim*.

Thursday 6

Wrote to Rose and F. He rang up: he's going to see *King Lear* on Saturday; has not had the parcel yet. Letter from French Merchant Navy man, in the paper, saying how well the British troops behaved in Marseilles.

Friday 7

His letter of 4th. Says the end of his beautiful dream is coming and we've had more little quarrels in a month than in all the time we've known each other. It made me very unhappy. I cried. '*You must forgive me if I hurt you, because my temporary disability makes me rather bitter! [...] My love has simply become fiercer, more mistrustful and above all I am more sensitive. Shall I tell you how stupidly jealous I was when I saw those young men who could dare to imagine they could share their life with you, simply because they were born on the right side of that wide expanse of water that keeps us apart. [...] Whatever I do, I shan't be able to stop loving you for many, many years to come – I dare not say 'forever' because I don't know what will become of me after I die. But if by any chance sinners are allowed to love, well, I'd still love you eternally. [...] But since fate and you have decided otherwise, I'll disappear from your life and you can be sure you'll never hear from me again. You cannot die of love: you can only live through it. And don't say I shouldn't love you, because that hurts. [...] Always remember that I have given you the most precious love I could ever feel and that I'll never take it back.'* He thinks I want to get rid of him and it is me who wants to separate. It's not true! I never said that. Wrote to him.

Went to AVF. *Mme* Kleber kindly asked after him. She talked about marriage and is of the same opinion as me. Met Hélène, a Parisian student, here for a month: she is an ardent Communist, most slovenly and no make-up. Oh! Cis, I am so sad.

Saturday 8

Letter from Cis, much more cheerful. He went to a concert of accordions at the canteen after he called me on Wednesday. He read *Les Femmes savantes* by Molière again and recommended it to me: *'You should read it because I'm sure it'll make you furious.'* Says Mrs Jones is *'a real good Samaritan'*: she brought him pancakes which were still very warm! *Prune* rang: he is going on Monday. F wants to write to him. *Prune* wrote to his WAAF.

Sunday 9

Called for *Prune*, in very high spirits. Sat out in the garden and discussed life in general. He has a very balanced and common-sense outlook. He also listens so patiently to one's problems. Showed us a picture of his crew: nice boys too. Going to Loughborough.

Loughborough: in Leicestershire.

Monday 10

Two letters from Cis. He met Wendy and her horrible electric machine again. He has abandoned his crutches. He doesn't see himself going back to bed, but however he will have to have the operation. Says the poem I wrote about him is a treasure: *'A little bit of your heart from the time when I caused you so much worry, poor little femme adorée.'* I feel he's sad again. *'Now that you're already so far away from me, you are once again the smile on the photo I say hello to every morning. You are once again my faraway Princess, to whom I can only express my love on paper. 'Don't make an idol of me!' – but how can I help it when hardly a minute goes by without a pang in my heart telling me you're no longer here? [...] When you're only a distant silhouette on the platform, that's the time when I smile so as not to cry. Let me love you the way I want, as someone to whom I have given myself without a second thought. I want to love you more in the short time that's left than in the whole of my life.'*

He rang up. Pat has not written to him. Had fish for dinner: he was very envious.

Tuesday 11

Party at hospital. Saw Mahon who now has both legs: it was lovely to see him walk. Wonder what all those men will do and how they will find jobs. Wrote to Cis.

Wednesday 12

Got a letter. He must do the washing up every day at noon, but not for long as he should have the operation next week. He might stay in bed for two months at the very most. He thinks that there may be a chance of his being in Liverpool for Christmas: it would be wonderful! Wrote to him. Heard Elisabeth Schumann.

Elisabeth Schumann: a German opera singer.

Thursday 13

In French class, listened to Dr Knowles' records: rotten selection, except for *Madame la Marquise*! Heard an excellent play on radio, *Return to Life*, about the RAF burns unit at East Grinstead. I am so happy Cis was not burnt. Got a long letter. He has found a dodge not to have to wear his awful clothes. *'You must stop writing 'Sgt' on your envelopes or you'll end up giving the game away. As I told you, thanks to my little trick, I don't have to wear those horrible convalescent suits and red tie. Write whatever you like, as long as it's not a lie, but I think that S/O (sous-officier) would be best. If possible I'll have my battle-dress dyed navy blue while I'm bed-ridden. Mrs Jones told me she would take it herself to be dyed. Then you won't make fun of my uniform.'* August is already so distant, which makes him nostalgic; he dreads his departure which is coming, so do I. *'I know that you, too, are already upset when you realize that our wonderful story is about to end, but sometimes I'm sad when it dawns on me that you can perfectly well get on with your life without me, whereas I don't want to think of <u>Life</u> without you. [...] We have shared hours together that no-one else ever had and no-one can ever take them away from me. Even if the only thing that remains is memories, they will be treasured, because not many others can ever experience such moments. As for marriage, since you seem to be talking of it from your own point of view, I must confess that, although my only wish was to spend the rest of my life with you, that huge word never crossed my mind. [...] Until you can prove the opposite, I will still be unconvinced when you say that parting from you will mean that I'll be happy in future. No, I never thought that you wanted to get rid of me. I only thought that for you, love was a wonderful adventure that you could go along with, when you are young, to taste it, but afterwards you would turn your back on it and never give it another thought, so as to live a sensible, untroubled life. Because love is a source of trouble; and I also thought that, for you, what made love beautiful was that it couldn't last. [...] I love you more than ever; I wish I could write this in letters of fire. I love you, you are my darling, my heart and soul, my beloved. My most loving kisses fly to you.'*

East Grinstead: West Sussex town (at that time) where a specialist burns unit, at
    Queen Victoria Hospital, became world famous for pioneering treatment of
    RAF and Allied aircrew who were badly burned and required reconstructive
    plastic surgery.
Sgt: sergent (sergeant). *Sous-officier:* non-commissioned officer. The sky-blue suit,
    with a white shirt and a red tie, was compulsory for the wounded, except for
    the officers.

Friday 14
Letter from F. He wrote to me from his bed on Wednesday. He was not
able to telephone that day as they had moved him into Ward 1 to get

him prepared for the operation. It must be today. He seems pleased that he's having the operation at long last, he was fed up with waiting. They are four in his room; he should stay there for two or three weeks. He heard from Pat who was thrilled with the present. '*Little Paul is all right and is growing almost by the day. Right now Pat's in St Helens with her mother.*' Sent him a telegram to wish him good luck.

Saturday 15

Battle of Britain anniversary. His letter of 13th: the operation was postponed for a day; he was ordered to stay in bed. So it is today, poor sweetheart. I am sad for him. I don't want him to be upset because of me. '*I love you my darling* petite femme, *and you'll never know how precious you are to me. If my love means suffering, well then, I'm willing to suffer, and you can be as reasonable as you want, but I know that your feelings are the same as mine. My love may be ill-fated, but as I've already said, nothing can deprive me of the wonderful moments it has given me. Whatever the future may have in store, I may have to remain silent, but not to forget. If I'd never loved you, I could never have forgotten your… well, let's call it your patriotism, since that's how you called it yourself. We are probably two opposites, but love doesn't care about such things. As two years haven't been enough to forget you, why would two centuries make a difference?*'

Sunday 16

Hope everything went well. Wrote to him. A year since Pat and Henri were married: how shocking it all seems!

Monday 17

His letter of 14th. He was delighted with my telegram. Says I must not worry if I don't hear from him for a few days. He finds me too sensible and thinks I'm afraid of suffering as Mummy did; but it has nothing to do with that! '*My explanations may be more complicated than need be. God forgive me if you've suffered because of that, but you are a girl with a heart as pure as a diamond – I'm quite serious – a heart that's full of splendid aspirations, and I can't bear to see someone like you try to smother all those beautiful, heaven-sent feelings because she has at the back of her mind the thought of a mother who had an unhappy love affair.'*

Wednesday 19

Wonder how poor Cis is. Wrote to him and sent him a parcel.

Friday 21

His letter of Wednesday: a pathetic little scrawl. He is not a bit well, he is in great pain. '*My darling, just a brief note to reassure you and prove I'm not dead. I'm sorry but I was unable to write until today. The operation wasn't very serious but very painful. Even now I'm just a bundle of nerves and restless – I can't remain in one place for more than two minutes. Again I am in plaster up to my waist and my right leg is bent and hangs out from the bed. At last my nerve is mended and now my foot is no longer numb but alive with feeling – but between you and me, this is something I could do without. I'll try to write a longer letter tomorrow but it's difficult: I can't concentrate, and can only hope the state I'm in is temporary. At any rate, tonight I only wanted to say 'I love you'. This is the only message I can send tonight. Do please forgive me. I kiss you, darling, and wish you were here by my side. I love you. Francis.*' Poor sweetheart! He enclosed an excellent photo of him in the room, taken the day before the operation. He sent the same one to his mummy.

Letter from *Prune*: he is keeping it up with the WAAF. Saw a wonderful film about the RAF and the USAAF: *The Way to the Stars*, so natural and real.

The Way to the Stars: a film directed by Anthony Asquith (1945). Motto of the RAF: '*Per ardua ad astra*' (Through adversity to the stars).

Saturday 22

His letter of 20th. He woke up in great pain on Sunday morning, poor Cis! '*My thigh was very painful and I could feel a shooting pain in my leg every minute or so, but I immediately felt something was different in my foot, and already I had some feeling. It's true that it hurts, but it's a normal sort of pain. Mrs Jones came to see me in the afternoon and brought me pancakes, but I didn't feel like eating anything. [...] Don't worry, I'm well looked after, with a special diet and chicken every day; in three weeks' time they'll change the plaster and I think that I'll be up and about in two months.'* On Wednesday, Mrs Jones brought him some records. They brought an Italian man to him, who does not speak either English or French: he is 34 and was made prisoner in Ethiopia. F says he looks jolly; he showed him the photo of his baby and can't wait to go back home: *'The father of such a baby can't be a nasty chap!'* He asks me to find him a book in Italian at the second-hand bookseller's; he will send me money. Wrote to him.

Monday 24

Got a very nice letter. He is much better. He was pleased with my parcel. *'I have received your long letter and could reply with arguments that would be just as long, but there's no point because they are the same, with different words. You see, I realize that civilizing you is a totally hopeless task (laughter). No, tonight I want to write you a pleasant, light-hearted little letter, in which my only topic will be 'love'. I can already picture you wearing that resigned look on your face, and I can also see that pretty little moue. Nevertheless I won't let myself be put off by this obstacle and I will go forward like any self-respecting knight in shining armour. Onward with my pen, onward with my ink, brave is my spirit, let sweet words fill this tender message of love, and dazzle you. Come forward you Muses and succour a poor lover trying to obtain a loving glance from his beloved. [...] Help me to tell her that there still exist some hearts that can love the same person forever. [...] Oh! If only I could see in your eyes that faint, sweet light that told me how you loved me, if only I could feel your loving arms around my neck, feel your lips kissing me, and hear your heart beating next to mine. [...] How I do wish you were here now to comfort me as only you can do. [...] At any rate don't be too cruel about my dreams, for dreaming is the privilege of the innocent.'*

Wednesday 26

Letter from F. *'I now have the sensation that my leg actually extends right down to my foot; it no longer feels as if there was nothing there, if you see what I mean. But it'll be twelve weeks at least until the foot actually reacts the way it used to.*' Hilda brought him tomatoes and an anthology of English poetry.

Thursday 27

Letter from F saying he is thinner than ever! '*Do you know what's actually made my waist slimmer? It's the plaster that encases it, so next time you see me I'll have a wasp waist.*'

Dédé is to enter Air France on 1st October.

Went round the shops for Italian books. I found two which I put into a parcel with apples and grapes for F. Mr and Mrs Dick came to say goodbye: they are moving to Surrey next Monday; their eldest son lives there with his family. I am so sorry: they are such good friends to me.

Friday 28

Two letters from F, one very funny. At last he received his own things from Elvington. '*Today I received the two flying logbooks and the money I'd left at Elvington on January 2nd, together with a note saying my personal notes would be sent as well – and not before its time. […] I hope nothing will be missing, especially dear old* Henry IV.'

Went to Parkgate in the car. Had tea there: scones with cream and jam. Passed West Kirby and Hoylake: shall always think of F in that connexion, dear little Cis! Wrote to him.

Parkgate: a small seaside village, in Cheshire.

Sunday 30

The Express train Perth–London had a terrible accident yesterday: forty-four people killed and eighty-eight wounded. Wrote to him.

October

Monday 1

Two letters from F. The one of 28th is rather sad: says he didn't dare ask me to marry him for fear of a refusal, and preferred to cling to his pathetic happiness. Poor little soul! 'Do you know what I'm thinking about? I'm thinking about the two of us in the past two years. I've come to think we are like two magnets that some evil people are trying to drag apart. My impression is that our love has only been a long series of successive struggles against each other, against ourselves and against everyone and everything. And do you know why? Because neither of us had enough confidence in ourselves. Moreover I'm sure there are lots of things that you didn't tell me and I didn't tell you, in order to protect each other. […] If I'd had enough confidence in myself right from the moment I knew that I loved you, I should have asked at once: 'Will you be my wife?' Since the answer would have been 'no', I would have had to disappear from your life. But all I did was to try pitifully to hold on to you, thinking that I could at least be happy for some time if I kept silent – well I was only being a coward. Why did it only dawn on me tonight? I've no idea, or maybe there are times when one is ready to be brave and face reality. […] I know that the day isn't far off when I'll find myself awakening from a long dream, and then all that I can do will be to read old letters or look at photos, but I want to be happy – happy, do you understand? How ironical! I want to enjoy every minute of my dream before I wake up, that's what the world owes me at the very least. Why, after all, I've the right to it like everybody else, and I will be happy. […] I love you so much, you know, oh yes, I do! I love you more than I can say; forgive me if I've hurt you tonight – maybe I ought not to have written.'

Fortunately, his letter of 29th is much less serious. He had just received my parcel and ate the grapes straightaway. 'As we say in France, 'One would think it was the good God himself in velvet trousers going down my throat!'' Alfredo was very pleased with the books and told him to thank me. F doesn't seem to get bored too much. Hilda visited him again. 'I was asleep when Hilda arrived, and can you guess how she woke me up? She tickled my toes. Of course my first reaction was to start yelling and I threw a pillow at her face. This was about to turn into a straight fight, but then she cried out: 'Watch out, Francis, I've got tomatoes!' That made me stop. We chatted for a moment, and, as you might expect, I finally started to tease her. As she knew about my weak point, she started tickling me again so I threw my blanket at her, or rather part of my blanket in her face; she wriggled and squirmed, but

*she was trapped and I only let her go after she'd said 'Sorry!'. Hurrah
for a French victory over Wales!'*

Tuesday 2

Back to university. Met an American sergeant who wanted the lecture-
theatre. He is on a ten-weeks engineering course until he gets back
home, with other Americans. His name is Jo Bouquard, of French, Irish,
German descent. He is married and lives in Cleveland, Ohio. Has been
to Coblenz, Roma where he saw the Pope, and Marseilles too. Wanted
me to take him on a conducted tour of Liverpool: Sheila nearly died
of shock! Went up to the hospital to see Sister Hogan and went round
the Nurses' Home. Letter from F. Says the last three weeks went by
quickly and they will change his plaster in six days. *'The other plaster
will be much less cumbersome and at least I shall almost look like a
human being – what with the leg that I have to keep bent, right now
I almost look like a frog that had fallen on its back!'* He asks me to
find a present for Hilda. *'This will be the only way I can show how
grateful I am. I admit it takes some courage to confront an old bear like
me. I'm sure there are plenty of girls who'd sooner spend their spare-
time doing something more interesting and above all something more
entertaining.'*

Wednesday 3

Went to see Miss Picton and found Hanna Schuma, now called Mrs
Connel: both charming. Two letters from F. *'I'm still lying on my bed of
suffering!!! Waiting for that blessed day when my legs can move again
in the way that, once upon a time, provided the delights of the* Folies
Bergères!' He wrote me a poem.

> *'I think of you when I awake
> And, from afar, I follow you with my eyes.
> I see you again when I fall asleep,
> In a mysterious dream.
> The only happiness my heart hopes for
> Is to have the sweetest confession of love
> From you.*

> *That's what I want to tell you.*
> *But alas! I am so afraid of you.*
> *When I watch your face,*
> *When I hope, at last, to see you,*
> *I tell myself in gentle tones*
> *To-night, I do so want her to be moved,*
> *I want, I want, with burning desire,*
> *To fall on my knees and tell her that I love her.*
> *It's this, it's this, that I want to tell you.*
> *But alas! I am so afraid of you.*

But I won't say anything, for I would again expose myself to a volley of sarcastic comments, illustrated with more or less genuine quotations by the author of Hamlet *and some other eccentrics. By the way, don't start imagining that this light-hearted banter is my own inspiration, for I'm quite capable of having that kind of thought, but not of turning it into verse.'*

What shall I do when he doesn't write anymore?

Miss Picton: German lecturer.

Folies Bergères: a famous cabaret music hall and symbol of French and Parisian life, where the careers of many French stars – such as Maurice Chevalier, Mistinguett and Josephine Baker – were launched. Dancing-girls generally wore revealing costumes that left little to the imagination.

Poem inspired by *La Romance de Maître Pathelin*, sung by Tino Rossi.

Thursday 4
Walked to Pier Head: saw heaps of French airmen.

Friday 5
Bought some ribbed wool stockings. Letter from F. '*Come off it*, Bébé, *and don't tell me life is purely a matter of chance; on the contrary I find it marvellously ordered, but the thing is, we cannot know what it has in store for us until we have lived it through. And at least those who died in that accident did not do so while trying to kill other people the way we were doing some months ago. We mustn't be afraid of death,*

*for death awaits every man from birth. To die only means to move
from one state to another, and, well, I may be cynical but all that's
new is beautiful after all. Lastly, do calm down, darling, you're much
too sensitive and I love you all the more for it. Good night, darling, I
fervently kiss those beautiful eyes I'm so fond of. I love you. Francis.'*
He has finished a swan for Mrs Dick and asked me for her address.
Wrote to him.

Francis refers to the accident of the train Perth–London.

Saturday 6

Two letters from Cis. He is going to have the plaster and stitches off
today. Says English are horrid to Alfredo and it is unfair as he can't speak
English and can't defend himself. How spiteful! Went to Ormskirk by
train with Sheila. We looked at the market and the church which has
both tower and steeple. Plenty of Polish soldiers and Italian prisoners.
Then went on to Southport.

Ormskirk and seaside Southport: two Lancashire towns north of Liverpool.

Sunday 7

Wrote to Dédé and Cis.

Monday 8

Letter from F. He was very disappointed on Saturday because his plaster
wasn't changed as expected. '*The hospital walls almost came tumbling
down when the Sister informed me this morning and I started bawling,
but I know I won't be anaesthetized so I'm happy.*' He is going to have it
off today. Says he had to perform acrobatics to have an X-ray and Mrs
Jackson, the doctor, drew a frog on his plaster. At the Leas, everybody
called him 'Admiral', because of his peaked-cap! Pat wrote to him: she
now knows for certain that she will never see Henri again. Poor boy! '*I
had a letter from Pat Martin; she's still in St Helens, and she heard news
about Henry, so to speak. He's buried in the cemetery in Dortmund.
Poor Pat, her very last hope has now definitely gone, but it's just as well.
She's so brave in spite of everything, and talks so much about her child.*

He is the one and only topic in her letters. I think her having this child is a great blessing, for she was quite shattered at the beginning. Henry – he was almost like a brother to me, and now he's only a memory, a heart-breaking memory at that.'

Wrote to him.

At university, we were constantly interrupted by lost Americans: they were all over the place! Three Yanks at our Social Science and Psychology lecture, one very objectionable. Met Jo again, who was looking for me. He's 28 and has no children. Asked him home on Sunday. Saw the *Monowai* bringing back prisoners of the Japanese: they got a marvellous welcome.

HMNZS *Monowai:* an armed merchant cruiser of the Royal New Zealand Navy, transferred to Great Britain in 1943 for conversion into an infantry landing ship; she operated as troopship HMS *Monowai* and was used during the landings in Normandy.

Tuesday 9

Letter from *Prune*: all over with the WAAF. Letter from F. Saw *La Kermesse héroïque*, with Françoise Rosay, Louis Jouvet and Jean Marais. I saw it too. Soon a year since F on leave. How much of a man he has proved to be. I must be grateful for being loved by him. At the *British* met Madeleine, a student from Paris, very serious, clever, industrious and shy.

La Kermesse héroïque (Carnival in Flanders): a film directed by Jacques Feder (1935).

Wednesday 10

Got a letter. He had his plaster changed on Monday at last. He's back in Ward 4. Is going to be in bed longer than he thought, I fear. '*I have the same plaster cast as before, but my knee is free, and under the knee there is a screw. They loosen it one turn every day until my leg is straight. But I'm afraid, after what Mrs Jackson said to me, it won't be three, but six more weeks I'll have to spend in bed. [...] My nerve was re-connected with a gold clip.'*

Wrote to him.

At university met two rather unpleasant Americans from Georgia, and a nice Canadian, called Harold Pinner, from Windsor, Ontario. Dock strike serious because of food situation.

Thursday 11

Sweet letter from F. Says Ward 4 is the best one in the hospital because there are only three or four wounded in bed. '*At any rate, the food is better; we can have tea or coffee with all meals, beer every other day, and what we enjoy the most is that those who can stand up are allowed to go out every day, while those who are in the other wards can only go out on Wednesdays, Saturdays and Sundays. I think we owe all these privileges to Mrs Jackson, the lady who operated on me and is in charge of this ward.*' Once again, it's he who is in bed and should complain, and it's he who cheers me up. '*You've been so wonderful ever since I've known you; you mustn't give up now. No, don't let things get you down! On the contrary, this is just the beginning for you, and don't worry, darling, for the moment I'm still here with you, and I'll do everything I can to help you. Goodbye for now! See you at 9 pm first and then again tomorrow! With a big kiss which, I hope, will calm you a little, and another one as proof of my love.*'

Posted him a parcel with cigarettes and a book for Alfredo. Saw another mercy ship with repatriated prisoners.

Saturday 13

Short letter from F. Mrs Jones looks after him very well: she brings him pancakes and tomatoes regularly; he even asked her to buy two shirts for him in Cardiff. '*I'll only be happy when I have one for each day of the week. Then you won't look at my collar in disgust anymore!*' The Singletons sent him a parcel with pears, apples, cigarettes, and also two chocolate bars from little Margaret, which he was delighted with. He's longing to see Pat again and meet little Paul. '*Yes, I hope Pat will still be in St Helens when I come to Liverpool, but, even if she's in London, I'll have to go there, as I'm dying to see my lively little nephew, because, don't forget, he' s a bit of a Marseillais too.*'

Sunday 14

Jo arrived on time. Everyone was very taken with him. Said he didn't like Marseilles as it was too dusty. He worked in the Tennessee Valley Authority. His wife is called Barbara. He had met her in Chattanooga where she lives. She is a Protestant, he is a Catholic. He talked about the American constitution and said he had voted against Roosevelt. He pronounces words so funnily. Stayed till 11 pm! Wrote to F.

Monday 15

Laval executed at 9 this morning: *sic semper tyrannis*!

Letter from F. He will keep the book for himself as Alfredo has already left. It's a pity because they got on well. He began another swan for the night-duty nurse, like the one he sent to Mrs Dick. At the *British*, met *le Vicomte* who is going back to France on Saturday. Said he had lost most of his friends. He looks much older and very worn. He was most warm in asking after F and wanting him to go to see him, if he was ever in Bordeaux. Such a nice man. I nearly cried when we left him, as he seemed another link snapped with F, which made me realize how soon he will be going too. Sheila most upset too. Dear Cis, you are so precious to me.

Pierre Laval: head of Nazi collaborationist government of Vichy France (April 1942 – August 1944).
Sic semper tyrannis: Thus always to tyrants!

Tuesday 16

More butter and sugar in rations. A year since F came on leave. Wrote to him.

Wednesday 17

Letter from F. Hilda came to see him on Sunday. He gave her the money order for his pay to send directly to the bank and the swan for Mrs Dick. He sounds in good spirits. '*I'm still the brilliant boy who, a year ago, still flitted around Yorkshire dances with a casualness that was matched only by his charm. Unfortunately, spiteful imps now prevent the world from enjoying his outstanding qualities.*'

He doesn't want to wear a forage cap; it would suit him though. 'No, *even to please you, I won't buy a forage cap! You can say I am contrary if you like, but you know that when I persist it is hard to make me change my mind. Anyway, I've spent five years in the Air Force and I've never worn one, so I won't start now, just when I'm going to be demobilized. Over!*' He seems to imply that I am rather a '*malade imaginaire*' and mentally lazy! '*There's no such thing as a mind inclined to melancholy. Why not admit you enjoy giving in to melancholy? It would be more appropriate. And you don't want to accept any responsibility, but then, where are all your ideas of independence? [...] Part of you doesn't want to bestir itself. Try to remedy that, and we'll talk about it another day.*' I am furious. All that because I told him I was tired, I often have migraines and I'm in low spirits at the moment. Wrote to him.

Malade imaginaire: hypochondriac.

Thursday 18

Got a letter from Dédé who is enjoying Air France, another one from Mrs Dick for F and one from him too. Says his leg is getting straighter little by little. '*My leg is slowly progressing towards the horizontal position and, when it does reach it, my 'yippee' will ring out throughout the hospital.*' He made his auto-portrait, slightly exaggerated, but just like him. '*As for my weaknesses, you forgot that I drink like a fish, smoke like a chimney, swear like a trooper, am the most unscrupulous and inveterate womanizer who ever existed, and last, that I think a lot of myself. Apart from these few piffling details, I admit I am a good boy. But if all the good boys like me were to be overwhelmed with parcels, England would be starving in less than a week.*' Sheila came and brought us some frozen cod which Peter gave her with his sweet ration: it was most welcome. Mr Steilman, from North Carolina, very boisterous in Social Science lecture: he complained to Jo that the English are unsociable! Sheila, Peter, Jo and I had a meal at Lyons. Jo worked his way through college at a 'supermarket': had never heard that word before. We went to the Playhouse to see the *Tragedy of Good Intentions* by Peter Ustinov: we all enjoyed

it. Jo came home and we talked about '*Yankeeland*', as Nelly would
say! Took him to the tram.

Lyons: a restaurant round the corner from the British Council.

Friday 19

His letter of 17th. '*Yes, a year ago, it was my last but one leave, and I didn't
think I'd be in bed a year later. I only imagined the worst or nothing.*' He
was surprised that I met *le Vicomte* again and said he always thought he
looked ill. Alfredo went back to his camp. He promised to write to him
when he gets home. F got a letter from Marie-Jeanne: she saw Anna,
Feriolo's wife, who told her they are separated. Cis can't get over it. I
shouldn't think it's Maurice's fault. Heard *Tristesse*.

Saturday 20

Woman in newsagents' asked after F. He told me something funny in
his letter of 18th. '*At lunchtime, for dessert, I was brought a nice plate of
peaches. But those peaches were swimming in a kind of yellowish sauce
which I didn't like the look of. Oh well, I thought, that's the famous
English custard once again. But no sooner had I tasted a mouthful
than I pushed my plate away, as if I had seen a snake in it. At the same
time, various loud screams – and some crude words – could be heard
throughout the ward, proving that the others were having the same
painful experience as I was. To tell the truth, the poor Waaf had made a
mistake and put mayonnaise on the peaches, and believe me, the mixture
was most unpleasant.*' He hasn't had his hair cut yet. '*I'd rather die than
entrust my gorgeous mane to the butcher who, in this very place, dares
to call himself a hairdresser.*' Pat is still in St Helens; she sent him some
magazines.

Met Jo, who was late, and his friend Dave Aaron Davidson, of Scots
descent, also married and with a quiet manner. He looks like Bing
Crosby. Went to an art exhibition in an 18th-century building, and
then commented on the architectural style. Then we took the Mersey
Railway to Birkenhead, and then to Parkgate. The boys seemed to
like it: bought postcards. Had tea in the Boat House, arguing about
Palestine, Roosevelt, Truman whom they like, and the Duke of Windsor!

Came back on the ferry, seeing RMS *Mauretania* with two huge funnels painted red: lovely.

Came home and had eggs. Daddy and the boys argued about socialism and schools, especially the American military academies.

Mersey Railway: underground.
Birkenhead: a town on the estuary of the Mersey.
Boat House: famous café and teashop in Parkgate.
RMS *Mauretania*: a transatlantic liner.

Sunday 21

Trafalgar Day. Jo came after lunch, talking about his very clever sister. He wants to find me a single American! Says English girls have nice complexions. This time last year I was arranging apples in the shelter with Cis.

Monday 22

Three letters from F. The one of Friday: critical of my 'hypochondria' again! *'There, there! My darling, I think you got the bit between your teeth in your letter. Everything would lead me to believe that it's you who have Latin blood in your veins. But this matter must be cleared up. You lost some of your temper, and you misunderstood me. I don't mean to say you enjoy gloomy thoughts, I only ask you not to indulge in them. If you can't dispel them, you can at least prevent them from upsetting you. As for the health question, I see you were annoyed, and I'm glad. Desperate situations call for drastic remedies! But once again, I mean that the more one focuses on pain, physical or moral, the worse it becomes. [...] You do need affection and understanding, which I have given you with all my heart, without even thinking. You say that I haven't, because I have scolded you a bit. Did you never get rapped over the knuckles by your* maman *when you were young? I love you as you are, as long as you don't do any harm to yourself, and I start from the principle that heart and spirit have a great influence on one's physical condition. It's not your fault if you feel miserable sometimes, but it's your fault if you focus on it too much. I'm sorry I made you cry again. I love you so much and I'm so worried about you. Up till now, you have*

*lived a sheltered life. I do so wish I could be sure that you will live
in peace and be happy when I am no longer here. […] I do so wish I
could be near you to tell you how you do have all the affection which
you talked about before. I'm yours, darling, with all my heart. Your
hands, Princess! I love you.'*

The last French airmen have left Elvington; the station has closed
down. I feel rather sad.

346 'Guyenne' Squadron left RAF Elvington on 20 October 1945, followed on
the 29th by 347 'Tunisie' Squadron. They returned to France to form the '2*l*e
Escadre' at Mérignac, near Bordeaux.

Tuesday 23
Polish liner *Sobieski* in. Wrote to Mrs Bouquard and F.

Wednesday 24
His letter of Sunday. It had been pouring for two days. '*You know,
when I'm in bed, the rain has a funny effect on me. I've already tried
to explain it to you, but I didn't succeed. I can only muse and dream,
and I could stay motionless for hours. What's even funnier is that I
like to go out for a walk when it's raining. People look so amusing;
they all look like ostriches, hiding their heads under their wings so
as not to be seen. I don't know why, but I'm thinking of our journey
to St Helens in the fog. The rain also reminds me of so many other
memories. I suddenly feel like nestling by your side, making myself as
inconspicuous as possible, and dozing off unnoticed.*' Sent him some
violets.

Thursday 25
Letter from F. Hilda brought him new shirts. '*Hilda came yesterday
afternoon and brought me the famous shirts and I'm jubilant, for
they have detachable collars, and that way, instead of washing the
whole shirt, I'll just have to wash the collar! I'm all the more happy
since my other shirts are dirty, and I wondered what I would put on
when getting up.*' Heard the wounded in his ward are going back to
Wroughton.

Friday 26

On Wednesday, he was visited by Laurette, a lady from the *Midi* who lives in Cardiff: she brought him grapes, oranges, figs and cigarettes. He was so happy to be able to talk about the *Midi* with her as much as he liked. The faithful Mrs Jones went to see him too, '*as dynamic as ever, accompanied by the inevitable tomatoes. She reminded me, for a while, of your* maman *or mine, because, when I was foolish enough to mention my shirts were dirty, she grabbed my bag and, to my shame, began to go through them. And what happened? She took them all away to wash them.*' He can't wait to be able to go out at night and have a bit of fun. '*It's pitch dark, and I do wish I could go out. My old night owl instincts are coming back. Good night, darling! I love you and kiss you madly, even if you have some lipstick on or fear* maman *can see us!*'

Saturday 27

His letter of Thursday. He was so pleased with the violets. '*First, I want to kiss you a thousand times for your flowers. How kind you are, my darling, and you know how to please me so well! You really are my Princess, you know, while I can only make you cry. It's wonderful; the violets haven't even been spoilt by the journey, and on my table I now have a bunch which makes the entire ward jealous! [...] You do things which really touch the most distant corners of my heart. I love you, Mrs Noah; I love you so much that I have come to the conclusion that love has no limit. I feel like dancing a cannibal dance, and then jumping up and kissing you madly all over, ruffling your hair, pulling your nose. Stop!*' The departure to Wroughton seems to be next week.

Went to Broxton for the week-end.

Broxton: in Cheshire.

Monday 29

His letter of 27th, very amusing. '*I suppose that at this very moment you must be singing bacchanalia with the customers at the hotel, whilst I'm tossing and turning on my bed of agony, tormenting myself as I keep thinking of you – and having no other beverage but that awful tea to gulp down. Frankly, I can imagine Mrs Noah only too well, dishevelled,*

a glass in her hand, beating the rhythm out of a song which the chaps,
being a bit merry, are singing their heads off to!' Since Saturday he has
been back in Ward 6, the first one where he came to, seven months ago
already. He's going to have his screw changed, and in two weeks' time
he'll have the plaster off. He thinks he will leave Church Village on 1st
November. Wrote to him.

Saw Jo and Dave who had enjoyed Edinburgh. They introduced us,
Sheila and I, to a US lieutenant whom they called 'Jack'! I was very
shocked by this: no English sergeant, nor a French one, would have
done that.

Tuesday 30

His letter of Sunday: sad at leaving the Joneses. Hilda, Edith and her
fiancé came to say goodbye in the afternoon. Edith's fiancé even gave
him a bottle of sherry. Hilda brought him his clean handkerchiefs back;
she will send the rest of his clothes by post, with tomatoes of course! *'To*
be honest, I felt a bit upset, for she has been so kind to me, and I teased
her so much. However I promised to send her postcards, in black and
white, and in colour as well! And when she left, I must confess, Mrs
Noah, that I kissed her hand at the moment of farewell. And that was
it – the last I saw of them was a hand waving a handkerchief out of the
car window. I'll probably never see them again, but, one thing is certain,
I will never forget them.' He felt so lonely that night, poor Cis. I do so
wish I had been with him. *'I really feel a bit sad and do wish you were*
here. You know so well how to soothe my sorrow, even the slightest
pain. I really need your arms round me tonight, I feel so lonely without
them. But I'm silly, really! Good night, darling! Oh God, I would give
anything just to be able to kiss my petite femme! *I love you and send*
you the sweetest kisses from my heavy heart.'

Wednesday 31

He was in better spirits the day after: he had had the screw changed,
and the sherry may have helped too! *'We had a feast last night, with*
the cost shared by the four of us – the only ones left in Ward 4. Well, we
had some tomatoes (essential!), ham, some lettuce, raw cabbage salad,
stuffed chicken (from Scotland), and fruit salad. Aperitif: a small glass of

sherry. Our drink for dinner: a big glass of sherry. Black coffee. Digestif: another small glass of sherry. Unfortunately, no cigars! It wasn't too bad, and that was my revenge on the pub!'

Bought his father some tobacco. Sheila and I had tea with Jo at university. Talked about education. Gave me some tobacco for Daddy and some chocolate for me.

Digestif: after-dinner liqueur.

November

Thursday 1
His letter of 30th. His departure has been delayed for a week; he'll have to say his farewells to the Joneses a second time. '*I don't know why, but I'm getting a bit bored at the moment; the days seem to go by more slowly, probably because I am beginning to see the day when I'll get up. You know, my leg is nearly straight, and next week, I think the end will be very much in sight. I'm a bit worried about my belongings, as apparently the squadron has left York. What I'm worrying about is my beloved* Henry IV *and whether those idiots have lost it.*' He sent me *La Révolte des anges*, with a cutting about women in the *Midi* who have meals in the kitchen with the children! Posted *M.* Uzay's tobacco. Peter, Sheila, Jo and I went to *Purple Dust*, by Sean O'Casey, at the theatre. Talked about the power of the King. Had supper at home. Jo washed up quite happily. Talked about religion and death. Poor F, I do wish he was here.

La Révolte des anges: a novel by Anatole France (1914).

Friday 2
Letter from F, with a photo of Jeanne, Jo and his sister whom he finds very pretty. Mrs Jones came to say her farewells to him on Wednesday, thinking he was leaving the day after. F says she has been a second mother for him: '*She washed my socks, which I do consider an act of heroism!*'

Prune came, looking very smart. He has arm-crutches. Went up to the hospital with him. He can walk faster than F. All pleased to see *Prune*. Said he had met Clark Gable and he was pleasant. *Prune* always seems to me a link with F. Daddy brought home two books for us to see: all about Hitler, beautifully produced; they had belonged to an SS storm trooper.

In 1943, Captain Clark Gable was assigned to a USAAF bomber squadron in Northamptonshire, to take part in the shooting of a combat film to promote the recruitment of air gunners. He actually flew five operational missions as an air gunner-observer on board B-17 Flying Fortresses, for which he was awarded the Air Medal and the Distinguished Flying Cross.

Saturday 3

His letter of 1st November. '*Tomorrow is All Souls' Day, and we should spare a pious thought for Jacques and Henry, my poor dear great friends, and for all who have departed. Anyway, I don't want to start reminiscing, it rather frightens me. God keep them both!*' In two weeks' time, he'll be out of plaster '*like a jewel out of its case*'. Wants a chess set: the Englishman in bed next to him offered to teach him to play to kill time. Has sent Sheila a little dog he has made. Dock strike ended.

Sunday 4

A year today since Henri was killed. Hope poor Pat and F aren't feeling too bad. Wrote to F and Rose. Jo came for lunch. Says his wife spends too much money: I anticipate trouble there! Talked about world politics. Jo has no international outlook. Thinks the Frenchwomen have indecently short skirts!

Monday 5

His letter of Saturday. '*Ten months ago, I spent my first night in hospital, and at that time I was out of the world. Yet I'd never have thought that, ten months later, I would still be in bed. At first I thought that I would lose my leg, and then that it was only a fracture and I'd be up after three or four months.*' Hilda brought him his clean shirts back when she finished work at the bank. He gave her something to post for me.

To kill time, he plays Battleships with the boy next to him. '*Good night, darling. May your sleep be full of beautiful dreams! As for me, I'm going to sleep, thinking that tomorrow there is an egg for breakfast!*'

Saw *Felix Roussel*, a graceful ship. Maurice wasn't on board this time.

Tuesday 6

Letter from F who sent me a lovely orange and green dog: it is a real masterpiece. On Sunday afternoon Hilda came back to keep him company. He said his farewells to her once again, wondering if it was really the last time. He wrote to me just after having listened to Tommy Handley whom he's very fond of. '*As for me, I still adore you like the far-away Princess of my dreams. I only dream about one thing, kissing your huge eyes. I only think about the very moment when I will meet you again. I only want to hold you very tightly in my arms to prove to myself that you are real. I love you in a word, ILY in another.*'

Saw *Johnny Frenchman*, shot in Cornwall. Françoise Rosay, excellent.

Tommy Handley: star of *ITMA* (*It's That Man Again*), a very popular BBC radio comedy programme which ran from 1939 to 1945.
Johnny Frenchman: a film directed by Charles Frend (1945).

Wednesday 7

His letter of 5th. He packed his bits and pieces and will go away by ambulance. I think his departure is today. At university met Mr Passo, an American soldier from Mexico: he looks like an Indian, speaks Spanish, German, and excellent French; gave us a Jitterbug demonstration. Sheila and I went to *Henry V*: I loved it. Laurence Olivier looked very fine in armour; Renée Asherson, delightful as Katherine; Esmond Knight, also good.

Henry V: a film adaptation of Shakespeare's play, directed by Laurence Olivier (1945).

Thursday 8

No letter: so F must definitely have moved.

Saw a Pole with a plastic surgery face. The other day, Sheila and I were buying records when we saw two Polish soldiers next to us: one was helping the other who was blind and with no right hand. It was so sad and I was very impressed. This Pole will always seem to me to represent the war.

Peter sailed for Vancouver. Hope he has a good trip: no need now to wish for a safe voyage. Heard Jean Sablon singing *Can I Forget You?* and *La Fille aux cheveux de lin*.

Can I Forget You?: a song from the musical *High, Wide and Handsome*, by Rouben Mamoulian (1937).

Saturday 10

Wrote to Jo's mother. She is a widow and a fervent Catholic. I think she doesn't like her daughter-in-law very much. Posted a parcel for Cis.

Sunday 11

Remembrance Day. Armistice Day: end of World War I. Wrote to F.

Monday 12

Two letters from him: one very cheerful, then another sad one. He is back at Wroughton. The journey was a bit long but rather cheerful. They went away in an ambulance convoy and sang all the way. '*Hilda was at Ponty when the convoy drove by, and I was able to wave to her through the ambulance's small window. I had told her approximately what time we would be there. [...] The ward here is gorgeous and small. There are only eight of us, a small radio, flowers galore, and four devoted Waafs truly at our beck and call. Alas! First of all, the Waafs aren't pretty, secondly, they think they're dealing with ordinary wounded airmen, so they woke us up at 5.30 am (sacrilege!) and seem to be very upset that we smoke after 9 pm. Well, in a nutshell, we must civilize them. Our doctor, Mrs Jackson, came along with us, and so did the beautiful physiotherapy officer. [...] Church Village is to be converted into a tuberculosis centre. Just before we moved, a convoy from the Far East arrived.*' He heard from Pat. '*Pat Martin wrote to me, and she's in London again. She's learning chiropody. She has already taken an exam and she says she'll soon be able to earn her living. So if you have corns on your feet, you'll be able to go and see her!*' His letter of 9th. I think he misses the Joneses and feels so lonely. He is the only Frenchman at Wroughton, once again. Luckily, there are lots of French books at the library. He's reading *Les Lettres de mon moulin* again: it reminds him of his beloved Provence which he misses so much. He also took *La Peau de chagrin* by Balzac. I sympathize with the poor WAAFs and nurses who look after him. '*All is fine here, but horror and putrefaction, we have to wash three times a day, at 6, 11 and 5 – I'll soon have no skin left. We've nearly lost all hope of making the Waafs and Sisters see reason. Their education has to be started all over again.*' Jeanne wrote to him: she saw Feriolo who has been demobilized and seems very downcast because of his wife.

Jo came: told us about his mother who had to work to keep three young children after her husband's death. He told me how he loved his wife, which was good to hear!

Tuesday 13

Letter from F. It is very cold and he yearns for his beautiful Provence more and more. '*Where is my Provence, burnt by the sun and dust, filled with a lovely fragrance of flowers, and tender like a lover's face under a clear, gentle sky?*' He's getting bored and seems rather depressed. '*As far as I am concerned, I'm doing well, but I'm getting a little bored. I can't wait to get up. The Sisters are too formal, and we really can't think about flirting with the scarecrows who act as Waafs. What's more, at Church Village I spent the week waiting for Sunday, whilst here the days are aimless and all just the same. I've devoured ten books since Wednesday, and I can hardly remember a word of each. I had that feeling already in Dijon, for no apparent reason. Funny how one can lose interest sometimes! […] I used to unburden my heavy heart to mummy. Perhaps you are one of my mothers. Is this the same man who was so jubilant and determined on hearing 'bombs gone' and who's now afraid, because he feels a bit lonely for one night?*'

Worked in the university café because it was so cold; they haven't yet repaired the glass in the windows. Saw a Russian film, *Lermontov.*

At the end of 1940, Liverpool suffered more than 300 raids from the Luftwaffe, and from I to 7 May 1941, intense bombings (the May Blitz) destroyed part of the city, causing serious damage to the university.

Lermontov: a film directed by Albert Gendelshteyn (1943).

Wednesday 14

His letter of 11th. '*Good night, darling! 8.30 pm, and all is calm. Patients, get some rest! A quarter of a century ago, today was a great day. Now, it's only one anniversary among so many others. Here, you can only value celebrations according to your stomach. I'm almost on my own in the room. Actually, there are only three of us; all the others have gone to the cinema. This afternoon I was allowed to go outside on the terrace, and they took my bed out. The weather was rather fine, although a bit cold. There is an airfield nearby, and I could see a single-seater glider flying. How graceful it was, a real bird! You would have thought it was drawing its elegant arabesques just for me. For a while I envied the pilot. At least he was flying, and there was no danger of his glider doing any harm.*' He's going to have the screw taken off soon. He is longing to get out and have a bit of fun after all those weeks he spent in bed. '*I'm dying to go out tonight, to throw myself into the light and the bustle, even to let it go to my head a bit. I feel as if I could spend all night up without being tired. I can feel a vague but growing desire for entertainment. I'd like to see a big dance, with bright or subdued illuminations, women and music; at last, my old instincts of debauchery are taking hold of me again!*'

Wrote to him. Heard *Brandenburg* and the *Academic Overture*.

Brandenburg Concerto: by Bach. *Academic Festival Overture*: by Brahms.

Thursday 15

Two letters from F. He's making gloves for me. '*I thought I could hide it from you, but, when you see them, you'll realize it was impossible, for the surprise might have caused a fatal shock. First, they are chamois leather: yes, my darling! But the disaster is that they are yellow: yes, my darling! The most beautiful canary-yellow the earth has ever seen. I'm sorry, but that's all that they had at the O.T., and you may be able to dye them or wear them over another pair; they might warm up those fingers which I dream of kissing. [...] Oh! I also made two rabbits, but not the same ones as the last: one is for my godson (I'm so proud of uttering the last two words) and the other for the little children at the crèche.'* He already ate the chocolate I sent him. He sleeps a lot. *'The old 'nervous wrecks' gang from Church Village have all ended up here. We took everything with us: doctors, masseurs, physiotherapy equipment, etc. We form quite a special little colony here. [...] Just before starting this letter, I nearly died laughing. The boy next to me had thrown more than half a packet of dry tobacco into the ashtray. I lighted it and began to blow on it. After a minute of that game, a thick smoke began to surround me, and I suddenly saw the Sister come out from behind the screen, snatch the ashtray out of my hands and throw water on it. The boy next to me was in stitches – she looked so funny – while I almost choked, and I actually thought she was going to call the fire brigade. Phew! I'm still holding my sides. Luckily she's nice, so afterwards she laughed with us.'* Says he won't go back to Hoylake as the Leas is closing on 1st December; he has no idea where the other convalescent centre will be. Perhaps it's a good thing he won't be at the Leas: it's so distracting. On the other hand, the news is good for his leg. *'Mrs Jackson came to see me today, and that's the end of the old plaster. I was supposed to have it off today, but probably the nurses were busy; so I hope it'll be tomorrow. Those people have no idea of the mental agony which one more day in bed can cause. Anyway, two more days for training and having my leg used to movement, and I'll get up. I'll probably be able to ring you up next week. Give me a kiss, darling, I'm happy! It came quicker than I hoped.'*

O.T.: occupational therapy.

Friday 16

His letter of Wednesday. He was in good spirits. *'No, I'm not sad anymore. You know those bouts of melancholy disappear like April showers. That's why I beg you not to worry.'* He had to wait one more day for having his plaster off. *'I was furious when the Sister told me this morning, and I threatened to cut it off myself, which made her roll her eyes: those foreigners, all the same! [...] Dancing? I don't think so, darling. Your punishment will be delayed. It'll take some time before I can dance, but the longer I wait, the happier I will be when I can.'*

Wrote to him. Read *The Way of Recovery*, a lovely book, very encouraging, by Squadron Leader Simpson.

Saturday 17

His letter of Thursday. Plaster off at last! '*Yippee! Here we go! The plaster is already only a memory. We parted this morning after lots of tears, and I hope we won't see each other again anymore. Well, well, I'm completely worn out. I feel as if I had been given a good hiding; my back seems to be a hundred years old, and I can't even sit. Moreover, my leg is reduced to the size of a bone again, but,* 'par le ventre de la mule du Pape', *I'm happy, as happy as if I had won the biggest prize of the National Lottery, and that's a good chance, or should I say, opportunity to pinch you a kiss. I don't know when I will be able to get up, but I hope it'll be very soon.'* He met beautiful Helen again, who was glad to see him again too. He does not wear the blue suit: everybody is in uniform. Says the Matron looks like Mrs Dick. '*The Matron came this morning, and, believe it or not, she didn't guess I was a Frenchman even after we'd chatted for five minutes, and then she asked where I lived. I said: 'Marseilles!' She answered: 'I beg your pardon?' So I repeated: 'Marseilles!' She answered: 'Where is it?' At that moment, I said: 'In the south of France!' and only then did she find out about my nationality. Hey! Haven't I got good grounds to swell with pride? Not for my nationality, of course, but for speaking such perfect English!'* It's good to think he's going to start walking again and we'll see each other soon, I hope so. '*It's funny, whether I'm sad or cheerful I seem to love you much more than usual. The result is that I kiss your dear face all over, as madly as I can. I say goodnight to you, assuring you that I will sleep well, and with no dreams. I love you. You are* la petite femme chérie *of my happiest dreams. Another kiss on your nose! I love you. Francis.'*

Heard *Pavane*.

'*Par le ventre de la mule du Pape!*' ('By the belly of the Pope's mule'): a typical *Provençal* expression, similar to 'by Jove!'

Monday 19

Letter from F. He seems in very good spirits. '*I started my mad escapades in the wheelchair again, and tomorrow I'll be able to have a bath, a real one.*' On Friday evening, he was able to go to the NAAFI cinema where he saw *And the Angels Sing*, with Fred MacMurray and Dorothy Lamour. He spoke French with a young WAAF, of Belgian descent, lying on a bed next to him, who had had a car accident. On Saturday night, he had a real feast. His bed-neighbour's parents brought plenty of food which they shared for dinner: raw celery, tomatoes, Spam, chips, pork pie, apple pie, biscuits, beer, brandy, and cigars! The boy's father knew Marseilles quite well. F found him very nice. '*You could not fail to find him rather touching, too, as he kept asking questions in a low voice: 'Do you think my son will recover? Will he be able to walk again? Etc. etc…' I thought of Daddy and Mummy, and in a way I'm pleased they couldn't see me in Dijon. Anyway, these two good people were so kind as to ask me for Christmas, if I was on my own. I told them I was not really alone, of course, and there was a little heart in England which was beating for me.*' He may go to Loughborough. He'll try to see if there is a centre nearer Liverpool.

Had long talk with Dr Hanna Schuma. Showed her F's photo. She advised me to choose someone sensible and reliable. She is Czech and I suspect she thinks Frenchmen are frivolous. Wrote to F. Jo came up home. Talked about cars and sums: it was dull!

And the Angels Sing: a film musical directed by George Marshall (1944).

Tuesday 20

The operation must have succeeded. Glad F is up. He had been up for two hours and a half and had just got back to bed when he wrote to me. '*My first take off, do you realize? I'm exquisitely tired and I love you. I kiss your little nose. By the way, I kissed your photo at least a hundred times in front of the Sister who desperately wondered if I wasn't mad. Tomorrow, the exercise will be a bit longer, and in three or four days it'll be all day. My leg works very well, the way a good old leg from Marseilles should. Only my ankle is a bit swollen, but it's always like that the first few days. I am beginning to feel my foot a little, not very distinctly, but I can feel it when somebody puts their hand on it. I walked a little in the corridor, and all the Waafs turned round, dazzled by all the gold trimming on my uniform – and I didn't even have my peaked cap!'* Wonderful! Hope everything will be ok this time. *'Now I'm going to leave you, I feel a bit dizzy. I love you, ma petite femme chérie, I love you, that's all! Just as in the poems or novels. A flood of kisses to take your breath away for at least half an hour. Je t'aime. ILY. ILD. Te quiero mucho. Francis. A kiss from me on all the Rigbian noses. I love you.'*

I think Jo is worried about his wife. Mary has met Ian Fraser who has got the Victoria Cross in the Royal Navy. They want to call one of the ferry-boats after him. At Hanna's lecture, Mr Kutchinsky behaved very badly and the lecture was interrupted: he was flirting with a student and lounged about in his chair! Jo is going to Lord Mayor's reception tonight. Listened to *Bal musette* and *De l'autre côté de la rue*.

Ian Fraser: cousin of Barbara's friend at university.

Mr Kutchinsky: an American. *C'est un p'tit bal musette*: sung by Frehel. *De l'autre côté de la rue*: sung by Edith Piaf.

Thursday 22

Letter from F, rather cheerful. He went to cinema again where he was settled into one of the best seats. *'Thanks to my gold braids and stripes, I was seated in the front, in a large seat, between a squadron leader and a pilot officer who looked at me with more curiosity than was necessary.'* He told me something funny about Jacques. *'Jacques was fond of* Miss Otis Regrets. *The poor boy used to sing it often, especially on the plane, which made* Chérubin *fly into violent rages and nearly made me die laughing.'* He says his father is very proud to show all his friends the tobacco I sent him and he's so grateful to me.

F rang up: sounded grave somehow. He's going for a fortnight to Chessington, near London. Is going to see Pat. Said he was trembling.

Miss Otis Regrets: ironic song by Cole Porter. 'And the moment before she died, she lifted up her lovely head and cried, Madam... Miss Otis regrets she's unable to lunch today!' And she was hanged!

Friday 23

Letter from Rose: 'Will you ever come to see us?' I wonder. Wrote to F. Suggested that he should telephone his parents when he is with us at Christmas. Must have moved today.

Saturday 24

Got the beautiful rabbit from F for the crèche children. Wonder if he has moved.

Sunday 25

Wrote to F. Jo came and we talked politics: he is as blind as a bat and can't see that America dare not stay out of European politics.

Monday 26

Letter from F, at last. Five of them travelled in a car driven by a WAAF. He's now at Chessington which seems a comedown from the Leas. '*What a disappointment! I thought all the MRUs were like Hoylake, but here we immediately lost our illusions. Imagine a big camp of grey, muddy huts, with personnel who only think about leaving as soon as 4 pm approaches. We had to protest to get sheets and a van to carry our bags. There was a boy with us, who was on crutches and had to go and find his blankets, etc., himself. What's more, we've been running around all afternoon from one office to another to register. Needless to say, when evening came I only thought about going to bed. I was literally exhausted; it's only normal, as, all in all, I was still in plaster hardly more than a week ago.*' He thinks he won't stay a long time in that centre. '*We came here to be used as guinea pigs to experiment with a new electric-treatment machine which, I heard, doesn't burn like Church Village's and gives much quicker results.*' The nearest town, Kingston, is only ten minutes from the village by bus, and London (Waterloo Street) twenty minutes by the electric train. He intended to go to see Pat on Sunday. '*I was so thrilled to hear you the day before yesterday, I was shaking like a leaf; it was so wonderful to hear you, and your voice hadn't changed. It was my darling again, and it seemed to me that the last time we'd talked was only the day before. You know, darling, I sometimes may have had doubts about myself and wondered*

*if I could love you as much forever [...] I'm sure I will love you as long
as God will let my heart beat.'*

MRUs: Medical Rehabilitation Units.

Tuesday 27

Wrote to F. Got a letter from Jo's wife, very amusing and nice, asking
me to go and stay in Chattanooga. Reception in honour of the
Americans. Jo came for me and we went down to Liverpool by car.
Students' Union looked quite good. Dave was there, Mr Kutchinsky
and Mr Passo too. I was introduced to hundreds of people, including a
jolly Yank who was going back home today. American Red Cross girls
nice. Unfortunate fracas with a rather forward officer to whom I was
not cordial enough! Jo showed me his wife's photo: she is very pretty.
The band was American. Lord Mayor made a speech. Lady Mayoress:
rather a battleaxe, as Cis would say. Lots of 'cousins across the sea':
speeches very dull. The Yank colonel said '*Lord* Mayoress' speaking
to the Lord Mayor's wife! We came home a bit early, then had '*cow-
cow*'. Jo stayed the night. I did enjoy myself. The Yanks' girls all wore
orchids.

Wednesday 28

Letter from F. He went to see Pat on Sunday. He sounds quite crazy
about the baby. '*I got on a train that took me to Wimbledon, and
from there, on a through train to Herne Hill. The whole journey,
including a ten-minute wait at Wimbledon, didn't last more than forty
minutes. Pat's house was rather a long way from the station, but on
my way I met a lady (with a Globule) who asked me with the most
perfect Parisian accent: 'Qu'est-ce que vous cherchez?' I told her, and
she took me straight to Pat's. I rang the bell, and naturally guess who
opened the door? Pat! She remained speechless for a while, and then
shouted: 'Mummy (her mummy wasn't there)! Mrs Singleton! Mr
Singleton! Come here everybody!' And there I was, on the doorstep,
wondering if that stream of people was going to collide with me on my
two crutches. Anyway, after that first impression, I made up my mind
and went in, and I immediately had to face floods of questions pouring*

from all sides. Well, I coped, with that panache which is so typical of me. Unfortunately, Paul was asleep when I arrived. He was vaccinated a week ago and had been a bit unwell. But, around midday, Mr Paul appeared. Oh! Darling, he is absolutely gorgeous, without exaggerating, chubby-cheeked, with huge dark blue eyes. I think he will look more like Pat than Henry. And you know, I took him on my knees, and he didn't cry. He looked at me with his big questioning eyes. But afterwards, we became close friends and had fun, and he expressed his approval with all sorts of lovely sounds. And he's so small I was afraid I might break him. He tried to catch my thumb, and his hand could only grasp half of it. He was very interested in the rabbit which I brought him and decided to call it 'Goo-Goo': anyway that's what he said whilst stretching out his little arms to it. He's a real sweetie, darling, and I wish I could have taken him with me. Pat will have him photographed, and I'll have a photo just for me. What's more, I let him play with my nose, which is a great honour. Pat looked glad to see me. She hasn't changed, as pretty as always, and childlike sometimes. The Singletons are kinder than ever, and I met their two grandmothers who exclaimed: 'Ah! So you are the young man whom we've so much heard about!' We had a lovely time playing, Paul, Pat and me. I also saw my little fiancée, Marguerite, and my little rival, David. They both seemed to wonder why I walked with crutches. Finally, around 10 at night, Mr Singleton drove me back here, and Pat came with us. I felt a bit of a lump in my throat, as that drive reminded me of others in York when Jacques and Henry were there. And that's all! I hope to go there again next Sunday. I think the week will seem very long. [...] I send you my maddest kisses, and one from Paul. I'm sure he agrees with me. I love you, my darling, with all my Provençal heart.'

'*Qu'est-ce que vous cherchez*': What are you looking for?

Thursday 29

His letter of Tuesday. He got three of mine, two forwarded from Wroughton. He's going to ring Mrs Dick. He thinks she lives about three miles away from Chessington. Seems to get very little time off. Wonder how long he will be in England.

Friday 30

His letter of 28th. He tried to phone me on Wednesday, but the telephone booth was occupied for a long time and afterwards it was too late. They will get two days off each week. Says he will come to see me as soon as he can walk better, and will be on leave from 22nd to 30th December. He's looking forward to ringing his family at Christmas. '*Your idea of phoning France is wonderful. Thank you for having thought about that, darling, you're an angel.*'

Wrote to him. I don't think he's walking very well.

December

Saturday 1

Letter from F. Seems to have adapted himself very well at Chessington. '*I'm now very well in with the physiotherapy girls. This morning I appeared at the NAAFI, surrounded by three young ladies and if the Englishmen's eyes were machine guns, your poor Mr Noah would now be riddled with bullets. They all want me to teach them French and all want me to sing J'attendrai. As I don't like rain, I could shy away till now. One of them is quite nice, with corn-gold hair and lovely blue eyes, but she's a bit plump! But as usual I'm very serious and pretend not to understand all the killing glances I'm subjected to (O modesty!). I think I will suggest that they fight, and the one who wins will get me as the prize, Me, the big Me, the one who is the very picture which all the girls are dreaming of, except for the nose!*' It's rather disturbing: he seems to be drinking. Says he's going to look for some pubs where you can find wine and cognac, which is not like him. Went to Pat Moore's to see the photos of the wedding of her sister with an RAF pilot who took part in Battle of Britain. AVF: no-one there.

Sunday 2

Heard Schubert's *Unfinished Symphony*, some lovely Handel, and Beethoven's *Emperor's Concerto* which did not please me. Hope F isn't drinking.

Monday 3

His letter of 30ᵗʰ. He will be here another four months. '*Three more days, and it'll be eleven months since I was wounded. If I had been told that before the accident, I would have cried my eyes out, for, when I thought about it, I expected the worst or nothing much, but without my injury, I wouldn't be here any more. No doubt my guardian angel is influenced by your beautiful eyes.*' He went out to a pub on Thursday night. '*I went into a bar. I drank a glass of beer. I asked if they had any food, as the walk had given me an appetite, and they brought me a huge sausage on a tiny slice of bread. I nearly laughed in the boy's face. Well, I ate it with as much dignity as a sausage will allow. With the same dignity, I got up and made an exit from the stage like Sarah Bernhardt herself. By the time I got back here, it was 10.30 pm. When I walked in, everybody started shouting out impatiently, asking me whether she was a brunette or a blonde. I said she was rather chestnut, as I was thinking of the sausage. That's all! I went to bed and slept till 8.30 this morning. By the way, do you know that, since I came here, I've only got up once for breakfast? It's too far, and it's too cold right now.*' Despite the physiotherapy, the movement of his foot is no better. '*I'm almost sure now that my foot is waking up, as it hurts me more and more, but the movement doesn't really seem to be getting back to normal. The P.T. girl told me it'll take four or five months,* Inch' Allah*!*' He obviously doesn't feel at ease yet, as he gave up going to the NAAFI dance on Friday night. '*As for me, I do so wish I could have gone and taken a look, but, firstly I would have been afraid of making everybody flee because of my two crutches, and secondly I think it would have done me more harm than good.*' He noted our address in Liverpool on the form for his Christmas leave. '*Only three weeks to go, and I'll be able to pull your nose again. You won't be allowed to tickle me, because, since the latest operation, my back has been even more painful. Besides, I know you wouldn't dare tickle a POOR WOUNDED airman. [...] Good night, darling! I love you, Mrs Noah, and if love is only an illusion, it is still so sweet to my heart. A thousand tender kisses to my petite femme chérie.*'

I'd like to make a Christmas *crèche* for him.

Wednesday 5

Got an amusing letter from Mrs Dick who kindly had F there, and another one from him saying he had enjoyed the Dicks'. They fetched him on Saturday at 5 pm and drove him back at 11. They took him to their son's, Kenny, where he met his wife, Pam, and their little James. He found Mrs Dick her usual lively and sparkling self. He does have difficulty in walking. '*No, I can't walk very well. Actually, it's worse than last time, but 'good things come to those who wait'.*' On Sunday he went back to the Singletons' where he spent another excellent day. He rhapsodizes over Pat's baby. '*On Sunday morning, I got up at 9.30 and at 11 I was ringing Pat's doorbell. This time, I was expected. At noon, Mr Paul appeared, and do you know that he recognized me? He smiled and offered me his little arms. I would do anything for this baby. We had lunch whilst Paul was sitting on my knees and trying to intercept what I was putting in my mouth.*' Marguerite was having a party for her ninth birthday. The house was full of children. '*At 7 pm, Mr Singleton took both Pat and me to a club which he is the chairman of, and where a riddle contest was on. Pat sat on the jury. We were in the first row. There were heaps of young girls who were just more than pretty, and I thought they were looking at Pat enviously, probably thinking she was the one who owned the heart of the jewel which I represent (no comment please!). As usual, my peaked cap caused a great stir. It was all over at 9. We had our supper, coffee, and then we had to think about returning. I said goodbye to Paul who was sleeping like a little angel, and once again Mr Singleton drove me back.*'

Wrote to him.

Thursday 6

His letter of 4th. He does sound miserable: there seems to be nothing to do. '*The days here are even more monotonous than in hospital, except Saturdays and Sundays. [...] It's been ten days now since I arrived here, and I only went to pubs three times. I don't think it is too much. Then, don't forget I am a Frenchman and cognac can't do me any harm. On the contrary, I think that the lack of it would do me harm. And I'm not haunting the pubs. [...] I don't do myself harm, you know. I drink one or two glasses of ale, that's all my stomach can manage, and I'm just looking, that's all! It's a bit of a change from my life here. Oh darling, do you think* maman *wouldn't allow me?*' My fears were exaggerated; he just needs to entertain himself. He's going to begin little shoes for Paul.

Friday 7

His letter of Wednesday. '*Today I tried to walk a bit without crutches. It was rather difficult, and a girl from the P.T. told me I looked very much like a lame duck, cheeky girl!*' He falls asleep under his blanket at each physiotherapy session, whilst his leg is exposed to infra-red light. He will soon finish my gloves. Thought of him coming on his last leave from Elvington, just a year ago. What he has gone through since then! I love him so much.

Something extraordinary happened tonight. It was Mummy's birthday. Went to cinema with Jo this afternoon. When we came back, Daddy and Mummy were playing bridge with the Nisbets. We were having supper, when suddenly Jo became white as a sheet, while we had just asked him for lunch with Dave on Sunday. He then was very ungracious about 'our critical attitude towards America'! All of us were stunned, and I was most upset. I would have never thought that a 28-year-old man would have been so childish when he's teased. He definitely has no sense of humour. Supper was rather wretched! We invited him very sincerely to visit us again, but he said he would phone and he was now 'anti-British' because of us!

The Nisbets: friends and neighbours opposite the Rigbys.

Saturday 8

Letter from F. They will have fourteen days for Christmas, and not ten: wonderful! Sounds rather optimistic about his foot. '*My foot is exactly the same as it was two months ago, but the doctor said this morning that it'll happen suddenly and I'll be even happier.*' He read an article about the Elvington Squadrons in a French magazine. '*I received at least twenty newspapers, all from Paris, and there is a magazine,* L'Aviation française, *with an article about Elvington. They mention Henry and his crew and the night they flew to Bochum, on 4ᵗʰ November, while I was dancing.*' He misunderstood what I said about him returning to France.

'*You're being unkind, darling, you know how much I would like to go to France, and you know I look forward to that day, but I also fear it, because from that day on I won't see you any more. Quite apart from my family, if you knew what France means to me, you wouldn't talk like that. Don't be cross, but there are some subjects which one mustn't joke about. I think obtaining a leave – and I'll try to get one after Christmas – would sort it all out. Your faithful Mr Noah, who was endowed by Heaven with a misshapen nasal appendage.*'

Went to concert with Beryl and Bert: *The Flying Dutchman*, *Till Eulenspiegel*, Purcell, and *Jupiter* from Holst's *Planets*. Conductor: Sir Malcolm Sargent; he was sinister-looking. Jo rang while I was out. No apology! He only said: 'Sorry I called!' That's all! Daddy said he was not a gentleman. We are as furious as ever.

L'Aviation française: a weekly aviation magazine, published between 1945 and 1948.

The Flying Dutchman: opera by Wagner. *Till Eulenspiegel's Merry Pranks*: by Richard Strauss.

Sunday 9

Two years since F landed in England. Sent him a telegram yesterday, and wrote to him today. Poor F, what he has gone through since he came, and how faithful he has been.

Monday 10

His letter of Friday. He can't stop talking about little Paul: he's fond of this child. '*Oh darling, if you could see Paul, you would be even more of a baby than I am; he is so sweet. I'm dying to see him starting to walk, and then we'll be able to play great games. I'm afraid that Pat's furniture might suffer or she might get an arrow when we're playing Indians.*' Better wait for him to make the *crèche*. '*We haven't got any of the things to make the* crèche*, darling. You need moss, santons, the cowshed where Jesus was born, and a mill. If I had clay, I could make some* santons*, but it takes too much time to paint them. You're a dear for having thought of that.*' On Thursday, an Irishman, who is in his room and was about to go home, was knocked down by a car: he came back with his leg broken again. '*Do you think one can say one suffered when seeing such cases? [...] No, I'm not in pain; the massages do me so much good, my ankle doesn't hurt any more at all when I walk, but this foot is so long in recovering. I had expected a bit too much from the operation. Like all patients I thought as soon as I got up, I'd be able to run. It's not at all like that in my case, and it's now that I really need to be patient, as this is a transitional phase.*'

Wrote to him and made up a parcel for the Uzays. Postman came, collecting money for poor old Dick who is ill.

Santons: manger figurines. Dick: the regular postman who always asked after Francis.

Tuesday 11

Bought books for F for Christmas. Saw James Latimer in Liverpool: they trimmed his leg again, poor boy! Listened to Yvonne Arnaud who played the piano, and saw *Tarakanova*, with Suzy Prim, Annie Vernay, and Pierre Richard Willm.

Tarakanova: a film directed by Fedor Ozep (1938).

Wednesday 12

Long letter from F. '*I found your telegram when I got back on Saturday, and thank you for that. I also thought of you and my first night in Liverpool. So much has happened since then, but above all, my love has endured till now. I love you more than ever, I love you more than I ever dreamt I would love someone. [...] Your second letter is so sweet; I don't know why, I nearly cried when I read it. You're too good to me, and for instance, if you talk about my qualities again, I will strangle you with your own skin! But apart from that, it was a wonderful letter. I wish I could have fallen at your feet and cried out that I didn't deserve such praise. I wish I could have kissed your hands and wept without knowing why. My only happiness is knowing you love me, and when you tell me in such a sweet and meaningful way, at the same time I feel stupid and wonder why.*' Dédé wrote to him: he's overjoyed about talking to him on the phone at Christmas, and

F is glad too. On Saturday he went to the cinema at Kingston, and on Sunday he went to Pat's again at Herne Hill. '*I turned up around 11.30, frozen stiff, as it was rather cold. I had a huge lunch, for Mrs Singleton knows that I never get up for breakfast. Then Paul arrived, his eyes still swollen with sleep; he looked so surprised to see the light. After lunch, we settled on the floor. He has a rattle and loves to throw it on the floor. Afterwards, he was pulling my ears and seemed to develop a taste for that game. If you only could see his lovely smile when I tickle him. When I begin to play with him, I can't stop, and Pat has to scold me so that I stop. We had tea towards 4.30. Paul went to bed. Mr Singleton set off to his club, and we stayed alone with Pat. We had a long chat, and you know, I think she feels terribly lonely. She is so cheerful in public that nobody notices, but she said it to me herself, and later took it back: if she didn't have her little boy, she would be terribly unhappy. And I've decided to spend New Year's Day with her. I know you are kind-hearted and you won't be cross with me for that. I do so wish, not exactly to cheer her up, but at least to take her mind a bit off her worries. You see, I am the only link which reminds her of Henry, and I think she is glad to see me. Do you understand me, darling? We have precious little time for us, and I apologize for having taken that decision without asking you first. Finally, I left her around 10 and came back in a taxi.*' I am disappointed; 1st January is the anniversary of our first meeting: I do so wish we had been together that day. Wrote to him.

Thursday 13

His letter of Tuesday: he intended to go to see *To Have and Have Not*, with Humphrey Bogart and Lauren Bacall. Says the English are insular: I agree! He thinks he will take the first train on 21st in the morning and will arrive at Liverpool in the afternoon. '*Only nine days to go, Bébé, and your sufferings will start! The days seem to go by slower as the date is approaching.*'

My godmother came to spend the night at home; she is going to a wedding tomorrow.

To Have and Have Not: a film directed by Howard Hawks (1944).

Friday 14

Letter from F. '*A Christmas tree, it'll remind me of my childhood. It's been such a long time since I sat up on Christmas Eve. You know, at home, we had a big fireplace, and Daddy was very clever at throwing curlpapers in the air, and, when they fell down, we thought Father Christmas was throwing them. But at home, we never saw Father Christmas, not like here; so the legend was all the stronger. I remember I couldn't wait to grow up so that my shoes would get bigger and contain more presents. And for a long time Dédé wondered how his tricycle had managed to go down the chimney.*' The film on Tuesday was rubbishy! He must go to the bank on Saturday. '*They completely forgot my pay this month, but I will earn £60 next month, which will make me feel rich.*' He'll be visiting the Dicks on Saturday, and Pat on Sunday, as usual. Wrote to him.

Saturday 15

His letter of Thursday. He seems well. He will phone before leaving to give me his time of arrival on 21st. '*But for heaven's sake, don't say anything to the journalists! You remember the crowd waiting for me when I arrived in Scotland!*' He met a doctor again who was at Hoylake with him. '*He said to the Waaf officer: 'He's one of my Hoylake types.' I do like him, because he's very friendly, and do you know what he said? 'He's a good worker!' talking about me. The poor girls who always see me sleeping stood open-mouthed.*'

He rang from the Dicks, but the reception was bad. He has got some money now. Sounded very well and cheerful. Hope he doesn't wear himself out. Bought Coty powder for 5 shillings: so expensive!

Sunday 16

Sheila and I saw *The Blue Angel*, with Marlene Dietrich singing *Falling in Love Again*. Wrote to F.

The Blue Angel: a film directed by Joseph von Sternberg (1930).

Monday 17

Letter from F saying he has stopped smoking. '*I haven't smoked for two days, or nearly, and it's the most terrible torture I've ever inflicted on myself, but, as always, I endure these ordeals stoically.*' I don't expect it will last long. He went to the hairdresser's, at last! '*Oh! Great news: today I had my hair cut. You will be pleased! I now look like a hen with a featherless neck; I'm cold and feel really weird. What makes me sorry is that it won't grow again in a week's time and I won't be able to annoy you.*' His knee is much better. '*It's almost straight, and I gained 5 degrees in two days. I can walk much better now.*' Almost every night he goes to see a show at the NAAFI and seems to enjoy himself. Wrote to him.

Wednesday 19

His letter of 17th. He enjoyed his day in the countryside very much on Saturday. The Dicks were very kind to him. They fetched him from Oxshott and took him to their house for lunch. Then they went for tea to Esher, a small village where they met Kenny, Pam, and little James whom F is fond of. '*Pam wore trousers! Those Englishwomen!*' In the evening, they played *Thank You*, which he found very amusing. On Sunday he was at Pat's. '*Pat helped me to wrap up the presents for the Christmas tree. So it's not me who will be congratulated for that. Paul is very well. We played for two hours lying on the floor. There must be something funny about me, as he laughed quite a lot. Then it was I who put him to bed, and don't laugh, I sang to lull him to sleep. He's even sweeter when he's sleeping. Pat came back with me here. We had a big taxi just for the two of us, as Mr Singleton's car had broken down. [...] You sound a bit cross about New Year's Day. You mustn't, darling. Pat really needs a bit of a change. She seemed so disappointed when I told her I was going away for fourteen days, I couldn't say no. It's a bit difficult, you know, and I owe that to poor Henry. No, it's her dad and mummy who are coming to London; she won't return to St Helens.*'

Thursday 20

Got a Christmas card from Pat, and another one from Mrs Dick. F rang up, very gay, and the line was clear. He's arriving tomorrow between 3.30 pm and 4 pm at Lime Street station. Feel rather miserable: I'm afraid it'll be the only and last Christmas we'll be spending together.

Friday 21

Letter from F. There was a big dance at the NAAFI on Tuesday for the centre closing at Christmas. He went with Venus. '*There were lots of hugs and kisses under the mistletoe. There even was a gang of people, a bit merry, who sang* La Marseillaise *for me. Poor Venus looked very embarrassed.*' It sounds he had great fun but he doesn't mention if he danced. '*When we got back, we found the room completely upside down: beds overturned, blankets all over the place, even on the roof, and sheets tied up. It was about 2 am when we got to bed, and no need to tell you that I had little naps most of the time today, interrupted each quarter of an hour by Venus who asked me to change sides, as I was under the infra-red light.*' On Wednesday evening he was invited at Venus' parents'. '*See you soon, darling! These two days will seem to me longer than ever. Best kisses from your Cyrano. I love you. Francis.*'

Got a card from Ardenne, from Guernsey, so that she has, at last, got back home, which must be wonderful. Went down to town to meet F. The train was twenty-two minutes late. Sheila was there, looking very glamorous, and was a great help. F looks much better and has a new French uniform. He does not walk very well. Fred, my canteen policeman, tried to get us a taxi, but only got a private car driven by a young man who would not take a sou; we were most touched. F looks very happy. I am so happy to see him again too, and so is everybody at home. Had dinner, then listened to the radio.

Saturday 22

Raced to the shops, doing well for sweets and oranges. F got up late. He has made a most beautiful pair of chamois leather gloves for me. He is clever. They are really yellow but I can have them dyed. Went to hospital to see Sister Hogan. Heard the beloved Rina Ketty on wireless. F as affectionate as ever, sweet and funny.

Sunday 23

Began to put call through to France: 6 shillings for three minutes! Decorated the Christmas tree; it was really fun and it looks lovely. Cis made his *crèche*, and that looks nice too. Telephone call did come through, but it was most unsatisfactory: F could hear Dédé but could not reply, so tantalizing. The operator said the lines to the South were bad. F so patient about it. Listened to *ITMA* and Christmas carols. Then we kissed each other a long time: very moving.

Monday 24

I did chores. Daddy, F and Patsy went to the shops. Went with F to Gran's for some nuts. Then we all went off to the Cassandra where we had a lovely lunch with fish. Heard *L'Enfance du Christ*, French Christmas carols from Guernsey, and *Il est né le divin enfant* which F parodied in his way: '*Il est né le divin enfant, il est né sur la Canebière!*' F very sweet, enjoying himself like a little child. He's so dear to me. We got a Christmas card from *Prune* with the RAF insignia.

L'Enfance du Christ (The Childhood of Christ): an oratorio by Hector Berlioz.
La Canebière: a famous avenue in Marseilles.

Tuesday 25

Christmas Day. Got up late and did all the chores. Cis was agitating to open the presents, and we did so. He brought lovely ones for us all, and especially for me: a gold pendant with pearls and peridots on a chain. I was so thrilled: it is the first piece of jewellery a man has ever given me. He also gave us Christmas cards from his mummy and Marie-Jeanne. I gave him books and shaving cream. He seemed so pleased. Said it was the best Christmas that he had had for ages. Went to Granddad's, and then we all went over to the Nisbets' for drinks, where we had a lovely time. There were two RAF pilots: one of them just got back from India yesterday; the other one was in Coastal Command. Came home and had lunch. Listened to the King's speech. Walked up to Bishop Eton's, but it was closed! Had a lovely Christmas dinner and F had the 3*d* bit in the pudding. Listened to the wireless: Richard Murdoch and Tommy Handley. Lovely Christmas. Dear Francis!

Granddad: Barbara's grandfather on her father's side.
Bishop Eton's: Roman Catholic church.
Richard Bernard Murdoch: another comedic BBC radio performer (*Much-Binding-in-the-Marsh*).

Wednesday 26

Boxing Day. Got up late. Did dusting and various chores. Party at Pat Tyler's, with RAF boys and WRNS like her. Everyone just about half-awake. We made F's face up and tied his hair with a bow! Had lunch and F went to sleep in the armchair, but without that horrible shuddering. Sheila came for the evening. Afterwards F said he wanted to marry me; he seemed so sad. Then he told me that I didn't love him as much as he did me. I don't know what I should do.

WRNS: Women's Royal Naval Service.

Thursday 27

Went to the library with F. Talked to Mrs Britten who said: 'Never marry a charming man!' F sulky this morning, but cheered up very much later.

Friday 28

Went to *The Three Caballeros* by Disney, then went to dinner at Reeces' with Beryl and Graham, and we had a very nice time. F bought a bottle of wine. I don't know if it was good or bad: I found it tasted like medicine! Beryl likes F very much.

Saturday 29

We went to the *British*. Sat in the canteen which was nicely decorated. F said English girls had no charm and took no trouble about their appearance if they were not pretty! He was amusing, and also said Frenchmen were more forward. Went to a children's party in the ball-room where there were a huge Christmas tree and a Christmas Father. The children were all foreigners: the little daughter of the Cunard representative in Paris, a little Chinese girl, Africans, and an Indian. Then we went off to the Royal. F annoyed because I asked for a cushion for him. I asked him if I had been any use to him, and he said: '*You helped me to be brave.*'

Sunday 30

Very foggy. Tried to telephone the Uzays again, but the exchange was closed again. Could not go to the Cassandra again because of the fog.

F fairly cheerful. I put on my white dress, then the black one: he was amused. We kissed each other, it was sweet. He told me that he loved me, despite my faults, and that he didn't want to leave me.

Monday 31

F had slept badly. He dreamt I had pinched his peaked cap. We gave him a little sweater because he was shivering. It was cold and foggy. Rang up Fred about reserving him a seat. F was so sweet and tender. Went to Lime Street station. Fred put F in a reserved carriage with a Scottish pilot officer and his wife. In the compartment he asked me if there was no hope about me marrying him. I said: 'No, I can't!' He said he didn't want to marry anyone but me and would go on asking me until he will be sure I was sincere. Poor Cis, he said it would give him pleasure, but also pain, to go home, and it was the best Christmas he had had since 1938. I was so glad. It was a wonderful Christmas for me too.

What a strange year! It started in such a tragic way, and at the end it all finished well. I wonder what will happen to Cis. I love him so much and I'm sure that no-one will love me as much as he. Wrote to him.

RIP: Henri, Jacques, Roger, Maurice.

1946

January

Tuesday 1

New Year's Day. Letter from Dédé: they received the parcel and were glad of it. F rang. The Scottish pilot officer and his wife were kind to him. Pat was there and I spoke to her. I thought about this time two years ago. I am so glad I met Francis. I love him so much and do so wish I could make him happy.

Wednesday 2

Wrote to him. He was shot down a year today. I'm thinking of him and of poor Jacques. I never thought he would be on leave again. What a pity he is not here!

Thursday 3

His letter of Tuesday, from Herne Hill. His train was two hours late. He thought Pat wasn't at the railway station; she had been for a cup of tea to get warm whilst waiting for him: the temperature in Liverpool is '*tropical*' compared to London! Mrs Singleton was impressed by the amount of food he enjoyed eating for dinner. He waited for the twelve strokes of midnight with Pat before going to bed. On Tuesday morning,

Paul was not very well; the doctor came and thought F was his father!
In the afternoon they went to the cinema, then in the evening they had
a family gathering with the Singletons. He sounds delighted with the
Christmas he spent with us. '*I do want to thank your parents again
for such a wonderful Christmas. I only have one regret, which is that
I can only express my gratitude with words. There are things that can
never be forgotten, and this is one. Thank you, too, my darling, who
manages to both love, and put up with, a chap like me! I try to show
you how grateful I am for that, but it would seem that so far I haven't
been successful. On the contrary, I definitely seem to have a delightful
gift for putting my foot in it – or rather, both feet. Forgive me, and if
this can be an excuse, no doubt love makes me silly, even sillier than
usual, and the result is rather appalling.*' He seems concerned that I
don't think he loves me, and says, now that the time is so short, we
must not misunderstand each other. '*I do beg you, we must not let the
slightest misunderstanding creep in. If I make a* faux pas, *let me know
at once. We haven't time to waste now, because each time I see you, I
have the awful feeling that (9 o'clock is striking, darling, I love you)
it is the last. Love me as much as you can, darling! I need your love
so much; it has made a real man of me, and it'll help me to remain so.
Good night, sweetheart. With my best kisses, my biggest kisses, and my
best wishes for a Happy New Year! May God bless you and guide you
through life's ordeals. I love you. All my best wishes to Riri, Mummy,
Patsy, Gran, Uncle Max, Sheila and all those I happen to know.*' He
goes back to Chessington today.

Friday 4

His letter of 2nd, from Herne Hill. '*There we are! A year ago I was
admitted to hospital. It's now 11.25 pm, and I suppose at that time
last year I was lying on the operating table, with the doctors wondering
whether they were going to cut off my leg or not.*' He did receive my
letter at the Singletons'. '*Anyway if I am all that you say, it's thanks to
you. Not only did you give me courage, but you inspired me to try and
do great things. Unfortunately I was not very lucky. I did so wish that
you would be proud of me. Without you, I would never have wanted to
recover so much, despite all the love I have for my family. I began the*

year saying your name, and I finished it far away from you by my own choice. Don't judge me too much from what I've done, and forgive me for having made you sad.' He had just come back from a show with Pat when he wrote to me. They went to *Gay Rosalinda*, which he enjoyed very much; he was glad to see how cheerful Pat was. Dédé wrote to him, saying he had cursed the telephone at Christmas and his poor father had trembled with emotion. He enclosed a cutting about his squadron which was decorated in Bordeaux, and the invitation to the medals ceremony which was on 24th November. *'I kiss you passionately with all the strength of my loving heart this evening – one year ago, it seemed to me the same evening was to be the last of my life.'*

Had my ears pierced: Mummy is giving me earrings for my birthday.

Gay Rosalinda: a version of Johann Strauss II's operetta *Die Fledermaus* (*The Bat*), music by Erich Wofgang Korngold, performed at the Palace Theatre in London.

Saturday 5
New Year card from Dédé. Went to AVF, then to a concert: *La Gazza Ladra, La Calinda*, lovely, and first movement of Beethoven's *5th*.

La Gazza Ladra: opera by Rossini. *La Calinda*: from the opera *Koanga* by Frederick Delius.

Sunday 6
Wrote to F.

Monday 7
Two letters from him. On Thursday evening, Mr Singleton and Pat took him back in the car to Chessington. Pat's parents will be in London next Sunday. Paul is better, but his teeth hurt him. Everybody thought of Cis for Christmas. *'The first thing I saw in my room was a huge pile of letters that were waiting for me. There were at least twenty, almost all of them Christmas cards, and even a parcel from the AVF with about two hundred cigarettes, some chocolate and a lovely little diary with the AVF seal.'* He also thought of Jacques on 2nd. *'So did Pat – that's funny.*

At this time last year we went to see a ballet with Pat, and a few days later I never thought I'd see old England again.' He's going to ask for leave for my birthday. I hope he'll be able to come. *'I don't doubt that you love me, darling. I've never had any doubts since the day when you told me so, but you know the wavering which a loving heart is subjected to. I'm rather afraid that you may not believe me. [...] I do love you, my darling, more than ever and less than always. I love you and send you my most tender kisses, messengers of a love which, God willing, will only end when I do.'*

Wrote to him. Listened to *L'Aiglon*: François good, also Thérèse and Metternich, but Duchess poor. Well translated.

L'Aiglon: a drama by Edmond Rostand (1900).

Tuesday 8

Saw many of the officers and men of the *Molotov* who are here to take over the Russian share of the German prize ships. They went about in groups. They look rather sallow and are generally tall. They wear long leather coats and cloth caps. The officers wear very long navy coats with no insignia, which makes them look like chauffeurs! Saw *Pièges*, with Maurice Chevalier, who is rather too old now, but he sang *Mon amour* and *Il pleurait comme une Madeleine*. Eric Von Stroheim excellent, and Marie Déa charming.

Molotov: a Soviet Navy cruiser.
Pièges: a film directed by Robert Siodmak (1939).

Wednesday 9

Letter from F who is feeling sad. *'It's about 10, and you're probably asleep, or almost. Are you thinking of me? Not so long ago, this was the time when we started to hope Riri and maman were going to bed for the sake of our half-hour skirmish. This was the time when I thought about all the words I was going to say to you and never did. How I was dying to kiss you when your face was so close to mine, and you knew it, you wicked flirt, boo! Your huge eyes seemed to me more those of a minx than ever. But I will kiss them again, those eyes, and make them pay for*

*the martyrdom I endured. And you may punch me as much as you wish
but that won't stop me. Oh! I love you so much, darling, and how I feel
it even more deeply when remembering all those little things. What a
treasure-trove of memories you have given me, if ever we have to part.
Please do remember that it's you, and you only, who could inspire such
love in me, such complete and utter love, which even in its sad moments
can still bring me joy! Don't leave me, darling, you're all I have. But I'm
stupid! I'm always afraid, even in those moments when I feel you closest
to me and have the impression that you are mine, mine only. Afraid of
what? I don't know, of some event that will take me away from you.'*
He was very proud of telling me that he had done a big wash. *'I washed
two pairs of socks, four collars, six handkerchiefs, three shirts, two
undershirts and a pair of underpants [...] and tomorrow I will iron;
but it doesn't mean you will get me to do the washing when I come
to Liverpool! Besides, it's all very, very badly washed!'* He went back
to London on Sunday and says Pat is looking forward to her parents.
*'She seemed very well, for I caught her singing during the day; it'd been
ages.'* Wrote to him.

Thursday 10
Saw some Russian women: tall, clean, but so stuffily dressed and badly
made-up. Two Russians at the *British*, on seeing the Poles at a dance,
said: 'Dirty fascist pigs!'

Friday 11
Worried about F. Wrote to him.

Saturday 12
Three letters from F: very good news. *'The doctor was very pleased
with my leg. He said that at that rate I'll have recovered earlier than
he had initially thought.'* He went to the NAAFI dance with Venus on
Tuesday night and even danced a bit. *'After some weak protest, I let
myself get dragged off with the promise of having an extra massage on
the day after. And you can believe me if you want, it didn't turn out so
badly! I danced, darling, for the first time in a year. It was only a waltz
at the beginning, but then there was some swing and a contest all at the*

same time. They worked it out by a process of elimination, and we held out for quite a time, but we had to give it up when the speaker said that all the escorts had to roll down their stockings and the partners to pull their trousers up; we found it was going a bit too far or, should I say, too high! Then came the last dance, and it was already over. I was so happy and so tired, I could have given Venus a kiss!' His peaked cap was stolen in the cloakroom, which he was furious about. He has great hopes of getting a two-day leave for my birthday: he said it was for a wedding!

Monday 14

His letter of 11th. He will be here on 22nd. *'That's it! The wedding is arranged!'* Lovely! Wrote to him, suggesting that he should wear a forage cap instead of his peaked cap!

Wednesday 16

Letter from F who is having a good time with Venus. On Saturday they went sightseeing to London and had a cruise on the Thames. They went to see *La Mort du cygne* and *Les Voyages de Gulliver*, then had dinner in a restaurant. The day after, he went back to Pat's and saw her parents at David's birthday party. They're going to live in London now. F played with the children a lot all the afternoon. Paul is doing well; he is growing up before one's very eyes.

La Mort du cygne: a film directed by Jean Benoît-Lévy (1937). *Gulliver's Travels*: a film directed by Dave Fleischer (1939).

Thursday 17

Nice letter from Rose, one from Dédé with lovely postcards of Berre and Marseilles, the *Château d'If*, *Notre Dame de la Garde*, and oil tankers. Also letter from F. *'Yes, slowly but surely my leg is getting better. Perhaps we'll even be able to dance on your birthday if you're not too concerned about your feet. Anyway, Venus told me it was an excellent exercise, providing I don't overdo it.'* I knew what he would say about the forage cap. *'Too late for the forage cap, my girl! I've already ordered another peaked cap. For the moment, I go out without a hat, which gives me the advantage of being taken for a civilian.*' He'll ring up tomorrow evening or on Sunday to let me know what time he's arriving. Wrote to him.

Saturday 19
His letter of 16th. He's suffering from the intense cold.

Sunday 20
F rang: he's supposed to be coming on Tuesday.

Monday 21
Two letters from F. '*I'm beginning to long to go back to Wroughton, as I can't wait to hear whether I'll be allowed to go to France or not.*' He has a new peaked cap but he doesn't like it as much as the previous one! He pretended to the physiotherapy girls that he was going to get married tomorrow and would only come back in a fortnight!

Tuesday 22
My 21st birthday. I arranged all my cards, including Dédé's one, and my presents carefully in the sitting-room: they looked lovely, as did my two birthday cakes. Mummy gave me some earrings. *Prune* rang up. A light lunch. Daddy came in, not having been able to find F, at which I grew very worried and was most upset. Margaret and I dressed. I put on my mauve silk dress, which we had made without coupons as the cloth had been slightly burnt by bombs, and lo and behold F arrived in a taxi, having missed the first train, poor sweetheart. All my guests were here: Sheila, Margaret, Mary Owen, Lester Nisbet, Beryl and Graham, Sergeant Trevor Tyler and Flying Officer Johnny Wintle, both from the RAF, and Cis of course. Unfortunately, Patsy was at school. Cis gave me a lovely real leather writing-case.

We all went to the Playhouse to see *The Moonstone*, which we all enjoyed, then to Reece's for dinner; Uncle Max joined us. We had a lovely dinner: soup, chicken, iced pudding, and coffee. I danced with F: it seemed such a long time since I did. He really dances quite well, and is walking much better. He was so tired naturally. Everyone drank my health, which embarrassed me. The band played *J'attendrai* and *Auf Wiedersehen*. Poor Trevor had to get back to London on the midnight train. It was a full house, as F, Sheila and Margaret, all stayed the night: we all went to bed about 1 am. Lovely day. Everyone was so kind to me. I hope they enjoyed themselves as much as I did.

Playhouse: theatre. *The Moonstone*: a 19th-century epistolary novel and play by Wilkie Collins.

Auf Wiederseh'n Sweetheart: sung by Vera Lynn.

Wednesday 23

We were all so tired. We took F to the station and thanks to my policeman put him on the train next to the dining-car. He seemed to have enjoyed himself. I wonder if he still loves me as much.

Thursday 24

Letter from *Prune* for my birthday. He's now flight lieutenant and to be aide-de-camp to a wing commander in Glasgow. Letter from Jo's wife: it seems she doesn't know we have fallen out!

Saturday 26

Letter from F. The return journey went well, despite four hours' delay. '*Now I must thank you for the wonderful time you gave me. What I appreciate most is that I was able to be totally happy without being alone with you, my glamorous sweetheart (phew!). Lots of times I felt like kissing you in front of everybody, but I restrained myself. At least, darling, if you were happy and enjoyed yourself as much as I did, God is with us. [...] Now, when you have finished your thank-you letters, write a little note to me and tell me you love me, and I'll be the happiest of men. [...] You were charming on Tuesday night, and I could have fallen in love with you a second time.*' The physiotherapy girls asked him a lot of questions which he answered with some '*no compris!*'

Mrs Dick came home for lunch. I was so pleased to see her again. F is welcome to her house again whenever he wants. Saw *Quai des brumes*, with Jean Gabin and Michel Simon.

'*No compris*': 'not understood'.

Quai des brumes (*Port of Shadows*): a film directed by Marcel Carné (1938).

Sunday 27
Wrote to him.

Monday 28
His letter of 25th. He's already gone back to the hairdresser's. '*The new one is all right, that is to say he doesn't cut too much off!*' He's coming back on Friday for the week-end. He'll have a seventy-two-hour ration card. '*I love you, dearest darling, woman or little girl, loving or motherly, I love you, because you are Barbiche, my* petite femme chérie. *A thousand kisses.*' Wrote to him.

M. Gouin: French Prime Minister. Let's hope he'll be more flexible than de Gaulle!

Félix Gouin: President of the third provisional government of France from 26 January 1946 to 12 June 1946.

Tuesday 29
Wrote to him.

Wednesday 30
His letter of Monday. On Saturday he went with Venus to the *Palais de la Danse*, at Hammersmith. '*It was more than superb! The hall was huge with two bands, and what's more, the dance session was broadcast. We danced from 3.30 to 7 pm, and I danced everything, including jive. Venus said I did much better than the first time.*' Then they had dinner at *Chez Auguste*, the French restaurant where he had been with Jacques. On Sunday, as usual, he visited Pat and took Paul out in his pram. '*As the weather was fine, all my resolutions about pushing a pram vanished, and, like any old dad, I pushed Paul who was thrilled to bits, and Pat didn't make fun of me! The little devil will make me do all sorts of things!*'

Thursday 31
Letter from F. He intended to go to see Mrs Dick this week, if he had the time. He thinks he'll set off to Liverpool tomorrow at midday and arrive at 7 pm if everything's all right. He had a letter from Patsy who is waiting for a full report about my birthday party. Concert: English music.

February

Friday 1

His letter of Wednesday. He had just written twelve! '*I'm sure Paul won't be pleased next Sunday, nor will Pat for that matter, but you know I am the prisoner of your charms and feel attracted to Liverpool like an* 'aimant' *(in both senses)!*' He doesn't know when he will leave Chessington yet. '*I have the feeling that I'm not about to leave here. I'm upset as I won't be able to ask for leave till I see Mrs Jackson, but that's a good thing in a way, for I'll be able to see you often, if you don't mind. Venus was ordered by the squadron leader to be cruel to me so as to straighten my leg again quicker, and every day she makes me scream as she presses down with all her weight. I begin to think that suffering under a woman's hand is not so gentle after all!*'

He came this evening. He walks well but looks tired. He is so sweet.

'*Aimant*' in French means both 'a magnet' and 'loving'.

Saturday 2

F did not get up till late. Went to see *Ten Little Niggers*, then listened to wireless: *Much-Binding-in-the-Marsh*, which F is fond of.

And Then There Were None: a film adaptation of *Ten Little Niggers* (original title). Agatha Christie's novel, directed by René Clair (1945). *Much-Binding-in-the-Marsh*: a weekly BBC programme about an imaginary and satirical RAF station, whose title was inspired by RAF Moreton-in-Marsh (Gloucestershire).

Sunday 3

F washed my hair! Took him to the station where he got the 4 pm train. He was very sweet and said he hated to go.

Monday 4

Wrote to him. Got a letter from Ardenne, from Guernsey. The Germans have vandalized their house, *Le Mont Saint*. There's plenty of make-up and silk stockings there, but they have had no soap for months.

Tuesday 5

Very nice letter from Morel. He is still in the Air Force and married. He seems happy. The rest of the crew are dispersed. He has had a bit of a crash again. Sent his letter to F.

Wednesday 6

Letter from F, long and affectionate. He thinks he will be back in three weeks' time. '*There is some of your lipstick on my handkerchief, darling, and if it wasn't so dirty (the handkerchief) I would keep it as a holy relic. I could say: I still have on my lips the sweet, burning feeling of your kisses, but would you like that? Now listen: would you please thank Riri and Maman for their unfailing kindness, and more concretely for the apple pie and the car. No, seriously, give them a big 'thank you' from me, and tell Riri that, if one day I discover an oil well, I'll be thinking of him. Good night now, and thank you, darling, for your love and all that it has brought me. I love you as much and as deeply as a Provençal can love, and believe me, that's something!*'

Dinner at Reece's with Lovat and his friends in the Merchant Navy: Gordon Rennie and his wife Bunty, both Scots, Ian Davison, from Newcastle, and his fiancée Noëline. Ian was very nervy. In the middle of January, last year, during a voyage in the Atlantic, his ship was torpedoed: he spent four days on a raft.

Thursday 7

His letter of 5th. He may be a *sergent-chef* shortly. '*Yesterday I got a form to fill in, you know: name, rank, date of my last promotion. It came from Headquarters, and I think it's about my chef stripes.*' He went to the NAAFI cinema on Monday and saw *The Thin Man Goes Home* again, with William Powell, for the third time! He tells me not to work too hard. '*Are you still tired? Your eyes were, last Friday. It seems to me you're working too hard, darling, and it's my turn to tell you don't push yourself too hard. You know the old maxim: slow and steady wins the race!*'

The stripes of a *sergent-chef*, flight sergeant.

Friday 8

Prune came to see us on two legs! He is tall. Walks fairly well and does not seem to tire easily. I am pleased to observe his gradual progress. He is fit for flying duties. Went to cinema and saw *Journey Together*, an RAF film about flying training. He said I had more boy-friends than anyone else he knew! Nice lad, pleasant and gentlemanly. Took him to the station.

Journey Together: a film directed by John Boulting (1945).

Saturday 9

Miserable letter from F. He misses Jacques so much. '*I'm not really sad, but a bit fed up and mentally tired of I don't know what. No doubt I am becoming jaded, and it's high time for me to see some new countries. I don't even feel like going to France any more, except to visit my parents. I seem to be going through a transition period. I think I've tried to enjoy myself too much lately, and in that case, enjoying oneself is not really that much fun, after all. I feel as if I can't breathe. I wish Jacques was here; he understood me so well.*' Luckily, he had a good time at the Dicks' on Wednesday. They are so kind to him and he likes them very much. If he had his way, he would come to Liverpool every week-end, but he knows it is difficult for Mummy because of rationing. He prefers to wait to have a new ration card, and he'll also have Friday afternoon off in two weeks. Answered him.

Sunday 10

Wrote to F.

Monday 11

His letter of 8th. He finds the time drags. He is so dear to me. Wrote to him. Short letter from Rose too.

Tuesday 12

Bought record *Can I Forget You?* by Jean Sablon. Hope *Prune* enjoys his first days at work.

Wednesday 13

Another miserable letter from F. He feels he is floating in a vacuum. '*I don't know whether my nerves are bad or not, but I feel I'm not as I was before the accident. I worry more easily, but that's nothing. I'm not upset by anything in particular, darling, it's just that I feel strange. Nothing gives me any satisfaction, or pleasure. Only with you do I feel relaxed. All that I do seems useless or wrong. I always hesitate before doing something, and when I've done it, I'm sure I should have done the opposite. I don't know what it is, I feel as if I was floating. It's easier to be brave when there's something to fight or overcome, but now there's nothing like that for me, only a vacuum. I know that there are people who care about me, and I'm grateful to them, but they don't fill the emptiness. Your job is giving you enough worries and trouble, and I should not talk to you like that, but who would I say it to, apart from you? I can cheer up easily when I go out, but it only lasts a few hours, and that's why I hate to stay here in my room. Well, I suppose it's one of my usual bouts of depression, and nothing to worry about.*' Last Saturday, he went to Chertsey hospital to see Ernie, a boy who was with him at Wroughton and Church Village, still in a wheelchair. On Sunday he took Paul out, as usual. He's supposed to ring me up tomorrow. He's afraid of being sent away and not having the time to see me again and would like to come to Liverpool this week-end. Wrote to him.

Chertsey: in Surrey, some twenty-eight miles from London.

Thursday 14

His letter of Tuesday. He was going to the NAAFI dance and sounded more cheerful. He's pleased to hear *Prune* can walk as well as before with his artificial leg. Asks if I spend half my time at the station, seeing people off and saying '*au revoir!*'

He rang: he's arriving tomorrow. Food ration news depressing.

Friday 15

His letter of 13th. He danced quite a lot on Tuesday, and finds it's getting better and better. '*Venus told me I had been perfect, but I think she exaggerated a bit. Anyway I felt much more self-confident. The dance lasted until half past midnight. The Hoylake doctor was drunk as a lord, and the lady who was with him was no less. When he saw me, he tried to speak French, but he couldn't, his speech was so slurred! In fact all the officers were more or less drunk, even the Waaf – the daughter of an air vice-marshal! I can't understand how anyone can get drunk on beer!'*

He came rather late, having had to wait for a taxi. He looks tired but can stand on his foot much better.

Saturday 16

He did not get up till very late. Then wrote to Antoine Morel. We booked at the Adelphi but Uncle Max said it was evening dress there again; so we booked at Reece's. Met Sheila and John. He got on well with F, although he doesn't like foreigners. They talked about Algeria. Danced a little with F. We had a very good time. F very sweet. I do love him.

Sunday 17

Woke him up late and made his breakfast. Took Wiener out in the park and talked about F's family. He does not seem over keen to return to France. Played records and he pretended to pinch £20 from me! Took him to station. Dear Cis, he is so sweet and so understanding.

Monday 18

Very bad headache and feeling tired. Wrote to F and made up a parcel for the Uzays.

Tuesday 19

Wrote to him.

Wednesday 20

Letter from F. He's coming back on Friday. Marie-Jeanne is waiting for him to come back to get married. She was shocked hearing that he goes out with Venus, and said, in my place, she wouldn't talk to him anymore! It sounds as if some of their neighbours do not believe he is an airman.

Thursday 21

His letter of Tuesday. '*Nothing special today, except for a little battle with Venus and Co where talc was used as munitions and I didn't have the upper hand at all, for I got back to my room white as a pastry cook, had to have a bath, and two hours later I was still sneezing. I hope to get my revenge tomorrow morning, but I'll have to take on those young ladies one by one, as three of them are much too much for me. I find it disgusting that women dare to attack me. I'll have to send a protest to my ambassador. […] By the way, my leg is completely straight now, and I thought my ordeal was over, but Venus is now focusing on my bending it and says that she will be fully satisfied only when I can fully do so.*' He feels time goes by faster now that he comes to Liverpool every week-end. '*No sooner do I realize I'm back than I'm already thinking about setting off again. I might put that differently, and say for example: I still have the taste of your latest kiss on my lips, and I'm already thinking about the next one!*'

Friday 22

Met F who was in good spirits. Went to Playhouse to see *The Recruiting Officer*, which he enjoyed very much. He said I was his '*raison de vivre*'. He's upset about what outsiders say about Frenchmen, and that his family are rather accusing him of malingering here.

The Recruiting Officer: an 18th-century comedy, by George Farquhar.
Raison de vivre: reason for living.

Saturday 23

Letter from Dédé. Daddy took me in the car to the shops and to change my library books. Woke F and made his breakfast. Went to the *British* and sat at our usual table. Talked about telling Patsy how to behave, and about English girls too. He said I was charming, at times! He had thought of breaking it all off and had not been able to do it. His ideal woman is someone who can cook, be a good hostess, and carry on an intelligent conversation: '*That is the woman's job!*' Went to Cassandra where we had a lovely dinner. The waiter said he would put us in a secluded corner, which he did. Told F about Sheila's adventures with James L, at which he was horrified. He said that one would only make such propositions to someone one was sure of, or a street-girl; I agree. He must be a nasty piece of work! He thinks Sheila should break it off with John, as she doesn't want to marry him. F very sweet indeed. I know that nobody will ever love me as much as he does. I told him, and he said: '*Thank you*!'

John was a friend of Sheila's brother who had died of meningitis in 1942. Her
    parents wanted them to get married.

Sunday 24

Woke F. He asked to be woken up early so as not to miss an hour with me. Went out in park. Pleasant day. F very sweet. Said the only way of getting rid of him is to tell him I don't love him any longer. Went to station. Stan there: nice man who is at Chessington with him. F very tender. I love him, despite my flirting. He left me 5 shillings for tobacco to send to *oncle* Jacques, the rural policeman. Bad headache. Dear Cis!

Oncle: uncle.

Monday 25

Still bad headache. Got tobacco for *oncle* Jacques. Wrote to F.

Tuesday 26

Went to Royal Institution to hear Alan Parker, of Quaker Aid. *Mme* Kléber there. Film about Toulouse and Marseilles: how brown the people are there! Made up parcel for *oncle* Jacques.

Quaker Aid: pacifist movement and relief organizers.

Wednesday 27

His letter of 25th. He's cutting down smoking! '*Today for me is the beginning of a period of penitence, for I've decided not to smoke anymore, except for one cigarette after each meal; I want to see if I'm up to it. Don't faint! If you did, you wouldn't hear me say 'I love you', for my love is stronger and more passionate than ever.*'

He rang. Wrote to him. French getting rather restive about Spain.

March

Friday 1

Went down to Mossley Hill station to meet F. Came home and made him some supper. Heard *Célestin et Célestine* and *Dis-moi le secret de tes caresses*.

Franco–Spanish border closed.

Mossley Hill station: local railway station.

Célestin et Célestine: a cabaret programme. *Dis-moi le secret de tes caresses*: sung by Tino Rossi.

26 February 1946: closing of the Franco-Spanish border, decided by the French government further to the execution of Cristino Garcia, a resistant who had fought with the Spanish Republicans.

Saturday 2

Bought oranges. Got F up. Went to *Johnny Frenchman* which we both enjoyed very much; it was even better a second time. Came home, got ready and went to the Adelphi. F told me I had '*farmer's instincts*', since I didn't want him to spend too much money! The head-waiter told us we could dance a little; so we did and it was very pleasant. We then went into the lounge where we met Beryl and Bert; the latter very quiet; F said '*half-dead*'! We all walked down together to Pier Head and came home with Beryl. The conductor on bus talked French with F. Cis gave us a studio portrait of himself. It is queer since they have erased all the lines and he looks exactly as he did when he first came: so young!

Sunday 3

He wrote a dedication of the photo for his father. Had lunch and played records. How sweet he is! Went to station and saw Stan and his wife who were pleasant. Stan's wife said last time, when they were all going to London, one of the Chessington boys had inferred that F was a seducer and went with women. He had been very upset, which accounts for his remarks last week-end, poor soul. The more I see F, the more he attracts me!

Tuesday 5

Tried to find food. Wrote to F.

Wednesday 6

Got his razor mended. His letter of Monday. He apologizes for any trouble his visits may cause. '*I think I have been rather thoughtless lately – I'm thinking about my visits to your place. It didn't occur to me that I might be a nuisance. I only had one thing in mind, which was that I couldn't stay here if I had any chance of seeing you. I now feel I definitely overstayed my welcome. I'm so grateful for what your parents and you have done for me that I wouldn't like to cause them any trouble whatsoever. [...] Please thank* Riri *and Mummy again, and tell them that, if a monument is to be erected in Marseilles, it will be dedicated to the Rigbys, the benefactors of a boy from the Midi.*'

Thursday 7

His letter of Tuesday. He's longing for Provence more and more. '*Last evening I heard an operetta from Marseilles on the radio:* Les Gauchos de Marseille. *It was wonderful and so amusing. For a while I could imagine myself under the sunny southern skies I know so well. I also noticed how different our humour was from yours. I wish I could have more opportunities to listen to French plays or the latest French operettas, otherwise I will seem so ignorant when I get back.*' He even gave up the NAAFI show so as to be able to stay on his own and listen in peace to the French programmes on the radio. The doctor is very pleased about his leg. Must get back to Wroughton on 15th to have some tests for three or four days. '*As from today, I'm growing a moustache, and hope that, when you see me, if you feel like voicing your disapproval, your good manners will stop you.*'

Friday 8

Letter from Rose, and one from F. He swam on Wednesday. '*My leg doesn't bother me at all, and I can swim as well as I could fifteen months ago. The only difference is that I now get out of breath so much more often. [...] Venus asked Mr Gilbertson for information, and he said that*

I should definitely have to come back here after four or five days at Wroughton.'

Went to meet him at Mossley Hill station. I don't like his moustache very much. Made him some supper. Brought me some chocolate. He's an angel.

Mr Gilbertson: the Chessington hospital doctor.

Saturday 9
F went to the dentist's to have teeth cleaned, as he is trying to give up smoking in earnest. Went to see *All This and Heaven Too*, with Charles Boyer. F fell for Barbara O'Neill! Went to the *British*, which was stiff with Poles, and saw Irene Owen. Then had dinner at the Cassandra. Walked up from Penny Lane, F teasing me about the British in Africa. We kissed each other for a long time.

All This and Heaven Too: a film directed by Anatole Litvac (1940).

Sunday 10
Went in the park. After dinner, washed up, with F pretending to be Serge Lifar again! Made him sandwiches and went to the station. Stan there again. Felt very sad and full of foreboding. I do so wish I knew what I have to do, he's so sweet.

Monday 11
Wrote to him.

Tuesday 12
Gens du voyage, with Françoise Rosay: you believe in whoever she portrays.

Les Gens du voyage (People Who Travel): a film directed by Jacques Feyder (1938).

Wednesday 13
Went to Ministry of Labour to get permission to continue at university renewed. Wrote to F.

Thursday 14

His letter of 11th. '*We may have two weeks off for Easter, and perhaps this is the chance for me to go to France.*' On the train, a Welsh WAAF called the English 'cold fishes'! Stan was speechless. Uncle Max offered to get a watch for F. I worry about my exams; my Psychology lecturer only gave me a 2 and a 3 for my presentation.

Friday 15

Letter from Dédé, and one from F. He saw *Kitty*, with Ray Milland and Paulette Godard, which he recommends me for '*the costumes and two wonderful scenes where we see them dancing the Gavotte*'. He bought a cellulose bracelet from a boy in his room, which he'll send to Patsy for her birthday. He's going to Wroughton today. Wrote to him and asked him what he frankly thought about my French.

I spoke to a boy who was a prisoner in the Tyrol. Said the Austrians felt quite different from the Germans and were very kind; the French prisoners worked for the Germans for fear of reprisals to their families.

Kitty: a film directed by Mitchell Leisen (1945).

Saturday 16

Very bad headache. Uzay's parcel returned. Letter from F of Thursday: he was asked to take all his bits and pieces away and he completed the necessary departure procedure, as he does each time he leaves a camp. Despite what Mr Gilbertson said to him, he thinks he probably won't get back to Chessington. He sounded rather gay. '*So many tears will flood the vale of Chessington! The moon and the trees will be silent witnesses to so many muffled sobs! My departure will leave such a great number of broken hearts and such a big vacuum! Like a great butterfly visiting the flowers that he loves and gathering the pollen from the open corollas, I flitted by in your lives. I was a ray of light in that misty cave, and with my departure darkness will return. Young ladies, never again will you see that charming, dark Mediterranean fellow who fascinated you! In their old days those of you who knew him will still be enraptured and speak about him in whispers, and those who never were acquainted with him will forever rue the day they did not throw themselves into his arms – those arms so welcoming to all who wore skirts (except the Scots!). That man will soon be leaving, and a huge, oppressive sadness will throw its black cloak over your frail shoulders. Amen!'* He went to see Pat on Wednesday. *'Paul is fine now, but the specialist who examined him two weeks ago said he had anaemia and had to go on a special diet. Pat looks terribly tired. That girl works too much, or at any rate she doesn't get enough sleep. [...] She has nearly completed her studies and will soon be ready to start her job. Paul can now sit up on his own and has also got into the habit of shaking his head, as if to say no. You just have to shake your head and ask him, and he does it too, all of it with babblings which, I suppose, certainly mean that he is laughing. He's also more and more fascinated by my shoulder knot, and I think I will have to give it to him when he can say what he wants. I would be sorry if I could not see him anymore, for I am really fond of the little rascal.'*

Shoulder knot (in French: *fourragère*): when the unit decoration of the *Croix de guerre* (which takes the form of a braided cord) is awarded, this is suspended from the shoulder of a uniform.

Sunday 17
Wrote to him.

Monday 18
F wrote from Wroughton. He got on a train for London on Friday morning with another boy. They had lunch at *Chez Auguste 'where there were chocolate* éclairs *for dessert again'*. They went to cinema, then got on the train for Swindon. At Wroughton he found four former Church Village chaps again; all the others had moved. He hoped that he could see Mrs Jackson the day after. *'Give me a big kiss as I do you, for I always feel a bit worried about anything new. I love you, darling, and send you my sweetest kisses.'*

Tuesday 19

His letter of 16th is depressing. He saw Mrs Jackson on Saturday morning. '*She was surprised by the way I can walk – very pleased, I mean. She asked me what I wanted to do, and I said: 'First, go on leave to France!' She seemed a bit embarrassed. Then she said I had to wait for a free bed in Ward 6 and she was going to consider my situation, for, she added, I was probably fed up with hospitals. All that is a bit vague, but I vaguely suspect that I could get back to my squadron for three months and then come back here, because she has already done the same for others. I'm also afraid that, when old Gilbertson said I was coming here for three or four days, he meant for three or four weeks, so I don't think I'll be able to make it to Liverpool for 5th April. In any case, I think next week I will hear what they're going to do with me.*' It's mad! He does not get enough to eat. '*The food is quite all right for those who're staying in bed, but, for those who like me can walk about, the diet is rather sparse. In just one single meal I could eat all the food we're given for a whole day.*'

Wrote to him. I am so afraid that he will leave me forever.

Wednesday 20

Psychology exam. I didn't have enough time and I became really panic-stricken: it's a disaster! I had worked so much though.

Letter from F. '*Mrs Jackson examined my leg with a new device; it's a kind of nerve detector or rather radio-detector. The only thing is that she pushed a needle some two inches long into my leg. I really thought it was going to come out the other side! Anyway my nerve is now definitely repaired and quite all right, but she says it's still too early to see the signs of improvement with the naked eye. The hospital's squadron leader is visiting us tomorrow, and I hope I will soon hear what they're going to do with me. They must hurry up, though, because yet another month like this will drive me completely dotty.*'

Feel miserable and tired. What shall I do when Cis is gone?

Thursday 21

Two letters from F. The one of 18th: at least, my French is not too bad. '*Your accent and pronunciation are perfect. Your spelling is very*

good. Your grammar is a bit weak, and above all you must watch your
vocabulary, as you're making up heaps of words, which would make
M. *Larousse's blood boil, like* 'tameuse de lions' *which, in French, is*
'dompteuse de lions'.' He is desperately waiting to hear what they're
going to do with him and says he's becoming neurasthenic. Wrote a
long poem about boredom. His letter of 19th. His father wrote to him;
he copied out a passage of his letter: '*Dear son, I received your photo*
which pleased me very much. I see that you really fulfilled my wishes
(he didn't want me to volunteer for the Air Force!). I was so thrilled
that I showed it to all my colleagues (I can picture the scene!) who were
delighted to see you have made so much progress (my foot!). I can't
wait for you to come back and see us, but as you are doing so well I
wouldn't like you to interrupt your recovery just for that. (Sic! Probably
the effect of the curt letter I sent about me getting back). Please say
hello to Barbiche (!) from me and to her parents as well, and thank her
for the tobacco, as it is so hard to come by at the moment. (Some more,
some more, some more…!) As for you, a big hug from your dad and all
the family.' He enclosed a little note for me from *tante* Rosalie, very well
written, with one of the violets she sent him. To kill time he plays cards
or Battleships with Jeannot, the Chessington Polish boy.

Wrote to him and suggested that he should look for a job in an embassy
or a consulate to stay in England. Don't feel happy about exams.

Larousse: name of a famous French dictionary.

Friday 22

His letter of 20th, rather melancholy. '*Dear heart, a year ago today, at*
this time, I was at Le Bourget waiting for a plane which would take
me back to old Albion and young Barbiche. Most probably, I didn't
think that a year later I would still be here. I'm afraid my letter will be
a bit too short to please you, for I haven't anything, anything at all to
say, except tender and soothing words of love which, you say, lose their
value by dint of being repeated too often. To my mind, they become
a little more meaningful each time, but we won't discuss that matter
tonight. Your photo has reappeared on my bedside table, so you're
watching me write.' Nobody bothers about him, he keeps on hanging

about. I'm afraid I will never see him again and I feel more and more depressed. '*I thought today I would eventually get to hear something about my situation, as Mrs Jackson phoned this morning, asking me to get ready to see her. But nothing happened, and now I'm praying with all my heart I'll see her tomorrow morning. If only I knew something definite, I wouldn't be so impatient, but being left in the dark is wearing out what little self-control I have. But it's time to say goodnight, and even to give you a kiss. It's also time to say 'I love you', an 'I love you' that's more passionate each night, although each night it seems to me impossible to be able to love you more.*'

Last exam, not too bad.

Saturday 23

Reduction in fat ration. Met Miriam who now wants me to marry F!

His letter of Thursday: still nothing new. '*You know, it's funny but I feel a bit oppressed too, something sad and burdensome, and I've been dreaming a lot lately, but once again I hope it's only my imagination. I touch wood and hope this is only one of those inaccurate forebodings.*'

Sunday 24

A year today since F came back from France: it seems much longer. Sent him a telegram.

Monday 25

His letter of Friday. '*Glad you like those few verses, but I don't make a regular habit of it. I do understand that you find my thoughts rather confused. Since I've been here, I've been totally bewildered. Thinking of both everything and nothing at the same time is more than confusing. As for writing some more verses, I'm liable to do so at any moment, but the next bout may just as well occur in a few months' time. Really I think the only attribute of a poet that I boast is… my hair!*' Glad he likes the idea of looking for a job in an embassy. '*It's very easy to think about a job in an embassy or a consulate, but I suppose there are heaps of people who are lining up just for that. Anyway, thank you for the idea, as it is something I would enjoy.*' Still nothing new about his departure. '*If I don't get a leave for France, I will certainly get four or*

five days for Easter, even if I'm still here, and you'll have a chance to feel
the tickling power of my moustache.'

Tuesday 26

 Mary's mother told our fortunes by tea-leaves. For me: a telephone
call, a new dress, a letter with a present, and a dance! For Sheila: a new
friend, very tall, and a holiday at the seaside!

   Letter from F. He bought a packet of cigarettes and a lighter in
Swindon: good resolutions over! Saw *Happy Landing*, which he had
already seen in France seven years ago, and also *Journey Together* which
I had told him about and he enjoyed very much. Met three French
sailors.

Happy Landing: a film directed by Roy Del Ruth (1938).

Wednesday 27
Wrote to him. Feel lonely.

Thursday 28
His letter of 25ᵗʰ. He got my telegram late: they were looking for
'*Sergent* Francis', thinking that Francis was his surname! He saw an old
Halifax taking off from the nearby airfield and says he wished he was
in it. It seems he's about to have a nervous breakdown. '*You know, I'm*
beginning to get really angry about my stay here. I wonder why I came.
Nobody has paid any attention to me this week; I'm not even given any
sort of treatment. All in all, I'm wasting my time. I can assure you that
if nothing happens this week, I'm going to jump at Mrs Jackson's throat
(figuratively speaking) and ask her what she intends to do with me. I
never saw anything more ludicrous. Furthermore, I can't even have my
shirts washed for fear of leaving the place before they are ready. But if
my hot temper gets the upper hand, some people are going to be told a
few home truths, and it'll probably end with a fortnight's confinement
to barracks, all the more so since my moustache will help me to look
fiercer. [...] I'm sure something new will happen this week, otherwise
either I will literally explode, burst with rage, or go crazy and call Mrs
Jackson 'Josephine' and tell her to kiss her little Napoleon, or possibly

*I will give myself leave of absence and get away from the hospital till I
feel like coming back! With this splendid, gay and optimistic forecast for
the coming week, I now kiss you as tenderly – nay, more tenderly than
usual if this is at all possible, and ask you please, don't worry about the
state of my brain cells, for my motto remains: 'Keep smiling – always'! I
love you, my beloved* petite femme.' Wrote to him.

Friday 29

Card for 1ˢᵗ April from Dédé: it must be a custom in France. Letter from F.
The weather was gorgeous; he was able to go out a little, which made him
feel quite good. He brought back a huge bunch of wild flowers to the Sister.
'*I dare hope this weather will last, for it's much less boring that way.*'
   Wrote to him.

Saturday 30

His letter of Wednesday, rather short: only a few words about a WAAF
speaking French and the weather. '*Mrs Jackson is still nowhere to be seen,
and the day I catch her she'll have a bad time of it. […] I have absolutely
nothing interesting to tell you and must keep some of my eloquence for
my next letters. That's all, Bébé! A kiss on your huge, beautiful eyes that I
keep dreaming of. I love you.*'
   Concert with Beryl and Bert: *Passacaglia in C Minor* by Bach, which
I enjoyed very much indeed, *Largo* from *New World Symphony* by
Dvorak, and *L'Après-midi d'un faune* which I didn't like. When I got
home, the family said that F had rung up and he would go to London this
week for a medical inspection. He thinks he will move to France for good.
I don't know what to think about it: it's an awful shock and so sudden.
He even doesn't know if he'll be able to come to see us again. It seems to
me he's dead a second time.

Sunday 31

Slept badly. Wrote to him, and also to Mrs Dick. Feel numb. What shall I
do without him? I feel as if I've known him for years. I don't know how
I will be able to do without him. I suppose I've been silly not to realize
this day would come. I will never be able to see him again, although I
need him and his love so much.

April

Monday 1

His letter of Saturday which accounts for what he said on the phone. It all seems a rush after weeks of waiting. '*My darling, this will come as a surprise to you just as it did to me. I'm afraid our forebodings were dead accurate. Yesterday I asked for a forty-eight-hour leave and hoped to be able to come and see you. My leave was already signed by Mrs Jackson, but she told me to go to the medical office first, to see if they didn't need me till Monday, and that was when I had a bit of a shock. In a word, this is the situation: on Monday morning I'm off to London Headquarters where I am to appear before a medical board which must decide on my case. At any rate, right now I am in the hands of the French Air Force, and the chances are that I'll be sent home as soon as possible. What is certain is that I'll never come back to this hospital again: Mrs Jackson assured me of that. I will certainly go to a convalescent centre in France, as she also said they were going to continue my treatment. These are the clear, precise facts! It happened quicker than we thought, didn't it? What is funny is that I feel strangely relaxed, as if something or some mechanism in me had stopped and was suspended. I'll ring you up tonight and I hope you'll be at home. Anyway if I have to go I will do all I can to get two or three days' leave before my departure, which I don't think they will refuse. I haven't written to you these last two days, for I was hoping to surprise you by arriving in Liverpool tonight. Et voilà, darling! I don't know what to say, I feel an utter fool. However, nothing is certain; perhaps I'll only be sent on leave, for there's still the problem of my treatment. I don't want to write anything more tonight, or I will get emotional, and that won't do any good. Don't worry too much! We have had so many false alarms so far. In any case, I'll phone you on Monday or Tuesday evening and let you know what's happening. Good night, darling! Smile and tell me you love me. Lots and lots of kisses, darling. Goodnight to everybody!*'

Francis arrived, having been for his medical board in London where they had no knowledge of him! He is going next Tuesday by plane to

Paris where he thinks he will be demobilized. Bad luck! Wonder if his leg will be ok. His moustache is very flourishing! He looks very well. I thank God that he has been able to come a last time.

Tuesday 2

Went to town and then to bank, seeing Mr Stewart, wanting us to go to the Grand National! F has put his remaining £60 into the *Crédit Lyonnais*. Went to the Food Office and got a food card for him. Bought different things like coffee and *Ronsonol* for F to take back to France. Sent telegram to M. Uzay and went for lunch; F eating a great deal. Went to the *British* where he did a bit of business with Patrick who sold him some clothing coupons. We sat at our usual table. Then we walked to the Pier Head and went over on the ferry to Seacombe, which was very pleasant.

Now I feel as if I am going to be executed: I know how condemned people feel. It's exactly the same as when Cis was at Elvington.

Ronsonol: petrol for lighter.

Wednesday 3

Went to town again to look for more things for F. Went to four different shops to try to get a suit: they are very hard to get. We finally ended up at the *Bon Marché* where a nice little man showed F a dark navy suit which fitted him perfectly. He looked very well in it, taller and very dignified. Had lunch there. An ex-RAF corporal, rather chatty, served us and asked F what Navy he was in and what his shoulder knot was! We got shirts, socks and such things. I was amused at playing the part of '*petite femme*'. He said that he didn't want me to visit him at home and that he would never come back to see us again: '*We must break off completely or not at all.*' I was most upset. Then he said he would not write, which upset me even more; I cried. Went to Southport. Said it was very like Aix-en-Provence. We talked about what we have done in the past. Had dinner at home, then we went to Gran's. F chose the watch for his birthday among a few Uncle Max had brought, which seemed to please him. He said that, even if things were all right in France, he would rather stay here.

Thursday 4

We were quiet all morning, both weeping. He then said he would do anything to make me happy, even come to see me again. Went to Chester; had a train compartment to ourselves. F said Chester was like York. Visited the cathedral. We sat down because F's ankle was swollen. Walked along the Rows, looking for a present for Nelly, then had a lovely lunch at Bolland's. F told my fortune in tea-leaves at the bottom of my cup: I will have six husbands, twelve children, and will survive them all! He was too tired to walk on the Walls. Got on the train home. F couldn't kiss me in the tunnel because of the light and lots of people in the compartment. Rang up Sheila; she asked me if I felt 'tragic'! Instead of going out to the neighbours' with Daddy and Mummy, we stayed at home and the great question of marriage came. F said I cheated myself and that I wanted both love and other advantages. Told him about the problems of religion, work and country again. He said the last two could be solved. Would I marry him if he stayed in England and had a job? '*I do so want you to be my wife.*' I said: 'Why not!' He told me that I will not wait for him. I know waiting is not my forte. He had wanted to talk to me like that so many times. At last, we decided to write to each other and wait until he had a job.

The Rows: wooden galleries on two floors with shops in half-timbered medieval houses at Chester.

Bolland's: a famous restaurant in Chester.

Friday 5

Got a letter from Civil Service about an interview for a job in London next Tuesday. I rang up Mrs Dick who can have us both, Francis and me, on Sunday. I am so pleased. We played records and then I ironed F's shirts and sewed. We sat out in the garden and F sewed his bear. We kissed a lot. He said I looked so small in his arms. Played *Can I Forget You?* and *Bella Raggazina*. Had dinner and dressed to go the *British*. I put on my long black lamé dress, with a red velvet jacket: F seemed to like it. We called for Sheila who had got all dressed up in a strapless blue evening dress. The dance was quite good with a Belgian band. All the French people there. F won a prize for being a volunteer.

I was a bit sad as it was the last time that we would be together at the *British*.

Bella Raggazina: sung by Tino Rossi.

Saturday 6

Went to the shops on bicycles; F rode very well. After lunch, Daddy, Mummy, F and I went to Parkgate through the Mersey tunnel. F was wearing civilian clothes. We walked along the promenade by the sea. Came home via Hoylake and saw the Leas. Then took Wiener out and went to Gran's. She and Uncle Max seemed very sorry that F was going. We drank his health. Came home. F was very, very sad; he hardly said a word. Then I said that I really wanted to marry him and he seemed very happy. He asked if I really wanted him to come back.

Sunday 7

F's last day at home. He packed his suitcase. We kissed for the last time at home. We were rather sad. Went down to the station with Mummy, Daddy and Patsy. Sheila and Clare were there; Sheila brought us a whole lot of food. We saw Stan and his wife. Mummy looked very sorry to see F go. The journey was pleasant, but F looked very sad. I did not feel so sad, as I know he may come back. We were helped by Stan and his friend at Euston station. Bus to Waterloo where F put his case in the Left Luggage Office. Then we got the train to Oxshott. Mr and Mrs Dick were there to meet us in the car. How kind the Dicks are! We kissed and did not want to leave each other.

Clare Cundall: another friend of Barbara's at university. Barbara had only been once to London with her mother, when she was 12.

Monday 8

Walked up with F as far as the pub, and then he went off to London. The Dicks and I went off to meet Pam and little James. F rang up from the station and came back. He does not now need to go until Wednesday: lovely! He doesn't seem to trust me very much and said I was still young. Mrs Dick thinks our project is a good idea. We went to the White Lion, a lovely pub in Cobham, where we met Kenny and Pam and had a lovely dinner. Had tea and talked about swapping wives for camels in Algeria! F and I took Smudge out and we kissed. We discussed the question of religion, and then he told me that he did not want to leave me: '*You are the only thing I have.*' I do not want him to leave me either. Then we all together had a great discussion about charm and old age! I wonder what's going to happen.

Cobham: a few miles from Oxshott, in Surrey. Smudge: the Dicks' dog.

Tuesday 9

F went off to French Air Force Headquarters in Prince's Gate. I helped Mrs Dick, then went to Waterloo station. The bomb damage is rather bad by Battersea. F met me at the station and said he would have to go to the FAF HQ again for papers. We went to *Chez Auguste*, in Soho, and we had some red wine which I liked very much. We discussed the great question again. He said he was not a real believer. I said that I did not want to be French and that once in France he should keep in mind my shortcomings. Went back to Waterloo. I was terrified of the escalator in the underground and had to help F to walk over the steel. He went off to the HQ again, and I stayed at Waterloo, watching the GIs' brides, rather vulgar, setting off for Tidworth. I got a taxi for Burlington Gardens for the interview; the five interviewers were all very pleasant. Met F who had been waiting outside for ages. He said he had an extra day. Went to the Academy Cinema to see *Une femme disparaît*, with Françoise Rosay and Claude Dauphin, and then *I Married a Witch*. As we came out at 9.15 pm, F said he never dreamed that I would be walking in London with him. Mr Dick came for us at Oxshott station. I gave F presents for Rose and Jeanne.

Battersea: power station.

Tidworth: US military camp converted into a welcome and transit centre for GI brides.

Une femme disparaît: a film directed by Jacques Feyder (1942). *I Married a Witch*: a film directed by René Clair (1942).

Wednesday 10

Got a taxi from Waterloo to Prince's Gate to get F's papers, via Buckingham Palace and Hyde Park. Put F's case into the Left Luggage Office at Victoria station and went to find the Army Travel Bureau. Had lunch at *Chez Auguste*. F said that my liking to be kissed was almost a vice! He also said that his family would not be upset about us as he was 24 and had no intention of staying in Berre, and that he would come back as soon as possible. I asked him if I would be a good wife to him, and he asked me if I would be happy with him. Went to the Army Travel Bureau and he got the papers. Went then to Madame Tussaud's, as F wanted to go; he liked Henry VIII. Went back to Waterloo. He likes the idea of representing a perfume or a wine firm. He is so good to me; I don't want him to make so many sacrifices. His only condition is to be able to go back home once a year. I am worried that *Mme* Uzay might be angry. F will write to Daddy. We waited at Oxshott and Mrs Dick joined us. Then we came home and sat by the fire, without the lights: it was lovely! F was so sweet. I don't feel too sad as I'm already thinking about his return, *DV*! He said it was impossible to behave badly with me. I hope he will still love me when he is at home.

DV: Deo Volente, God willing.

Thursday 11

We left Mrs Dick: she has been so kind and understanding. Then we went to Waterloo. F asked me to come and stay on holiday with him if he couldn't get back here; he said his family fully expected it. Feeling very sad, we went to Euston to leave my case, and then to Victoria where we got a rotten lunch; it was so sad. We got a nice porter. We did not say much. F asked me to thank Mummy and Daddy, not to work too hard or listen to discouraging people. He looked as if he would cry. We said we loved each other, then we kissed passionately. And the train left. I wept bitterly.

****

We kept on corresponding for some time. The following summer, I went to Berre where Francis' family gave me a wonderful welcome. Then, our ways drifted apart for ever. At Christmas, Daddy and Mummy received a card from Cis saying: '*With my best wishes for 1947 and to tell you, that, whatever happens, I will never forget you all!*'

And I will never forget you too.

Barbiche

Happy the man who, like Ulysses, has made a wonderful journey!

16th-century French poem by Joachim du Bellay.

Postscript
The French Heavy Bomber Squadrons in Great Britain 1943–1945

In 1943, after the invasion in North Africa and the operations in Tunisia, the Allies decided to integrate *Groupes* 2/23 'Guyenne' and 1/25 'Tunisie', two units of the French Air Force from North Africa, into RAF Bomber Command. The first 'Guyenne' aircrews arrived in Liverpool in early September 1943.

The British required that all flying personnel had to be up to RAF standard, and all had to re-take full training courses at specialist schools, before being put together into aircrews and declared operational, that is to say fit to carry out war missions.

From this time the RAF squadron numbers '346 and 347' were born, and the first crews of 346 'Guyenne' Squadron arrived in mid May 1944 at RAF Elvington, followed a month later by crews of 347 'Tunisie' Squadron. Located ten kilometres east of the city of York and commanded by a French colonel, Elvington was the only RAF Station to be operated by French personnel and had about 2,300 French airmen, air and ground crew, which earned it the name of 'Petite France' among the inhabitants of the area.

On 1 June 1944, 346 'Guyenne' Squadron was the first to begin operations. On the night of 5/6 June, eleven crews took part in the D-Day operations with their Halifax aircraft, bombing the German gun batteries of Grandcamp-Maisy, in Normandy.

A Halifax bomber crew comprised seven men: pilot, navigator, bomb aimer, wireless operator, flight engineer, mid upper gunner, rear gunner, and to ensure continued operation, the RAF planned for two crews per aeroplane. This required thirty-two crews for each squadron, that is to say a total of sixty-four crews at Elvington. Reinforcements arrived each month to replace those who had been shot down and to supplement the ground crews.

The two French Squadrons took part in 131 actions, either together or individually, amongst which were 123 bombing raids (118 for 346 'Guyenne' and 111 for 347 'Tunisie') and 8 petrol supply missions to Belgium.

Their targets were mainly the Ruhr synthetic petrol and weapon factories in Germany and the launching sites of V1 and V2 flying bombs along the North Sea coastal area.

In eleven months of operations, 216 men were killed: 175 on missions, thirty-three in training and eight in bomb-loading accidents.

RAF Bomber Command lost 55,573 aircrew during World War II, among them the 216 French airmen of 346 'Guyenne' and 347 'Tunisie' – one in two were killed.

About the Authors

Barbara Harper-Nelson (*née* **Rigby**)
In 1946, after passing her BA Lettres, Barbara taught, then did market research. She opened a library and information centre for the College of the Sea for Merchant Seamen in Liverpool, and organised postal educational courses for them. In 1952 she joined the Women's Voluntary Service, doing welfare for British servicemen in Malaya during the Emergency. She joined the Women's Royal Army Corps in 1954 as a staff officer and served in Hong Kong, Malaya, Edinburgh and HQ London District.

In 1958 she joined the Colonial Service and was posted to do community development work for African women in Kenya. In 1960 she married Major John Harper-Nelson, King's African Rifles in Nairobi, who was then posted to Uganda.

She emigrated to Australia in 1962. She served on the West Australian Council of Social Service, was archivist for Kalamunda and Districts Historical Society, and was honorary Life Member of Returned and Services League.

Geneviève Monneris won Best Documentary at the IWM London Film Festival 2012 for *De Lourds Souvenirs, 24-12-1944*, a film about her father's aircrew (the 347 'Tunisie' Squadron), made with her son Thomas Lesgoirres.

She is the author of two other documentary films, *Apart from that, everything's ok!* and *Henry and Pat, December 1943 – November 1944*. They were made in memory of the French squadrons in RAF Bomber Command, and have been screened at the Yorkshire Air Museum and London Imperial War Museum.

Her father, André Guédez, was a mid upper gunner in the crew of *lieutenant* Leroy (347 'Tunisie' Squadron). Their Halifax was shot down on Christmas Eve 1944 above Düsseldorf. Five men were killed. André Guédez and François Duran, the flight engineer, were the only two survivors. It was the only French crew missing that night. The next French crew to be shot down was that of *lieutenant* Cottard, including Francis Usai, on 2 January 1945 (part of the same squadron).

Michel Darribehaude is a Senior Lecturer in British Civilisation Studies at the Université de Toulon (France).

Christian Darribehaude, his father, was a wireless operator in the crew of *capitaine* Brion (346 'Guyenne' Squadron) and flew thirty-three missions from June 1944 to January 1945. His mother Irene, *née* Looker, was born in Liverpool and served there as a WAAF at RAF Coastal Command's 'Western Approaches' Headquarters from 1941 to 1945. So she was one of the 'guardian angels' watching over the safety of all those men who, like Christian, André, and Francis, sailed in a convoy to Liverpool ...

Irene and Christian married at the war's end and lived in France, happily ever after.

The Yorkshire Air Museum & Allied Air Forces Memorial

The Yorkshire Air Museum & Allied Air Forces Memorial at Elvington near York is one of the largest history of aviation museums in Britain. It is the sole Allied Air Forces Memorial in Europe and the Chiefs of the Royal Air Force and French Air Force are permanent Vice Presidents. The Museum occupies a twenty-acre parkland site on the largest original World War II RAF Bomber Command Station open to the public and the former base of the only French heavy bomber squadrons of World War II. The museum has over sixty historic aeroplanes and vehicles with over fifteen exhibitions and receives around 100,000 visitors per year. It is a registered charity and a nationally accredited museum with around 150 registered volunteers, a small professional staff and a permanent French office. The Museum undertakes historic research, aircraft engineering, displays, and works closely with French museums and the embassies of our two countries. Ian Reed has been its director since 1999 and was awarded the *Ordre National du Mérite* by the President of France in 2013.

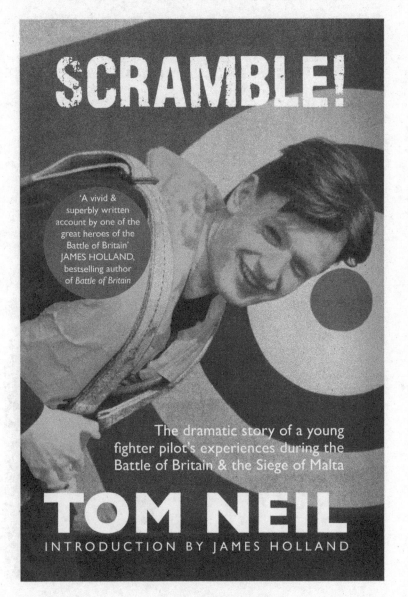

Also available from Amberley Publishing

THE SECOND WORLD WAR IN THE AIR
IN PHOTOGRAPHS

1944

L. ARCHARD

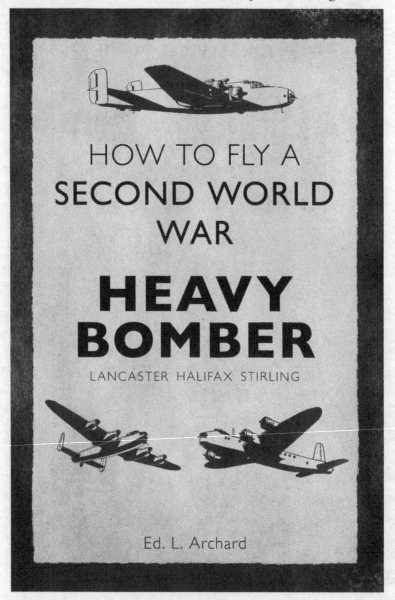